SIXTH SENSE

SIXTH SENSE

THE WHOLE-BRAIN BOOK
OF INTUITION, HUNCHES, GUT FEELINGS,
AND THEIR PLACE
IN YOUR EVERYDAY LIFE

Laurie Nadel

WITH JUDY HAIMS AND ROBERT STEMPSON

PRENTICE
HALL
PRESS

New York   London   Toronto   Sydney   Tokyo   Singapore

Acknowledgment is made to the following for permission to reproduce copyrighted material from the sources named:

Be My Guest, by Conrad Hilton (Prentice Hall, 1957, 1958). Reprinted courtesy of Prentice Hall.

The Collected Works of C.G. Jung, translated by R.F.C. Hull, Bollingen Series XX, Vol. 8 (Princeton University Press, 1960). Reprinted courtesy of Princeton University Press.

The Structure and Dynamics of the Psyche, by C.G. Jung (Princeton University Press, 1969). Reprinted courtesy of Princeton University Press.

Memories, Dreams, Reflections, by C.G. Jung (Pantheon Books, 1961, 1962, 1963). Reprinted courtesy of Pantheon Books.

The Penguin Dictionary of Psychology, by Arthur Reber (Viking Penguin, 1986). Reprinted courtesy of Arthur Reber.

Anatomy of Reality: Merging of Intuition and Reason, by Jonas Salk (Columbia University Press, 1986). Reprinted courtesy of Columbia University Press.

Special thanks to *Natural History* magazine, which first commissioned and published Laurie Nadel's interview with Ralph Coe in an article called "Lost and Found Traditions," July 1986.

Prentice Hall Press
15 Columbus Circle
New York, NY 10023

Library of Congress Cataloging-in-Publication Data
Nadel, Laurie, 1948–
Sixth sense : the whole-brain book of intuition, hunches, gut
feelings, and their place in your everyday life / Laurie Nadel, with
Judy Haims and Robert Stempson.
p.   cm.
Includes bibliographical references.
ISBN 0-13-502899-X
1. Intuition (Psychology)—Problems, exercises, etc. 2. Intuition
(Psychology) I. Haims, Judy. II. Stempson, Robert. III. Title.
BF315.5.N33   1990
153.4"4—dc20   89–28660
                                          CIP

Designed by Irving Perkins Associates, Inc.

Manufactured in the United States of America

10 9 8 7 6 5 4 3 2

First Edition

For our children:
Charly, Jennifer, Stephanie, Craig, and Matthew

ACKNOWLEDGMENTS

So many people believed in this book and gave me their support and good wishes that I can't begin to acknowledge them all.

First, I would like to thank my agent Madeleine Morel, who believed in me and this book from the very beginning. It was Madeleine who nurtured the concept, edited the original proposals, reviewed the manuscript, and helped me through each stage of the editorial process. I would also like to thank my editor Gail Winston, who helped me to organize the manuscript. Gail's editorial judgment and commitment to the book was invaluable in motivating me. Special thanks to Elena Oumano whose editorial judgment and sensitivity were a wonderful help. Thanks, too, to Elizabeth Perle and Marilyn Abraham.

I also would like to thank my coauthors Judy Haims and Robert Stempson for their superb contribution of insight, information, and intuition. I'm sure they didn't quite know what they were getting into when they signed on at the beginning of this project but this book could not have taken shape without their help. My thanks, too, to P. J. Dempsey, who suggested that the three of us collaborate. P. J.'s belief in this book was invaluable in getting this project launched.

For taking the time to review the proposal and manuscript, I would like to thank Barbara Coats and Steven Leeds. Barbara is the most gracious editor with whom I have ever worked. I am especially appreciative of her friendship. Steve Leeds, who has spent the past year teaching me neurolinguistic programming, has given me the tools to use when creating NLP exercises for intuitive development. Steve's concern, patience, intelligence, and sincerity are both remarkable and inspiring.

To the scientists who took time from their busy schedules to speak with me, I also say thanks. Each individual took the time to explain complicated scientific concepts in words easy enough for me to understand and, at the same time, made me feel welcome and respected. I am grateful to Robert Beck, Jan Brice, Dr. Eugene d'Aquili, Norman Don, Willis Harman, Stephen Hinkey, Dr. Robert Jarvik, William Kautz, Stanley Krippner, Dr. Leigh Lipton, Dr. Paul MacLean, Jean Millay, Edgar Mitchell, Charles Onorton, Andrija Puharich, Ernest Rossi, Dr. Oliver Sacks, Dr. Jonas Salk, Dr. Sherman Schachter, Dr. Mary Schmitt, Dr. George Solomon, Dr. Roger Sperry, Russell Targ, and Vince Wiberg.

At CBS News, thanks to all my friends, especially Gayana Gashian, Megan Marshack, Renee Weinstein, Gil Quito, and Chuck Sinkier who never stopped caring and offering their help. Special thanks go to Donna Dees, Susanne Meirowitz, and Dan Rather. Harris Salomon of ABC News has gone out of his way to dig up information, sources, and unlisted phone numbers so many times that I cannot begin to thank him.

I am also grateful to all those who gave me interviews and information: Stephanie Abarbanel, Rod Bicknell, Simon Boughton, Marilyn Bruno, Scott Burnell, Karen Buckley, Patty Canova, Jair Cardoso, Rob and Robin Clark, Carol Colman, Thomas Condon, Francis Ford Coppola, Alice Corring, Elaine de Beauport, Sonia De Chacon, Kimberly Ebert, Mary Edgerton, Barry Fernald, Lillian and Al Fink, Jane Finnegan, Peter Fellows, Genevieve Geer, Jean Hacker, Charlene Harrington, Darryl Hill, Fred Hodges, Mary Ann Huff, Arianna Stassinopoulos Huffington, Cynthia Bain Kress, Gay Larned, Dorothy Laub, Matthew Lesko, Stephen Levy, Laura Lofaro, Dan Miller, Martin Mordkoff, Roy Murphy, Bill Murtha, Eric Nadel, Carol O'Biso, Tim O'Shaughnessy, Helen Palmer, Joan Pankosky, Jagdish Parikh, Lee Paxson, Michael Ray, Arthur Reber, Edith Rubin, Donna Samet, Sandy Samet, Stuart Siegel, Nancy Sharpnack, Jack Smith, Mike Steckman, Jeff Stein, Ron and Gretchen Taylor, Tom Trebelhorn, Barbara Vettell, Marilyn vos Savant, Sharon Weathers, Earl Weaver, Tim Wernet, and Eric Yaverbaum.

I am very grateful to Ned Herrmann, his family, and staff, all of whom gave so generously of themselves. In particular, I would like to thank Ann and Margy Herrmann, and Sylvia McDaniel.

Writing is a tough and lonely business, and, as Dorothy Parker pointed out, it's a wonder anyone would choose to do it when there are other gracious professions around like, say, cleaning out ferryboats. There is no way I can express my thanks to those friends who kept me company, boosted my morale, urged me to keep going, and even got me to laugh from time to time. For friendship above and beyond its usual meaning, I profoundly thank Vicky Secunda, Helen McNeil, Sue Watt, Maggie Kapel, Kathleen McLane, Patty Harris, and Julie Zalat. For allowing me to share my insecurities and for helping me to change them into more resourceful states, I thank all those who shared NLP training with me: Malka Ahearn, Doug Boltson, Jose Guijarro, Haley-Zee, Rich Heddleson, Rachel Hott, Adele Letterman, Louis Railer, Theo Scolnick, Abigail Sperber, and Dr. Frank Stass. My special thanks to Ray Quezada, whose understanding, warmth, and friendship are a tremendous gift. I would also like to thank Harlene Brandt, Karl Brandt, Kim Moinester, Rosemarie Shaffer, Josephine Brown, Michael Brown, and all those who helped me keep my life in order.

I am sad that my father died as I was finishing work on this manuscript as he encouraged me in so many ways. There is no way I could have undertaken this project without the help of everyone in my family, especially my husband, Phil Van Dijk, and my daughter Charly. For Phil, my writing this book was particularly trying at times. I know it was hard to live with someone who was physically present and mentally absent for extended periods of time. Along with the isolation, Phil shared my frustrations as well as my excitement. Were it not for his insistence that I join the twentieth century, I would still be using a manual typewriter instead of a computer. I could not have done the research, writing, and editing required without his good nature and patience to sustain me.

CONTENTS

PREFACE

I have been exploring intuition—personally and professionally—ever since a startling event changed my life.

In February 1975, I was looking for work in San Francisco. I had been staying with a family near Palo Alto, about an hour's drive from the city. One afternoon, I borrowed a car so that I could go into town for an interview with a magazine editor. My appointment was for 3 P.M. and as I approached the city limits around 2:30 P.M., I realized that I did not have a map.

I had never been to San Francisco. The freeway exits whizzed by as the downtown spires loomed closer. I had no idea where I was or what exit I needed to take. There were no gas stations in sight, nor was there anyplace along the road I could stop at and ask someone for directions. Suddenly, I sensed that I should get off at the next exit. The feeling was so strong that it was as if someone were in the car telling me where to go. This feeling that I should get off the highway became more insistent. Whizzing along at sixty miles an hour, I eased off the freeway and onto the ramp. Nothing looked familiar. How could it?

Suddenly, I was prompted again. This time, I almost thought I "heard" instructions: "Turn right at the next light." I did, but still had no idea where I was. "Go two blocks up the hill and make a left," were the next directions. Then, the instructions speeded up. "Right turn at the stop sign. Left turn at the light. Two blocks, then right. Left at the stop sign." I drove confidently through streets I had never seen, weaving my way through traffic jams as if I knew where I was going.

After about twenty minutes, I slammed on the brakes. "Laurie, what are you doing? This is absurd," I scolded myself. "You have absolutely no idea where you are, but you're driving around as if you do."

I pulled into a gas station to ask for directions. The office I was looking for, the attendant told me, was very close by, just a few buildings away. I was stunned. How had I known how to drive through San Francisco without a map and reach my destination? It occurred to me that if I had not applied the brakes when I had, I would have continued to follow this amazing guidance system and would have arrived at the magazine office's door right on time. I was uncannily close enough as it was.

Later, I tried to analyze what had happened in the car but came up with no rational explanations. All I could attest to was that I had somehow navigated through unfamiliar territory by following some kind of mental radar that had given me accurate, understandable directions. How did it work? Where did it come from? Was it part of me or was it an external force? If it was an external presence, then who or what was it?

As a journalist, I was used to asking questions, but I wasn't sure how to start finding the answers to these in particular. I wanted to understand the basic *W*s that I was trained to look for: What? When? Where? Why? and Who? I also wondered if—and how—I could learn to access this source of information whenever I wanted.

If every journey begins with a single step, then I had somehow leapt into brand-new territory, literally, without a map. I intended to find out how I had arrived there. As intensively as I would begin scoping out the subject of an article, I began research into intuition, ESP, and metaphysical philosophy. I began a program of yoga and meditation, working my way through several schools and correspondence courses. I became a student of the Self-Realization Fellowship, the organization founded by Paramahansa Yogananda, who brought yoga to the United States in 1920. During that time I began to see auras, the shimmering electromagnetic fields around every living thing. I took a course in the aura given by a physicist. I studied and published an article on therapeutic touch, a hands-on healing technique in which you feel a person's aura, or energy field, with your hands to promote natural healing. I also learned how to do *Reiki,* an ancient Japanese healing technique whose name means "universal life energy." I spent several years working with The Course in Miracles and studying the work of Alice Bailey, an author of metaphysical books. You could say that I acquired a comprehensive range of New Age credentials.

I found all these teachings to be effective tools for developing intuitive awareness in different ways. I also discovered that the current applications of scientific research into how the brain works supports many metaphysical approaches. The main difference between the scientific and metaphysical approaches is that to develop your intuition using metaphysical techniques, you need to believe in a spiritual philosophy. However, to develop your intuition as an intelligence—an innate mental ability—you do not have to believe in any particular spiritual framework. All you have to believe is that you have a brain and that you can learn how to use more of it.

For two years after the incident in San Francisco, I was compelled to find answers. What had really happened that day? Did I have hidden powers? Was this magic? Was I going crazy? Even as I strengthened my intuition, I continued to question whether my perceptions were real. Apart from this unusual occurrence, my life showed no signs of disturbance. I worked, saw my friends, and continued my daily routines. Nonetheless, I could not forget about what had happened nor could I stop thinking about it. Several months after my trip to San Francisco, I entered counseling with a woman who incorporated Jungian and Gestalt techniques. Unlike traditional, Adlerian, or Freudian-based psychotherapy, her combined Jungian/Gestalt approach helped me to understand that my intuition was a natural, helpful part of me. It helped, too, that this particular therapist valued her own intuition. "You are like a radio that cannot get stations," she remarked after our first session. "You must first ground yourself by understanding and working with your own emotions." Emotional interference, she explained, is one of the main obstacles preventing us from recognizing communication from our intuition. As we clear out conflicting emotions, we become better able to recognize the source of our many different sensations and impressions. She also counseled me to analyze those options that apparently came to me spontaneously and not to accept every intuitive flash without first checking it out.

Now I realize that she was effectively advising me to use both my rational and intuitive abilities. I appreciated her efforts at the time, but, now, years later, I am especially grateful for her common-sense advice. Having discussed the role of intuition in therapy with many psychotherapists, I realize now that to balance intuition with reason was absolutely the best advice I could have received.

As I attained greater insight into the relationship between my intuitive perceptions and rational thoughts, I also became better informed about what had happened during that first intuitive experience. The key to understanding it seemed to lie not in querying the nature of the intuitive signals themselves but in examining how my mind and brain had functioned when I was "picking up" those directions in the car. Although the signals had, at first, seemed to be coming from someplace outside me, they could have been absorbed and projected by my intuition, which has the ability to acquire information by means other than conscious, rational processes. My intuition could have presented that information in auditory form to my conscious mind. Instead of hearing words giving me directions, I could just as easily have seen a visual image or flash, or felt something in a kinesthetic form, such as a physical sensation somewhere in my body.

After several years, I developed a personal technique for getting in touch with my intuition in stressful situations, which I call "relax, center, visualize." I take a couple of deep breaths to relax and mentally project myself to my "personal center." My personal center is an image from nature, a place where I know I always feel relaxed and calm. I'm not a magician and intuition isn't magic. With practice, anyone can learn how to do this. It is simply another way of using your mind.

When I began to work on this book, I was able to accept my intuition most of the time. The information it gave me invariably proved accurate. Even though I knew how to call upon my intuition when I needed it, I still had to know more. What was intuition? How did it function in the mind? In my interviews with many of the scientists, authors, and psychologists who were involved in studying the mind and the brain, this theme—the need to know *how* you know—recurred in many discussions. It appears that many people who consider themselves intuitive or who value their intuitive awareness are also persistent and curious. They feel compelled to search for information about the nature of the mind and are not content to accept easy answers. Dr. Paul MacLean, the neurophysiologist who first proposed that we all have three brain systems—the triune brain—says that he has been asking questions about how his brain works since he was three-years-old. "I think the brain is intelligent enough to realize that you have a very short time in this life," he said. "Especially if these questions are burning. I can't remember when I didn't have them. I think you're built that way." Neuroscientist Dr. Roger Sperry, who won the Nobel Prize in 1983 for discovering the separate functions of the left and right hemispheres of the top brain, the neocortex, is also motivated by his own need to know, he says. "I entered neuroscience because the brain is the origin of mind/consciousness. I was attracted to the search for answers. Mind has always been the big secret."

It's a secret that I would not presume to say I know, although I understand more about my own mental processes—especially the intuitive process— as a result of working on this book. In the course of conducting research, I have found that my understanding of intuition has shifted through several states of knowing—not knowing, believing, and wondering.

Six months into the research phase, I began to doubt the wisdom of my taking this project on altogether. With some fifty interviews under my belt, I began to realize the enormity of the subject I had chosen as well as its elusive complexity. After dozens of interviews with scientists, educators, and psychologists, as well as teachers, actors, realtors, businesspeople, police and military officers, and housewives, I noticed that, in keeping with the ephemeral nature of my subject, the more I learned about intuition, the more elusive its essence became.

How had I gotten myself into this? How could I ever write a book about something that's over in a flash, something for which few people have words? Think of it! How many times have you described yourself as having "just a feeling" or "one of those hunches?" My research confirmed that I had chosen a topic that was essentially nonverbal. In fact, intuition occurs in a part of the brain that has no language.

No matter how much information I obtained, I was continually reminded that intuition could not be grasped or forced to remain still while I examined it. I seemed to have come full circle in my efforts. Yes, it was possible to define, clarify, and access intuition when I needed it. Yes, it was possible to develop exercises that would make that process "user friendly" and to write those exercises down so that intuition, despite its nonverbal essence, would be accessible. Yet I had to concede that no matter how thoroughly I refined my descriptions, something about intuition itself seemed beyond my reach. Scientist and author Willis Harman eloquently summed up my dilemma for me when he said, "I don't think intuition is something you define. I think it's something you learn about as you grow in age and wisdom."

Although I am now comfortable with the elusiveness of intuition and with talking about my intuitive experiences, it took me more than ten years to come out of the intuitive closet. I decided to open up and talk about my first experiences because public opinion was changing. More people were admitting that they, too, had experienced different forms of intuitive and psychic perception. In 1987, the National Opinion Resource Council published the results of a survey showing that two-thirds of the participants believed in psychic phenomena. Around the same time as the publication of the survey results, ABC television broadcast the miniseries "Out on a Limb," about Shirley MacLaine's first psychic experiences. The survey and the miniseries are indications that more and more people in this country are now accepting these kinds of experiences as real.

At first it was not easy for me to say that my life had changed as a result of that drive through San Francisco in 1975. Even after years of seminars, courses, and meditation, I still believed that my intuition was weird. Like most Americans, I was brought up to respect only what could be explained logically. After thirteen years of working to develop my intuition, I still felt uncomfortable letting people know that I was "into that stuff." And while my intuitive, unconscious mind had, over the years, rewarded me generously with flashes of insight, feelings, and information, I still had a tendency to denigrate my intuitive flashes. As I came to accept my intuition, I helped heal the rift between my objective mind—the one that I was raised to consider "real" and more important—and my subjective, inward-seeking mind. Writing this book enabled me to penetrate some of my internal, invisible borders. As a result, my outer and inner worlds have synchronized.

Without knowing it, my investigative approach was being done in the spirit of what is called the new science. "If you really want to know something, or to know about something, you become one with it," Willis Harman explained, describing the new science of consciousness. "You learn about intuition by turning inward. That doesn't mean it's not scientific. You, the observer, are going to be changed by the observing process. Because you'll change your whole life. Otherwise, you won't learn any-thing."

As part of that learning process, any discussion of intuitive development must cover attitudes, values, and fears. Most of us are brought up to be suspicious of experiences that have no rational basis. When intuition comes to us spontaneously, we sometimes cut and run, frightened by its potency. Trained in measurable, sequential thinking methods, we distrust the random, spontaneous, and effortless flow of intuitive input. We tend to argue with ourselves when it appears, calling it just a foolish feeling.

In actuality, intuition and reason form a coprocessing system that enhances our intellectual abilities. We need both intuition and reason in order to survive, writes Dr. Jonas Salk in his book *Anatomy of Reality: Merging of Intuition and Reason.* The next step in human evolution is taking place now, and Dr. Salk characterizes it as is an evolution in consciousness. In order to solve the problems threatening humanity, we have to overcome the inner obstacles that prevent us from becoming whole-brained thinkers. We need to become thinkers who use all of our abilities, not just our ability to think logically.

We also need to see the connection between human consciousness, of which intuition is a part, and the physical world. Space is frequently called the final frontier. For most of us, that means planetary exploration by trained astronauts. But many people see astronaut Edgar Mitchell's decision to leave NASA so that he could become more involved in consciousness research as a symbol of a new movement to explore inner space. "The space age was an exploration of the unknown," observes Judy Haims, one of the coauthors of this book. "Once we went there it seemed like the logical next place to go was inward. We're still exploring space and time, but it's some other space and some other time. What else is there that we don't know?"

This book is as much a part of that question as it is a part of the answer.

—Laurie Nadel

INTRODUCTION

Whether you are reading this book to learn how to develop your intuition or simply to get information about intuition in general, we would like to assure you that your intuition works perfectly right now. There is nothing in this book that will "make it work better."

However, we can guarantee that by reading and doing some of the exercises, you will develop your ability to identify, value, and trust your intuition. You will also be able to feel more comfortable about accepting information that comes to you intuitively. We can also guarantee that, with practice, you will be able to get in touch with your intuition when you need it, instead of wondering if it will signal you at the appropriate moment.

Learning how to recognize your intuition will require that you remove some of the obstacles keeping you from reaching the intuitive part of your mind. Some of these obstacles may be as simple as your saying, "That can't be true," when you get a hunch or a gut feeling. To become more attuned to your intuition, you first have to go inside yourself and observe your beliefs, thinking patterns, and responses. You also have to become sensitized to your own feelings so that you can distinguish and identify your intuitive states. Unless you are willing to use yourself as a point of reference, you will find that much of this material will be useless as far as developing intuition is concerned. You can focus your attention on the intuitive part of your mind, but you need to be aware that your intuition functions simultaneously with your other mental processes. Therefore, learning how to home in on it involves training your entire mind.

While there are aspects to intuitive perception that are fairly universal, your own intuition is unique. It communicates with you in an original, personal way. In becoming aware of how it speaks to you, or how it looks or feels, you will be training your mind to see, hear, and feel information that ordinarily lies below your threshold of consciousness. This means that as you become more comfortable with your intuition, you will have more of your total mind and brain power available to you. You can regard developing your intuition as a goal in itself, or you can look at it within the framework of learning how to make the most of all your mental abilities.

THE TEN-STEP PROGRAM

In organizing this book, we will be showing you how to become more familiar with the components that make up your intuition. We will also show you how this information fits into our Ten-Step Program. As you read and absorb this material, you can then apply it to the Ten-Step Program presented in chapter 15.

We concede that the idea of a Ten-Step Program for intuition seems to be a contradiction in terms because intuition does not occur in any sequential order. Nonetheless, our experience has shown us that it is possible to delineate some of the essential steps involved in developing it. This sequential format develops your intuitive abilities simply by making you more conscious of the mental process involved in intuitive thinking.

The Ten-Step Program is meant to serve as a guide. But if you do not find it helpful or find the sequential structure antithetical to your concept of intuitive functioning, then by all means do not feel compelled to use it. Explore the Ten-Step Program and other material in this book as you please. Use whatever is helpful to you.

In Part I, we will take a large subject—intuition—and give you ways to break it down into smaller, more manageable chunks that are easy to assimilate. Part II of this book will discuss intuition in education, psychology, and corporate training. Part III is a workbook section with exercises. In Part IV, we will present you with the opportunity to examine the larger field of which intuition is a part—namely, the mind, or consciousness. Breaking down intuition will make it easier for you to define and identify those times when it occurs in your life. Examining the subject in totality will give you an overview.

PART I

DEFINING AND IDENTIFYING YOUR INTUITION

*"My father always used to tell me
that I had no brains. You can't imagine how
relieved I am to find out that, in fact, I have three."*

—ANONYMOUS

CHAPTER 1

Knowing How You Know

DEFINE INTUITION FOR YOURSELF

The first step that you need to take to develop your intuition is to define it for yourself so that you can recognize intuitive states when they occur. This may seem elementary, but you will find that it is worth taking the time to make sure that you have a solid understanding of what intuition means to you. Remember that although there are characteristics that are common to intuitive perception, there is no objective standard for intuition. Your own intuition will look, sound, and feel different to you than it will to anybody else.

Defining intuition is so important that Robert Stempson begins his intuition development seminars at Programs for Human Development (PHD) in Greenwich, Connecticut, by asking participants to come up with their own definitions. These have included a way of knowing, a hunch, an inner radar, and a deeper self-definition. Julian Rowe, a participant in one of those seminars, defines intuition as "listening to yourself with love instead of with mind." He adds, "Intuition is when I *know* what I should do." For Andrew Moddafferi, another seminar participant, intuition is "in essence, the quiet voice of my deepest desires, the part of me that reveals my true purpose and unique function in the universe." Stempson defines intuition as "a very subtle voice, feeling, or sense that pokes at you, tugs you, and nags at you. It is important for you to identify how your intuitive 'voice' speaks to you and where it resides in your body. By

3

noticing it and practicing being connected to it, you can develop a strong intuition."

Defined by *Webster's Dictionary* as "the immediate knowing of something without the conscious use of reasoning," intuition is an integral part of your thinking process. It is also one of the least-understood aspects of how the mind works.

The word *intuition* is derived from the Latin root *in,* meaning "in" as it does in English, and *tueri,* which means "look at." This description gives you some indication of how the intuitive process works: By looking *in*ward, you can also *look at* some experience or issue and thereby see it from a different perspective. By reaching *into* your intuition—an aspect of your unconscious mind—you can come up with new insights or methods. By listening to the inner voice of your intuition, you can hear new answers.

Philosophers, musicians, artists, and scientists throughout the ages— from Archimedes to Einstein—have used intuition to create their greatest achievements. Albert Einstein, who fully acknowledged this powerful, nonrational element in himself, said, "The really valuable thing is intuition."

You don't have to be Albert Einstein to be an intuitive person. All of us possess intuitive abilities and can learn how to harness them to help us solve all kinds of problems—creative, emotional, intellectual, and practical.

EVERYDAY INTUITION

Intuition can also be simply described as "knowing without knowing how you know." We believe that you know more about your intuition than you think you do and that you have experienced it at least once in your life.

Have you ever had a hunch that you would get a job for which you had not yet applied, or that you would succeed at a project before it got under way? And then your hunch proved correct? Actor Stu Siegel walked into an audition for a Polaroid commercial and knew as soon as he sat down that he had the part. "I felt this warm feeling rush across my shoulders and chest," he says. "I felt completely relaxed and secure. Before I even opened my mouth, I knew I had it."

Perhaps you once had a strong feeling—for no apparent reason—that something terrible was going to happen. And subsequent events proved you were right. When Jeff De Chacon was getting ready to leave for a conference in Miami, his wife, Sonia, suddenly felt uncomfortable about his upcoming trip. The owner of a travel agency, she was not generally nervous in regard to travel. That time, though, "I had a very bad feeling," she says. "I couldn't explain it. I didn't want him to go but I couldn't tell him that. He wouldn't have listened to me. Instead, I just I told him to be careful." After an evening of partying a few nights later, her husband was a passenger in a car that crashed into the curved wall of the Fountainbleu Hotel in Miami. He was thrown eighteen feet into the air and was almost killed. "I should have paid attention to that feeling," Sonia says. "I should have insisted that he cancel his trip."

You may have had a gut feeling that you should simply pay attention to something. CBS News anchorman Dan Rather says that when Salman Rushdie's controversial novel *Satanic Verses* was signed to be published in the United States, a friend of his commented, "This book could be trouble." Says Rather, "From that first second, all kinds of flashes went off and my gut feeling was, 'This sounds right to me.' " Although he made a note to look into it, Rather didn't follow through on his intuition because of other pressing news. "I asked someone at CBS News to check it out and I should have followed up. But I didn't and I have been cursing myself ever since," he says.

Have you ever had a "flash" in which you suddenly saw an image of someone or of an event about which you had no rational knowledge? Stage manager Charlene Harrington was working on a film when she suddenly had a flash of her brother underneath a car. "I could see the car falling on him. When I finished work on the set, I rushed out to his place to see if he was okay," she says. "He was all right, but scared." While his sister was on the set, he had jacked up the car to change a flat tire and it had fallen on him.

If you recall having seen, heard, or felt something similar to the above examples—even if you rationalized it as a coincidental or insignificant occurrence—then you already know more than you think you know about intuition. In fact, even if you don't remember, recognize, or acknowledge any time in which you knew something that you could not explain logically, you have been using your intuition throughout your life. How do you know when someone whom you cannot see directly is staring at you? How do you know when someone is lying to you even when you have no factual evidence? These are all examples of how you use your intuition.

INTUITIVE AND RATIONAL THOUGHT WORK TOGETHER

Contrary to what you may believe at first, developing intuitive abilities does not require that you give up rational thinking. If you prefer analytical and rational methods, you may find it helpful to think of intuition as a form of coprocessing with reason. Intuition can provide you with another source of information that you can verify objectively. Dan Rather gives a good explanation of how that works. "I believe in hunches, gut feelings, and intuition," he says. "I also say to myself, 'A good reporter follows his hunches but doesn't report them.' " By that he means, a good reporter checks out his hunches to find out if the facts back them up. For Rather, this combination of hunch and logic proved invaluable in the 1970s when Henry Kissinger was national security adviser. Rather had been covering the White House and sensed that Kissinger wanted to be secretary of state. "Putting together various fragments of information and intuition, I asked myself, 'Do I think this is going to happen? If so, when and how is it going to happen?' In my mind, I sketched out a hypothesis." In his spare time, Rather made more than one hundred phone calls trying to disprove his hypothesis. "I couldn't disprove it," he recalls. "But I couldn't prove it either." Eventually, one of his sources got back to him and suggested that Rather check further into Kissinger's activities. Rather did. As the result of his hunch, followed up and confirmed by persistent legwork, Rather broke the story that Kissinger was going to become secretary of state.

INTUITION IS A NATURAL MENTAL ABILITY

Like the ability to read, speak, calculate, and think in logical form, intuition is a natural mental ability. You could even call it an intellectual skill. Like other skills, you can learn how to use intuition when you need it. When you want to balance your checkbook, you "go" to the part of your brain that knows how to perform arithmetic functions. Likewise, you can "go" to the part of your brain that works intuitively. The arithmetic and intuitive processes are different but all you basically do to activate your intuition is shift your point of focus or attention to the part of your whole-brain system that knows how to work intuitively. Then get out of its way and let it do the work.

Intuition works effortlessly. Relaxation is essential for you to receive strong impressions from your intuition. Throughout this book we will emphasize the need for you to be comfortable and relaxed to get the most out of the exercises.

YOUR UNTAPPED RESOURCES

Simply reading this book and absorbing some of its information on intuition will enable you to use more of your total mental capabilities. Not only will you become more conscious of how your intuitive processes work, but you will also gain new insight into other parts of your mind.

You will also find out why you may be having difficulty trusting your intuition. Learning to trust your intuition is one of the most important steps in developing it. You will discover how your values, attitudes, and fears may be holding you back. For example, the myth of "women's intuition" is a preconception that prevents many men from using their own intuitive abilities. In fact, men do experience all forms of intuition, although they usually refer to them as hunches and gut feelings. In the course of our research for this book we found no significant difference between men's and women's experiences of intuition, with one exception. Men tend to describe their intuition in terms of physical feelings, whereas women tend to talk about intuition in terms of emotional feelings.

THE CLIMATE OF OPINION IS CHANGING

In the past year alone, we have been asked by people in positions as diverse as an aide to South African Archbishop Desmond Tutu, a senior publishing executive, and a deep-sea diver how they can use their intuition on the job.

For many years, executives and managers have emphasized logical, fact-based decision-making skills. Today, even conservative professions such as finance accept the value of intuitive decision making, and many corporate seminars teach intuitive management approaches. "The turnaround in the last six or seven years is really quite amazing," observes Professor Michael Ray of the Stanford University School of Business. Management styles are changing to reflect a new respect for intuitive thinking. A worldwide business project to promote intuitive thinking and behavior as a business skill is under way. The International Management Institute (IMI) of Geneva is conducting the project to investigate ways in which executives can develop and use their intuition to come up with new concepts and strategies. The chairman of the IMI Intuition Research Project and its network, Dr. Jagdish Parikh, articulates this new trend in international business: "Computer technology has taken away a lot of what management used to be about: analytical, logical problem solving. Now, necessity is the mother of intuition. Not only is it a practical necessity in business, it is a compelling urge. Intuition is a gateway for businesspeople to get involved in the inner dynamics of the human system. Human potential in thinking and creativity remains untapped to a significant extent."

The Federal Reserve Bank of America has been exploring intuitive forecasting models, too. In 1988, the Fed published a research paper titled "The Seasonal Structure Underlying the Arrangement of Hexagrams in the *I Ching*," written by Larry J. Schulz and Thomas J. Cunningham. The *I Ching,* like tarot cards or astrology, uses intuitively derived information for determining possible outcomes to specific situations. In the Federal Reserve Bank paper, it was used to track agricultural and climatic conditions that could be of help to commodities traders. The Fed has not taken up casting the *I Ching* in its boardroom nor is not likely to in the future. But publishing this research is a sign of some acknowledgment that intuitive models can be useful in financial forecasting.

The following are other indications that the climate of opinion toward intuition is changing:

- Stanford University's School of Business teaches intuition as part of its "Creativity in Business" course taught by Michael Ray and Rochelle Myers.
- Surveys show that many chief executive officers rate intuition as one of their most prized creative assets.
- Government experiments on intuition show that intuitive skills can be learned.
- The scientific community is beginning to change its views on the role of intuition and consciousness. Cognitive psychologists, behavioral scientists, and biologists are starting to accept that mind, or consciousness, is a valid starting point for scientific research.

OLD VALUES DIE HARD

Despite these developments in business and science, for many people old values die hard. Most of us are conditioned not to make full use of our intuitive abilities. In fact, many of us are conditioned not to rely on them at all. From earliest childhood, we are praised and rewarded for performing mental feats involving logic, memory, and other measurable cognitive skills. The entire foundation of our traditional education system is predicated on the belief that these skills are superior to other mental abilities such as imagination and intuition, which can be experienced qualitatively but which do not lend themselves to the same kind of quantitative measuring as do memory and logic. In other words, intuition cannot be tested and measured in the same way as arithmetic can be tested.

Thus you learn early on in life to program your mind to use only a limited part of its ability in performing all its tasks. It's as though you were taught how to drive with the advisory to use only your frontal vision and to exclude your peripheral vision.

MULTIPLE INTELLIGENCES: DE BEAUPORT'S MODEL

Elaine de Beauport, who founded the Mead School for Human Development in Greenwich, Connecticut, has identified thirteen intelligences, including intuition. They are identified on page 10. "It's important to realize that intuition is an intellectual skill," says de Beauport. "It is a brain state that you can shift to. All brain states are natural." De Beauport teaches adults how to use their network of multiple intelligences in all areas of their lives. "By shifting your energy to another brain state, you can activate your brain's mental abilities," she says.

This may seem like a radical idea and, in fact, you were probably conditioned to believe otherwise. You may even have been cautioned against acting on your intuition. Many of us are advised or pressured to ignore, denigrate, or discount intuition as imagination, dream, or fantasy, but intuition is a valid way of getting information about the world. Intuitively derived information is important not only for its content but for the insight it provides into how the mind works.

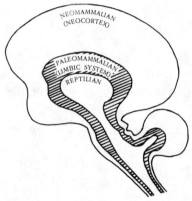

THE TRIUNE BRAIN—
USE IT OR LOSE IT

ELAINE DE BEAUPORT'S MULTIPLE INTELLIGENCE SYSTEM

NEOCORTEX

Rational
To perceive the reason for, the cause and effect of, sequential process, deduction, summary, and conclusion.

Associational
To perceive randomly, to expand information through random connection, to perceive connections between and among, to juxtapose, to improvise.

Visual/Imaginal
To perceive in images.

Intuitional
To know from within, direct knowing without the use of reason.

LIMBIC SYSTEM

Affectional
To be able to be affected by, to recognize and develop closeness with a person, place, thing, or idea.

Motivational
To be close to one's wanting or desire, to know what one is close to, and what moves one to action.

Mood—Pleasurable/Painful
To be able to create vibrational mood states and shift from and into vibrational states along a pleasure-pain range, from depression through anger to ecstasy.

Oral
To be aware of and able to guide vibrations connected with the oral area.

Nasal
To be aware of and able to guide vibrations connected with the nasal area.

Sexual
To be aware of, receive, originate, and give off vibrations of attraction.

REPTILIAN

Basic
To be able to move toward and away from, imitate, and inhibit other ideas, actions, processes, and people.

Routine
To be able to recognize, create, and sustain repetitive rhythm.

Ritual
To be able to recognize, create, and sustain repetitive rhythm enhanced by art, music, drama, thought, or action.

THREE BRAINS, NOT TWO

Elaine de Beauport bases her multiple intelligence theory on The Triune Brain Model (see p. 10) proposed by Dr. Paul MacLean. The chief of Brain Evolution and Behavior at the National Institute of Mental Health, Dr. MacLean discovered that all of us have three brains, not two, as was formerly known. He calls it the "triune," or "three-in-one," brain. Each brain system is physiologically and chemically different from the others. The left and right brain that people refer to are actually the left and right hemispheres of your top brain, the neocortex (see p. 12). Your other brains are the limbic system and the reptilian brain, whose functions are outlined below:

Your Triune Brain

- The reptilian, or primal brain creates patterns, habits, routines, and instinctive behavior, as well as your sense of territory and safety.
- The limbic system (paleomammalian), your most chemically active brain, is the site of origin for all your emotions.
- The neocortex (neomammalian) is divided into the left and right hemispheres, also known as the left and right brains, as described below.

All these brain systems give you information about the world around you. When we talk about whole-brain thinking this implies the use of your three brains. If you shut out your emotions (limbic), or ignore your need for safety (reptilian), or ignore your intuition (right neocortex), you won't have as much of your own brain power available to you. Logic (left neocortex) is important, but you cannot expect a single mental process to do everything. Although seventeenth-century French philosopher Blaise Pascal knew nothing about the triune brain, he wrote in his book *Pensées*, "Two excesses: to exclude reason, to admit nothing but reason."

LEFT AND RIGHT NEOCORTEX

Your left hemisphere is considered the dominant one by neuroscientists because it is the center of language. The left and right hemispheres are believed to function independently of each other but they maintain parallel

THE CREATIVE BRAIN
(The right hemisphere/left hemisphere theory
combined with the triune brain theory)

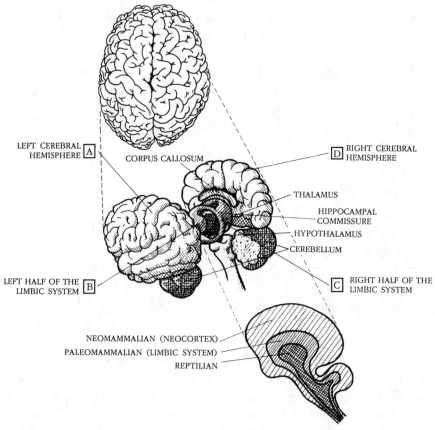

LEFT CEREBRAL
HEMISPHERE [A]

CORPUS CALLOSUM

[D] RIGHT CEREBRAL
HEMISPHERE

THALAMUS

HIPPOCAMPAL
COMMISSURE

HYPOTHALAMUS

CEREBELLUM

LEFT HALF OF THE
LIMBIC SYSTEM [B]

[C] RIGHT HALF OF THE
LIMBIC SYSTEM

NEOMAMMALIAN (NEOCORTEX)
PALEOMAMMALIAN (LIMBIC SYSTEM)
REPTILIAN

Copyright © 1988 Ned Herrmann

states of activity. That is, your left hemisphere can balance your checkbook while your right hemisphere listens to music.

Like the reptilian brain and limbic system, your right hemisphere is nonverbal. It cannot keep time or measure space although it can create and move mental images. Unlike the left hemisphere, which perceives information in steps and pieces, the right hemisphere perceives in wholes. If we asked you to come up with a mental picture of a shoe, your right hemisphere would give you an image of the whole shoe. Asked "What is a shoe?"

the left brain will give you its composite elements. It will tell you that a shoe is made up of a sole, heel, leather upper, laces, etc. It cannot give you a complete visual image of the whole shoe.

Because it lacks language, the right hemisphere often communicates to the left hemisphere directly through the corpus callosum, a mass of more than 200 million nerve fibers that connect the two hemispheres. Or your right hemisphere may signal the limbic system, and you may experience a physical sensation or an emotion that you describe as "a gut feeling" or "a sense." Whether it communicates directly to the left hemisphere or via the limbic system, the right hemisphere sends nonverbal data that your left hemisphere processes verbally. When you see someone for the first time and don't trust him, your intuition may be signaling your limbic system, which in turn is producing a gut feeling you translate as, "I don't know why but I don't trust this person." Language can be the left brain's attempt to express something that has no words. The left brain is limited because language cannot encompass nonverbal, nonsequential, intuitive perceptions.

It is important to realize that both your left and right brains are always working and that you can think intuitively and rationally at the same time. This may be hard to believe because you have been trained to think in terms of choices. For the most part, you have been educated to believe only what the left brain understands and perceives, which means that your thinking preferences are probably out of balance. To begin correcting that imbalance, it may be more useful for you to say, "My rational, logical mind sees it *this* way and my intuitive mind sees it *that* way." You can learn to allow your left brain put your intuitive insights into words and then let your feelings help you gauge whether your sense of the situation is right. In other words, your intuition can provide you with information to which your rational mind would not have access and your rational mind can put that information into words. Your rational processes can verify your hunches and gut feelings at the same time you bear in mind that you can make the wisest, most effective decisions when you have gathered the most information.

This whole-brain approach to thinking may be new territory for you, initially unfamiliar and uncomfortable. It requires that you surrender your beliefs in an either-or choice and begin to accept apparently contradictory ways of knowing. But whole-brain thinking allows you to take in more information than you would if you used only one processing system.

Remember, your brain does not approach receiving, storing, and retrieving information as a competitive experience and neither should you.

SUSPEND RATIONAL THOUGHT

Although rational thought is a necessary part of whole-brain thinking, to learn to use your intuition effectively, you must first suspend rational thought for a while so that you can relinquish your attachment to it as the only valid mental experience. This prospect may scare you. After all, you were probably brought up to believe that nonrational means irrational. Irrational, in turn, implies emotional, out of control, and possibly even crazy. Perhaps you told yourself that you were crazy when you had a flash, heard an inner voice, or felt a sensation in your gut about an event, person, or situation in which your intuitive impression conflicted with an external reality. Judging your nonrational mental abilities so harshly creates obstacles that prevent you from harnessing your mind's full power. Try instead to welcome, value, and nurture your intuition by suspending those judgments for a while. Let yourself find out how your intuition can help you even if you do not understand how or why.

FREE-FORM THINKING

Releasing some of your preconceptions about the need to be logical at all times gives you a chance to suspend the control of your conscious mind while you enter a mode of free-form thought, visualization, and association of images and ideas. Free form does not mean vague, disoriented, or disconnected, although that may be the interpretation your rational mind imposes. Actually, free-form thinking enables you to connect with other areas of the mind, the uncharted unconscious areas that are rich in image, symbol, and meaning.

Now you can bring to the surface of conscious perception new images and insights that can propel you into a new way of looking at the world. Visualize, if you will, a pond from whose depth and stillness rise intuitive impressions. Watch as they emerge and break the water's surface—your conscious awareness.

As you develop greater intuition, you can begin to examine how you view your own thinking process. Instead of pushing to come up with the right answer or fiercely concentrating on a problem to the point of frustration or anxiety, you can learn to let go, instead, to become still and focus on an inner compass point for directional guidance.

As you become more adept at doing this, you will develop a deeper respect for your mind's versatility, including its ability to locate and retrieve information in different forms. Images, feelings, thought forms, words, and picture sequences will start appearing with greater clarity so that your conscious mind can recognize and evaluate them. As your intuition sharpens, you will find it easier to relax and allow your intuitive mind to work in its own way, without consciously grasping for means to "help."

INTUITION FOR SKEPTICS

We like to think of this as a manual on intuition for skeptics. The whole-brain approach presented in this book is based on pioneering research in the fields of education, psychology, and neuroscience. It is based on the premise that intuition is a powerful mental tool you can learn to use without changing your personal beliefs or adopting a metaphysical framework.

KEEP A LIST AND ESTABLISH A POINT OF REFERENCE

As you read through the following chapters, keep a list of any intuitive experiences that you have had and note down any identifying characteristics. Consider these cases as points of reference so that you can learn to identify your own intuition. By recognizing an intuitive experience that has occurred in your life, you can acknowledge another such experience the next time it happens. This is one way for you to touch base with yourself and become familiar with your patterns of intuitive response.

As you become more familiar with the types of intuition that you have experienced, you will also begin to notice how frequently and in what form they tend to occur.

- You may find that you get intuitive flashes. An intuitive flash is a visual form of intuition in which an image passes through your mind very quickly.

- You may find that you process information from your intuition in the form of an inner voice. An inner voice is an auditory form of intuition.
- You may have gut feelings. A gut feeling is a kinesthetic form of intuition in which you get a strong physical sensation or an emotional feeling about someone or something.

In addition to processing intuitive information as a flash, a voice, or a gut feeling, you may find that you tend to have certain types of experiences that we will describe in the following two chapters. As you read about these different cases, we would like you to make comparisons with the types of intuition that you have experienced.

If you take the time to define and identify your intuition, and then use your list of experiences to establish a point of reference within yourself, you will find it easier to validate your future intuitive perceptions. You will be able to say, "Oh, this feels like the time when I had that gut feeling about my new boss," or "This dream looks and feels just like that other one that came true," or "The last time I heard that inner voice, I didn't pay attention and I regretted it." Instead of pushing your intuition aside, you will be more likely to value and trust it. Once identified, the intuitive experiences you have had in the past can serve as a bridge for those that will occur in the future.

MIND OVER MIND

Intuition is a gift, an inner power that you can turn to whenever you need it. Creating intuitive power is, in a sense, a process of learning how to use both conscious and unconscious awareness by transposing "mind over mind."

We often say that intuition functions like a satellite dish. It picks up signals from the unconscious that it then transforms into images, feelings, words, or impressions that it projects onto the screen of your conscious awareness. You can then decide how or if you want to act as a result of having looked at, heard, or felt those signals. As you become more proficient at tuning in, you will probably find that you rely more on your intuition for advice and creative ideas as do many scientists, business leaders, and artists.

CHAPTER 2

Intuitive Knowing with Precedent

To help you identify your intuition when it occurs, we are going to break it down into two categories: intuitive knowing with precedent and intuitive knowing without precedent. Intuitive knowing with precedent refers to intuitive states in which there is a precedent for your having acquired intuitive information through the five primary senses. Intuitive knowing without precedent accounts for those states of intuition in which there is no precedent for your having acquired information through your five senses.

Scientists and engineers often attribute their insights to sudden flashes of intuitive knowing with precedent. This type of intuition often synthesizes information that is stored in the unconscious memory and presents it to the conscious mind in a new and original way.

Dr. Robert Jarvik, inventor of the Jarvik-7 artificial heart, recalls how his intuition came into play when he was working on a power system for his artificial heart. "It used a miniature pump which had to perform in forward and reverse rotation," he says. Dr. Jarvik and an engineer developed a computer model to work with the power system. When Dr. Jarvik asked the engineer to use the model to check a certain type of design approach, he ran it on the computer. The computer predicted that the performance would be miserable. "I just knew that wasn't right," says Dr. Jarvik. "I said, 'I know it intuitively that it will work, so build it.'" The engineer reluctantly built the new model and found that "it worked much better than any of the other systems that we had built before," notes Dr.

Jarvik. And the engineer? "He was angry. He had worked for months on the previous computer models and couldn't see their limitations."

In cases where you simply know something but cannot explain how that information got into your brain, you are dealing with what we call intuitive knowing without precedent. For example, when Dr. Sherman Schachter, director of the New Hope Guild for Emotionally Disturbed Children in New York City, met a psychiatrist colleague at a cocktail party, he said, "I just saw your latest book. *The Anatomy of Dreams,* isn't it?" His colleague turned noticeably pale and said, "It hasn't been published yet. I haven't even named it. But yes, I have been thinking of using that title. And no, I had not discussed it with anyone."

Intuitive knowing with precedent is easy to accept. Even logical, conservative thinkers are prepared to acknowledge it and say that they have experienced it. They can explain how they got the intuitive information in a way that is acceptable to them. But these same logical, conservative thinkers have trouble accepting the idea that intuitive knowing without precedent exists, or that it is even possible because they cannot come up with a sensory-based explanation. However, both types of intuition fit *Webster's* definition of intuition: knowing without the conscious use of reasoning. In *The Penguin Dictionary of Psychology,* Arthur Reber provides the following definition of intuition:

> *Intuition.* A mode of understanding or knowing characterized as direct and immediate and occurring without conscious thought or judgment. There are two distinct connotations which often accompany this term: a) that the process is unmediated and somehow mystical; b) that it is a response to subtle cues and relationships apprehended implicitly, unconsciously.

The following illustrations further explore a definition of intuition.

SCIENTIFIC SOLUTIONS AND HYPOTHESES

Intuitive insights are behind many great scientific breakthroughs. Among the earliest intuitive insights on record is Archimedes' discovery of the principles of displacement while he was taking a bath. With a cry of "Eureka!" which means "I have found it!" in Greek, he jumped out of his tub and ran naked down the street, shouting the good news. Archimedes is remembered today not only for his discovery of the principles of displacement, but for the manner in which they came to him. The phrase "Eureka experience" has entered our language as one of the terms most commonly used to describe similar flashes of insight. Dr. Paul MacLean, the neurophysiologist who discovered the triune brain, says, "More often than not if you can plug a question into your noggin and then forget about it, you usually have this Eureka experience months later. That's what intuition is all about."

Aside from Archimedes in the bathtub, perhaps the best-known example of a scientist who intuitively perceived a theory is Albert Einstein. From the time he was sixteen, Einstein puzzled over what would happen if someone tried to capture a ray of light. According to several published accounts, Einstein daydreamed that he was riding on a beam of light that he followed in his mind's eye back to its point of origin. He then spent years formulating the mathematical equations that would elevate his daydream to the status of one of the most famous theories in the history of science: the theory of relativity. Einstein placed a high value on his intuition, and wrote, "The intellect has little to do on the road to discovery. There comes a leap in consciousness, call it intuition or what you will, and the solution comes to you and you don't know how or why."

Ned Herrmann, president of Applied Creative Services, Ltd., a company that organizes and presents whole-brain creativity workshops, comments, "Einstein was very intuitive. He was also highly visual and very much oriented toward his ability to visualize, such as riding on a beam of light." Herrmann believes that Einstein's intuition "was crucial in positioning him to have such a visualization." What's significant is that Einstein believed in his intuition. "He honored that part of himself instead of saying, 'That was ridiculous. Who the hell are we kidding here?' " Herrmann says.

You may not be able to tell whether it was creativity, intuition, or visual thinking that was primarily responsible for Einstein's coming up with the theory of relativity. Probably all three were, though. Visual intelligence and intuition are not the same but they do work simultaneously and in conjunction with each other to such a great degree that it is often impossible to separate them. Creativity and intuition are often inseparable, as well, but you can be creative without being intuitive, and vice versa. For example, imagination, often an element in creativity, is different from intuition. "Imagination is more an idea than it is a knowing. Intuition is a way of knowing," explains Herrmann. For Herrmann, an idea is something that you put together with other fragments into an identifiable whole, whereas "intuition is knowing without knowing that you know, without demanding proof of knowledge, but being very secure in the understanding that there's something there." Unlike an idea, intuition tends to resist analysis and rational probing. An intuitive insight or concept can often turn out to be an unexpected success when logical signs indicated that it would probably fail.

SIR ISAAC NEWTON'S INTUITION

Like Einstein, Sir Isaac Newton worked out his proofs and conducted his experiments to verify what he had first determined intuitively. Although Newton, who discovered the laws of gravity after observing an apple fall from its tree, is considered one of the foremost rationalists of the seventeenth century's Age of Reason, he also ranks among the most intuitive of Western scientists. Economist John Maynard Keynes delivered an essay called "Newton, the Man" in 1946, on the occasion of the Newton Tercentenary Celebrations at Cambridge University in England. He made the assertion that Newton owed his success to "his muscles of intuition." Keynes further noted that Newton's powers were "the strongest and most enduring with which a man has ever been gifted." For most people, intuition occurs instantaneously and is often over before you realize what has happened, but Newton had the ability to extend that period of immediate knowing. This, said Keynes, was one of the abilities that contributed to his genius. Newton "looked upon the whole universe and all that was in it as a riddle, as a secret which could be read by applying pure thought to certain evidence," Keynes wrote. A colleague once described Sir Isaac as "so happy in his conjectures as to seem to know more than he could possibly have any means of proving."

FOR COPPOLA, INTUITION IS A "MOMENTARY LIGHT"

Director Francis Ford Coppola relies on his "intuition, love, and feelings." "In every creative situation or in problem solving, it has always been the little momentary glimpse that encouraged me to keep looking in a certain direction," he explains. "I'm sure the solution is there since it had intuitively been presented to me. It comes up when I try to solve a serious problem in a movie. It's as if I'm in the dark and I suddenly put on a flashlight for just a second to see where the steps are. That little momentary light lets me see where things are. I can then work in the dark a little more because I've had a flash of the spatial set up. I feel more comfortable about working and devoting my resources to working because I have had a hunch that it was there. I've never had that intuitive kind of method turn out not to be valid."

Intuition provides Coppola with more than insight and method. Because he has learned to value it, intuition is a reference point, something he can rely on. "I'm comforted by the fact that it's there," he says.

A FORM OF UNCONSCIOUS PROCESSING

Dr. MacLean describes intuition as a form of unconscious processing. "Intuition is what the brain knows how to do when you leave it alone," he says. As a young man, he once tried to draw a squirrel monkey. "I'd get closer and closer to what I wanted and then the next day it would be terrible," he remembers. "One day I was explaining something about the squirrel monkey to a colleague. I was blind in my right eye for sixteen years and I'm therefore not used to using my left hand. I had a piece of chalk in that hand and I drew a picture of a squirrel monkey on the blackboard as I was talking. The drawing was just right. Isn't it amazing that the brain is smarter than we are," he concludes. It is important to respect the brain's natural ability, Dr. MacLean observes. "It's awfully important to have information coming from your inside world at the same time as things are coming from the outside because if you don't, you're not an individual."

Dr. MacLean was able to effortlessly draw that squirrel monkey because his unconscious mind had absorbed and processed information about it prior to his unsuccessful attempts to draw it and prior to the intuitive experience that resulted in a successful drawing. He points out that although the information you need is stored somewhere in your brain, you do not actually remember it. Nor can you retrieve it from your memory as you would a name or a date. You must let go and allow your intuition to take over and do the job. "What you're talking about here is your experience plus your reading, of which you very often will forget the specifics. You are using your intuition," he notes. "There has got to be some precedent for something if you're going to be intuitive about it."

DOES INTUITION MAKE YOU UNCOMFORTABLE?

If you have responded to some of the above examples of intuition by calling them coincidences, or lucky mistakes, you may be one of those people who are simply uncomfortable with the idea of intuition. If so, you may wish to take a few minutes to consider the following questions:

- How do you respond to explanations that do not follow sequential or logical form?
- Do you tend to reduce events to statistical probabilities?

If so, then please bear in mind that your response is only a sign of your mental preference. Different people have different preferences of thinking style, so bear in mind that yours is not the only valid response. As noted earlier, rational thinking is just one of many mental processes functioning in your whole-brain system at any time.

Intuitive knowing is qualitatively different from other mental processes. It reflects your sensitivity to internal messages as well as to your external environment and can be described as an openness to flashes of insight that come as wholes. In terms of brain activity, it's a combination of chemicals called neurotransmitters and neurological, electrical connections called synapses that form a complete concept or thought.

If your sense of reason has been disturbed by our examples and interpretations thus far, you may find that you feel even more uncomfortable as you read the next chapter. There, we will present you with examples of intuitive knowing without precedent: that is, cases where there is no explanation for someone's having acquired the intuitive information through the five primary senses. Many people are skeptical and wary when first encountering this aspect of intuition because there is no rational explanation for how it occurs. Dr. Jarvik voices this skepticism in the following comment: "There's a line that you cross here between what is an intuitive understanding, a valid mental process, and what enters the realm of predictiveness where there's no relationship between the information and the prediction. That gets into something about which I feel very distrustful and skeptical."

But the part of your mind that believes such knowing to be impossible is the part of your mind for which it is impossible. The sequential, analytical left neocortex finds it hard to accept as valid any mental process that has no logical ground.

CHAPTER 3

Intuitive Knowing without Precedent

Have you ever experienced an instantaneous knowing, sudden recognition, or a strong feeling about a person or an event? Or have you simply "known" something without being able to explain how you acquired that information?

As registrar for the American Federation of Arts, Carol O'Biso was invited to address a conference at the Metropolitan Museum of Art. The coordinator told her that she would be speaking with another registrar whom she had never met, a woman named Eileen McConnell. O'Biso was chatting with some colleagues when a group of people she had never seen entered the room. She walked up to one of the women and extended her hand, saying, "Hi, Eileen. I'm Carol O'Biso." "I thought you didn't know her," the coordinator said, staring hard. O'Biso remembers, "I felt myself getting sweaty and thought, 'Jesus, I don't know Eileen. What did I just do?' Then Eileen said, 'That's okay. I'm very intuitive, too.' "

Arianna Stassinopoulos was doing research for her biography *Maria Callas: The Woman behind the Legend* when she woke up in the middle of the night. "I suddenly knew that Callas had undergone an abortion," she recalls. "I had not seen it written anywhere nor had anyone told me or even hinted at it. But in this state of what I call 'natural knowing' I realized that it was true. A while later, when I was having lunch with Callas's agent's wife, she mentioned a trip to London that Callas had taken. 'Was that the time she had her abortion? I asked. How did you know?' she exclaimed. Naturally, I was not about to reveal my sources!"

In cases like the above, there are simply no sensory-based precedents to explain how the information was acquired. This is why we categorize these experiences as examples of intuitive knowing without precedent.

INTUITIVE OR PSYCHIC?

Intuitive knowing without precedent can also be called psychic intuition. The difference between this type of intuitive knowing and psychic knowing is a question of degree. We believe that psychic knowing is a stronger, finely honed intuitive sense. But it is nonetheless a natural mental ability. In fact, the two types of intuition, with and without precedent, are so closely aligned that it is often hard to tell for sure which one you have experienced.

"It's very hard to separate intuition as it's normally described from its psychic counterpart," says physicist and author Russell Targ. "Intuition is normally thought of as a sum total of everything that we've experienced in our life and is stored in unconscious processes. Then that becomes available to us. It's as though your consciousness is a peel of the orange and all the data that comes in is the inside of the orange. So you have experience, which is data acquisition, and on the outside you have analysis of that data. The acquisition and storing is something of which you are not particularly aware." Targ believes that "intuition can have the two parts, the unconscious processing, which is what your intuition is most of the time, and psychic functioning."

Psychic is a loaded word for many people, implying mysterious, supernatural connections. Yet *Webster's Dictionary* defines it initially as, "of the psyche or mind" and then as "beyond known physical processes." The operative word in this definition is *known*. Human knowledge of this domain is limited, just as human knowledge of planetary movement was limited during the time of Copernicus. Standard sequential explanations for psychically derived information do not work because we simply don't yet have adequate information to explain how such things occur. The scientific data have not caught up with the phenomena. "Science is in its infancy," observed Albert Einstein, who also said that he believed in mental telepathy and in the existence of a reality outside the one that we presently understand.

Is psychic functioning an aspect of intuition? Both psychic and intuitive knowing conform to *Webster's* definition, "knowing without the conscious use of reasoning." But the source of that information, which *Webster's* defines as "beyond known physical processes," is what semantically differentiates psychic from intuitive perception. The idea that you can know about an event before it happens or describe an object that you have never physically seen may well defy your understanding of how space and time are measured. But instead of saying "that's impossible," you may wish to consider the possibility that space and time themselves are bounded by your ability to conceptualize them. Because your right neocortex (the top brain) does not measure space and time, is it not also possible that your brain's intuitive abilities can function outside the space-time continuum that only your left neocortex perceives?

Rather than blame the phenomenon of intuitive or psychic knowing for failing to conform to our knowledge of space and time, we need to redefine our notion of space and time. "Evidently modern physics is incomplete and inadequate to describe that kind of activity," Targ says. "There's no doubt that there's something incomplete about modern physics."

Intuitive knowing without precedent often concerns something personal to you. If you have a strong gut feeling that you should not drive on a particular day and you ignore it only to have an accident, then you failed to pay attention to your intuition. When you find yourself suddenly have a strong gut feeling about someone you have never seen, you are probably experiencing intuition with a strong psychic component. While it is acceptable to sense things about yourself, it can be frightening to get a flash of psychic information about someone you don't know. Ann Hutchins, a manicurist, remembers the time a customer was talking about going on vacation with her husband. "I knew as soon as she said she was going that her husband would not be coming back with her. Three weeks later, I found out that her husband had died on that trip. I felt creepy." An intuitive person may experience similar psychic incidents from time to time, but a psychic person experiences them on a regular basis. He can also make a conscious decision to use this finely honed intuition at will. Certainly, the number of people in this country who openly acknowledge having had some personal psychic experience is growing. In the 1986 study by the National Opinion Resource Council (NORC) in Chicago, 67 percent of Americans surveyed reported having had psychic experiences compared to a 1973 poll by NORC in which the number was 58 percent.

Stanley Krippner, an author and professor of psychology at Saybrook

Institute, supports the inclusion of psychic input into any overall discussion of intuition. He warns that our cultural and social conditioning make it difficult for us to accept such phenomena. "Some cultures will encourage people to act on hunches, to pay attention to dreams, to look within for an answer," he says. "These are processes that we lump under the term intuition because they do not follow the cause and effect, logical, step-by-step reasoning that we promulgate in our culture. Intuition comes to us through some arational process. If it proves valid, then we have made some sort of breakthrough that we can attribute to intuition."

DEMYSTIFYING INTUITIVE KNOWING WITHOUT PRECEDENT

Now that we have discussed what you don't know about this form of intuition, how can you demystify it so that the intuitive process becomes easier for you to work with? Again, the easiest way to start is to define and identify this type of intuition by breaking down this larger subject into smaller units of experiences that share certain components. Continue using the following true cases of psychic intuition as a point of reference to help you define and identify your own. Continue making your list of similar experiences that you have had, or think you may have had in the past, no matter how insignificant or trivial they may have seemed to you at the time. Perhaps you were thinking about someone to whom you wanted to speak and that person called you, or you had a feeling that something was going to go wrong with your car and it did. Instead of ignoring or discounting events like this, take note of them. They are the basis of defining and identifying your intuition.

HUNCHES WITH AND WITHOUT PRECEDENT

When talking about intuition, most people say they have hunches and gut feelings. Hunches can occur with and without precedent. So can gut feelings, which generally take the form of a go-ahead signal or a warning. While you cannot always tell for sure which type of intuitive knowing is at work when you get a hunch or a gut feeling, in some instances it is pretty clear:

- *With Precedent.* Engineer David Haysom was crossing a busy street in San Francisco when, he recalls, "I had a strong feeling that something was coming at me." As Haysom grabbed his nephew and pulled him across the street, two cars collided right where he had been standing. Haysom offers this explanation: "I must have unconsciously picked up signals that something dangerous was about to happen. Perhaps out of the corner of my eye I noticed something strange or heard the squeal of brakes."

- *Without Precedent.* George Garcia, who is completely deaf, cannot attribute his survival to hearing people apply their brakes. Garcia was crossing an empty street at 1 A.M. He recalls that "the light was green but as I started to walk I felt as if someone was pulling me back and I stopped." A car suddenly zoomed around the corner and through the intersection, barely missing Garcia. Had he not sensed that he was in danger, he surely would have been hit.

For Garcia, intuition is the sense that compensates him for his lack of hearing. "Deaf people have to become intuitive," Garcia explains in sign language. "From the time they are babies, hearing people pick up sounds all around, which gives them information. A deaf baby has nothing coming into his ears. He has no words. He has to point to show what he means." Because deaf people do not hear, "they feel and they have to develop a sixth sense to make up for the one that is missing."

PAYING ATTENTION TO HUNCHES

You can probably remember feeling that something was going to happen at least once in your life. Along with that feeling, you may have had a sense of urgency. One of the characteristics of a hunch is the sense that you have to act on it right away. One example of a common, everyday hunch is the feeling that you need to call someone immediately. When you do, he tells you that he was just thinking about you and tells you something that you need to know at that moment. Another type of everyday hunch is the feeling that you have to go someplace immediately. Lee Paxson, a retired entertainer, had been trying to borrow a book from her local library for several months. Every time she went to the library, the book was out. Although she had seen it listed in the library catalog, she had never seen it on the shelves. One morning, she had a hunch that this particular book was sitting on one of the library shelves. She told her husband, "I have to go to the library right now. That book I have been looking for is on the shelf."

"How do you know that?" he asked.

"I just 'saw' it in my mind's eye," she said, "and I'd better rush over there."

When she got to the library, the book was right where she had mentally seen it. The librarian told her that it had come back that morning, just a few minutes before Paxson had received the flash about where to find it!

The strongest element of a hunch is the sense that you had better act on it immediately. Many people have told us that when they have ignored their hunches they often have regretted it later on.

It's no mystery that hunches are the basis of good detective work in real life as well as in fiction. Former New York City police officer Jane Finnegan insists that hunches are an essential part of staying alive on the streets. "Male cops won't discuss this, but you don't just use your five senses. As a cop, you use this intuitive sense all the time," she says. Finnegan once walked up to a man and said, "You've got a gun." Her suspect was not behaving in a suspicious manner and there was nothing she could point to that led her to single him out from the two hundred other people milling around on a Harlem street corner. "I don't know how I knew but I knew this guy had a gun, and I was right," she says. Another hunch enabled Finnegan to locate a suspected drug dealer in hiding. "Suspects seem to have more relatives than the Kennedys and there's no way that you can figure out logically which one will be housing your man. In an extended family a suspect might have fifteen aunts," she says. While working on one case, Finnegan came into work one morning and looked at a long list of one suspect's relatives. "I said, 'Let's go visit this aunt.' The suspect was sitting there eating breakfast. He asked, 'How did you know where to find me?' 'That's a good question,' I said. How could I pick the right one out of those fifteen aunts? There's no logical way," Finnegan says.

People who deal with money, whether by trading, investing, or gambling, frequently talk about their hunches. In the case of someone who has years of experience, it's pretty hard to say whether a particular hunch is a seasoned judgment call or whether it's a form of intuitive knowing without precedent. In the case of one inexperienced investor, however, playing a hunch without precedent paid off. Computer salesman Theo Alexander and his wife had several thousand dollars invested in the stock market. For several months, they had been considering selling their shares. Neither of them had financial training or inside knowledge of the market. One afternoon, Theo told his wife to locate the stock certificates because, he said, "We have to sell them today."

"Why?" she asked.

"I have a hunch we'd better do it today."

"Do you know something in particular?"

"No. It's just this feeling," he said.

Theo unloaded their stocks by closing time that day, picking up a $2,000 profit. Selling them the next day, when those stocks plunged sharply, would have yielded a comparable loss.

At the Stanford University School of Business, Professor Michael Ray often suggests that students sharpen their hunch abilities by standing in front of an elevator bank and sensing which elevator will arrive first or where you will find a parking place in a crowded mall. Henry Schwartz, a banker who maintains that he "doesn't believe in that stuff," found nevertheless that he was able to get a hunch when he needed one naturally. Schwartz, who lives in New York City, where parking places are scarce, had been circling a block for half an hour in the middle of the night, when, he says, "I decided to use my intuition. Suddenly, I had a hunch that I would find a parking place four blocks away, even though that particular street has a hospital on it and is usually impossible for parking. I drove right over and there it was!"

Sometimes a hunch can propel you in a direction you would not ordinarily go. It can be so strong that you feel as if someone is telling you something, or as if you are being guided to follow an invisible compass. Al Siebert, a psychologist who is also the publisher of the *Survivor Personality* newsletter in Portland, Oregon, found that following a strong hunch changed his beliefs about the power of intuitive thinking. Siebert says that his training as a traditional psychologist did not include any preparation for what happened to him when he sat up in bed wide awake one morning at four o'clock with a strong urge to go to the beach. Siebert put on his clothes and rain slicker and was starting out the door when he thought, "Hey, why don't you take your knife and leather gloves with you?" He never carried a knife and only wore his thick gloves for gardening, but he followed his hunch and set out equipped. When he got to the coast, he turned right and started walking north. But as he walked, he remembers, "I kept wondering why I was here. I kept having the feeling that I was going the wrong way. The feeling wouldn't stop so I turned around and walked in the opposite direction. At that point, I knew I was being led to something but I didn't know what it was." Siebert scoured the shore looking at the debris when he saw something move in the surf. As he got closer, he saw a dark bird with an orange beak entwined in deep-sea fishing tackle. One wing couldn't flap and it could not move its legs. The plastic line was deeply cinched up all around its neck and body and there was a sinker and hook dangling around it. Smiling to himself, Siebert took out his pocket knife, opened up the small blade, put it in his mouth, put on his leather gloves, and crouched down. "I extended good feelings to the bird. I touched it a little bit, then put my left hand around its neck gently and it relaxed. Then I took the knife and very carefully cut the strands around the bird," Siebert recalls. It took him about five minutes to free the bird, which scrambled out to the waves and paddled away.

Siebert pondered the incident for a long time. "I was aware as I was walking up the beach that some intelligent force in the universe had been able to scan out and locate me a few blocks from the beach and lead me to the bird so it could be freed."

GUT FEELINGS

Like a hunch, a gut feeling has a predictive element: Your "gut" is telling you that something is going to happen. Many people say that when they get a gut feeling it is usually a first impression about someone or a warning. Former police officer Jane Finnegan recalls driving into work one afternoon listening to the news on the radio. She was reassured because it sounded like the streets were calm. "But by the time I had driven about half an hour, I had this unbelievable feeling, which was saying, 'Don't go to work. Don't go to work.'" Finnegan was crossing the Williamsburg Bridge from Manhattan into Brooklyn when the feeling got so strong that she went to the first phone she found, called in, and said that she was taking an emergency day off. Then she went home. That night there was a bad riot in Brooklyn where her partners and some other friends were seriously injured.

By paying attention to her gut feeling, Finnegan believes that she avoided being seriously injured that night. On the other hand, Angela Carpentier talked herself out of her bad feeling about driving to the beach with disastrous consequences. Carpentier had called her friend Gillian Conner the night before to say, "I have a very bad feeling that I should not drive tomorrow." The next day, however, she said, "I don't know what came over me. It was just a strange feeling but I feel okay now. Let's go." Conner tried to persuade her to trust her gut feeling and stay home, but Carpentier said she didn't want to give into it. Instead of calling it a "strange feeling," she began to call it a "stupid feeling" and insisted that she and Conner go to the beach as planned. As they were driving there, a drunk driver ran through a stoplight, crashing into Carpentier's side of the car. She was thrown from the vehicle and was taken to the hospital in a coma. She remains paralyzed to this day.

Both Finnegan's decision not to go to work and Carpentier's decision to drive show a clear connection between a gut feeling and an event. There are times, however, when you pay attention to your gut feeling and do not, therefore, verify the consequences. You may have avoided an accident or stayed out of trouble but you have no way of knowing. Judy Haims notes that when you have a strong gut feeling that is signaling you not to do something, only you can decide whether or not to trust it. She recalls one time when her teenage son wanted to go boating at night with a group of friends. "I knew that he was careful and a good swimmer and normally I would have said yes. But I had a sense of swirling darkness, fog, and icy water and I felt a chill go down my spine." Haims told him that she didn't want him to go and explained that she had this feeling, although there was no logical reason for it. He told his friends and they all decided not to go. "We'll never know if my intuition prevented an accident," she says, "but I think in a case like this you're better safe than sorry."

GUT FEELINGS HAVE A KINESTHETIC COMPONENT

Unlike a hunch, which takes the form of immediate knowing, a gut feeling has a strong kinesthetic component. You may get a physical sensation somewhere in your body or have an emotional response. Although the term gut feeling describes a sensation somewhere in the abdomen or solar plexus, you may find that your gut feelings are located in another part of your body. Your fingers may tingle or your throat may suddenly get warm.

Several men have told us that their gut feeling is a sensation around their chest area. George Garcia, the deaf man who had a hunch that he should get out of the street, says that his are located in his chest and the back of his head. Sharon Weathers, a children's-book editor, says that during moments of intuitive insight, she has felt "slightly nauseated in the chest and abdominal area." While in a Paris supermarket, Weathers had this gut feeling as she approached the cash register. "I knew when I had this feeling that my wallet would be gone. And when I looked in my purse, it was."

A SCIENTIFIC THEORY ABOUT GUT FEELINGS

Have you ever met someone for the first time and although you had no reason to dislike him something in your stomach felt weird? Even though you couldn't explain it, you had a gut feeling not to trust that person. Ernest Rossi, the author of *The Psychobiology of Mind-Body Healing,* believes that when you have a gut feeling "you are picking up cues and getting molecular responses." The specific molecule in question may, in fact, be a neuromodulator in your brain called cholecystokinin, or CCK. Candace Pert, chief of Brain Biochemistry at the National Institute of Mental Health, was the first person to theorize that CCK may be the signal for what we call gut responses.

CCK is a hormone that is active in the digestive process but it also connects with a nerve that modulates learning and memory in the brain. "CCK is released from the large intestine when we've had a good meal and the fatty acids and the amino acids hit the small intestines," Rossi says. An immediate effect is that CCK connects with one of the nerves that, in effect, modulates memory and learning. CCK is an example of an informational substance. "In an evolutionary sense, it's important," Rossi maintains, "because when we have had a good digestion, the organism needs to send some message up to the brain to say, 'That was a good meal. Do another one like that.'"

When you feel an emotion, the first place you usually feel it is in your gut. Seconds later, you feel heat in your cheeks as you begin to blush, possibly because other informational substances such as vasoactive intestinal peptide (VIP) released from your gut dilates those blood vessels in your face. Informational substances such as CCK and VIP can activate the brain where they trigger specific receptors, affecting moods and emotional responses. "When you meet someone and get that gut feeling, the body will stir and you will say, 'I feel terrible.' That's how the information gets up to your conscious mind." You may say, "I don't know why but there is something about this person that I don't like." You connect with the kinesthetic element in the body first; your conscious mind picks it up afterward.

FIRST IMPRESSIONS ARE GUT FEELINGS, TOO

First impressions and deciding whether or not to trust someone when you first meet him is almost always a gut decision. How can you logically make a determination about someone whom you have never before seen? Trusting those first gut impressions can be critically important, especially when you have to make a decision to proceed with a particular job or client.

That discomfort can serve as an early warning signal, if you pay attention to what it is telling you. Les Hogan, production coordinator for a small Hollywood movie company, spent a lot of his time dispatching trucks and vans around town to pick up, off-load, and strike various movie sets. "I used to work with one particular trucking company," Hogan says. "The dispatcher there was always polite, helpful, and friendly. No negative vibes, you know what I mean? He was always ready to send someone out at a strange hour to help me out, but I never trusted him. I couldn't figure out why since he was one of the nicer people I dealt with at work." But when an impending teamsters' strike threatened, Hogan's contact suddenly said, "You know these Hollywood producers make millions and we don't get any cut in their profits. So if we have to break a few fingers or a few legs to get in on some of that, well, we have to do what it takes." Hogan got off the phone as soon as he could and sat there, his hands shaking. "I knew from the first I shouldn't trust him," he says.

Hogan was not in direct or immediate danger. He realized his initial sense of wariness about the dispatcher may even have protected him. "Had I trusted that guy because he was nice, I might have started hanging out with him," he says. "That gut feeling told me to stay away."

LEARN TO LOCATE YOUR GUT FEELINGS

Learning to locate your own gut response is essential if you are to be able to identify and acknowledge your intuition. One way is for you to pick a time when you have had a gut feeling and observe your mental image of that experience. How did you look? How did you sound? What physical sensations did you have in your body? What emotions did you feel? How was this particular gut feeling similar to others that you have had? The key to developing your intuition is developing your self-observation skills. The more specific you can be in describing the components of your gut feelings, the easier it will be for you to acknowledge and trust them in the future.

SYNCHRONICITY AND DÉJÀ VU: A GLITCH IN TIME

Synchronicity is a spontaneous physical event preceded by an intense emotional or mental activity about that person or event. For example, you can't stop thinking about someone whom you haven't seen in twenty years. You miss your regular train and that person suddenly appears behind you. Such combinations of thoughts, feelings, and dreams that connect to physical events can be explained logically by calling them coincidence. But anyone who has experienced synchronicity, the term first used by Swiss psychologist Carl Jung, knows that there is something startling about the quality of the mental or emotional event that precedes the physical event.

Synchronicity and déjà vu, the feeling that you have lived through something once before and know what is about to happen, both feel like a glitch in time. For a moment, time seems to distort. It may slow down or expand. Déjà vu is particularly common among children, so common that most of us forget how often we encountered it, as we have forgotten many other intuitive perceptions from our childhood. As with synchronicity, déjà vu confounds your sense of chronology by seeming to superimpose a future event onto your awareness of the present. It's as if you have suddenly become a piece in a puzzle that only you know how to insert to complete the picture.

Synchronicity occurrences are particularly dramatic and often give you the eerie feeling that you have stepped into the twilight zone. Charlene Harrington was working as a stage manager on the set of the television series "As the World Turns" when suddenly she began to think of a colleague whom she had not seen for five years. "The thought that came to me so strongly out of the blue was, 'Is she still alive?' It was weird," Harrington says. No one at the television station had spoken about her for several years. She seemed to have disappeared from work one day five years earlier after learning that she had cancer. Harrington had no compelling reason to suddenly think about her now. "The most compelling thing about this thought was that I could not get it out of my mind," Harrington recalls. "It haunted me and I kept asking myself, 'Why am I thinking about this woman?' " One week later, she went to the airport to assist her cousin who was traveling with a small child. They had been waiting for over an hour for the flight to be called when an airport worker came over to her and said, "Aren't you waiting to board flight 217? The gate has been changed to gate five." Harrington obtained a special pass to get through the security checkpoint so that she could walk to gate five, which turned out to be at the far end of the terminal. "I walked to the far end and when I got there the gate was dark and empty," she recalls. "A woman wearing a headscarf was sitting in the corner. She turned around and it was my former colleague, the woman about whom I had been thinking all week. I got chills."

There can be a serendipitous quality to a synchronicity experience, as Elizabeth Boyer found when she was broke and out of work. When a newspaper blew against her legs, she picked it up and saw that her former boss was now working at a company in town. "Isn't that interesting?" she thought, going to a phone booth to call him. "It's so nice to hear from you," he said. "I didn't know who I would find to work with me here. Can you work for me again?"

"The unconscious does not have the same timetable as the conscious mind," observes Genevieve Geer, a Jungian psychotherapist. "We do get strange things that happen. Everyone has had a clock that stops when somebody dies. I don't know why."

Synchronicity, it seems, has its own causality. "It threatens something very profound," Geer notes. "It threatens logical, linear thinking. If you want the basis of Western thinking since Descartes, it is 'I think therefore I am.' This is very linear, but it is no longer going to be our main mode of processing information. The rest of psychology is catching up with Jung, who first talked about synchronicity."

Whether you interpret synchronicity as significant or merely coinciden-tal will depend a great deal on your own thinking style. As we have explained in connection with other intuitive experiences, if you are very logical you may be disturbed by our description of synchronicity because it threatens your model of reality. Psychologist Dan Miller observes, "The process is one of acceptance. You can see two events going on and say they have nothing to do with each other. Or you can say, yes, although they seem to be unrelated, I know that they are related. My intuition tells me that."

DREAMS

Dreams can have both kinds of intuition, those in which the precedent of acquired information is apparent and those in which it is not. As we mentioned in the previous section, a dream can signal synchronicity or contain other precognitive aspects to it.

Television news producer Judith Rogers awoke one morning at six o'clock, shivering and frightened. She had just dreamed about the final scene of Sam Peckinpah's movie *Deliverance* in which the hand of a drowned body is seen clutching at the air while the river swirls around it. She had not seen that movie recently, nor had she reacted strongly to it at the time. She had made no plans to travel or go swimming, nor could she find any connection between events in her life and the dream that she described as "disturbingly sharp and penetrating." Arriving in the newsroom, she learned it was a slow news day but joked that "someone famous will die this afternoon and it will get busy." At 2:30 P.M., someone called out for her to read the news wire: Sam Peckinpah had just died.

Although many people say that intuitive dreams have a special clarity, some dream researchers believe that mundane, boring dreams can contain as much intuitive material as do startling, lucid dreams. But you are more likely to notice intuitive information in lucid dreams because their sharp visual and emotional quality makes them more memorable. If you remember a dream, you are more likely to ponder its meaning and discover its intuitive elements. However, the quality of the dream does not indicate whether you have received valid intuitive information. That has to come from verification. In other words, the dream has to come true.

In a lucid dream, the images tend to be brighter, larger, or in clearer focus, and you are often aware that you are watching the dream even as you are participating in its unfolding. In such a dream, you are the writer, director, starring actor, and the audience. When you awaken, you know that this particular dream was different and important. Albert Santiago, an accountant, was looking for an apartment when he dreamed that he was in a house that had interior windows and a huge bed. "I was talking to a man in the dream. He was tall with a cleft chin and he was wearing red. He told me he was sad because he was guarding the crosses." Five days later, Santiago answered an ad in the newspaper and found himself at the same apartment he had seen in his dream. It had the same interior windows he had dreamt about, windows that belonged to a section of the house that used to be the porch. The apartment had the same huge bed about which he had dreamed, and the landlord, who was wearing red and white, was the same man he had seen in his dream. Santiago says, "Down the hill was a cemetery and I understood why I had dreamed about him guarding the crosses. The thought of being so close to the cemetery depressed me and I didn't rent the apartment."

Like gut feelings, dreams can sometimes warn you of impending trouble. As with a gut feeling, when you pay attention to a disturbing dream and act on it, you may never know if it would have come true. Dorothy Laub had a dream that warned her about one of her friends. "It was a terrible, terrible dream where she was on a hill calling to me. I knew if I went to her something horrible would happen. The dream was so vivid that I discontinued my friendship with her."

Dreams can offer intuitive solutions. One of the best-known examples is the story of Friedrich August Kekulé von Stradonitz, a nineteenth-century Flemish chemistry professor who had been pondering the structure of the benzene molecule. In a dream he later described as "acute," Kekulé dreamed of dancing atoms that formed a snakelike chain. The snake then grabbed its own tail and continued to spin. Kekulé wrote up his discovery in scientific terms and also described how he first saw the solution. His advice to fellow scientists? "Let us learn to dream, gentlemen."

Elias Howe had been trying to design the sewing machine for several years. His first attempts failed because he had placed the eye in the middle of the needle. One night he dreamed that he was taken prisoner by a savage tribe whose leader threatened to kill him unless he finished his machine immediately. From the terror of his nightmare, Howe noticed that the savages' spears had eye-shaped holes in the tips! Howe jumped out of bed and immediately carved a needle based on the images of the spears he had dreamed.

Women scientists and inventors have dreamed solutions, too, say Ethlie Ann Vare and Greg Ptacek, authors of *Mothers of Invention: From the Bra to the Bomb, Forgotten Women and Their Unforgettable Ideas*. Eighteenth-century mathematician Maria Agnesi, whose formula for duplicating the volume of a cube is called "the witch of Agnesi," solved mathematical problems while sleeping. Agnesi would write them down immediately upon awakening and would then be surprised later on to see how accurately she had put down her conclusions in that half-awake state.

Whether you are dreaming of snakes, a place to live, or a tribe of savages, "the unconscious is always creating. It's very generous," says Ernest Rossi, the author of *Dreams and the Growth of Personality.* "New things are being created at every moment, especially in our dreams. Often when you go to sleep you have a tough problem. The next morning, the solution seems obvious to you. What's the big deal? The big deal is that your unconscious had to process it."

Becoming aware of your personal dream symbols and learning how to remember dream elements help bring all aspects of your unconscious, including your intuition, into focus. Thus learning how to work with your dreams can help you become more aware of your intuition. "Due to the very neuropsychology of dreams we are forced to be creative every night," says Stanley Krippner, coauthor of *Dreamworking,* who conducted a dream research project at Brooklyn's Maimonides Medical Center in the 1970s. "When we have REM [rapid eye movement] periods at night the lower brain centers begin to fire neurons more or less randomly. These neurons hit visual centers in the brain and the brain has to make sense out of this stimulation. It does this by pulling together memories, images that we have from our past and putting them together in more or less creative ways. We are forced to pull together information to meet the physical demands of the dream process. This type of stimulation, synthesis, and recall is very important to intuition."

Krippner recommends working with dreams to enhance problem-solving abilities and creativity, citing studies showing that people who recall dreams and do work with them score higher in certain creativity and problem-solving tests. "Nothing works for everybody and one cannot guarantee that working with dreams will help make you more intuitive. But it seems to be part of the total package that characterizes an intuitive person," he observes.

The best technique for developing dream awareness is keeping a dream journal. Of the dozens of books on the subject, *Dreamworking* offers substantial information combined with insightful dream journal exercises.

GATEWAY INTUITIONS

We call certain intuitive experiences "gateway intuitions" because they are actually gateways to a new depth or dimension. When you are having a gateway intuition, you are acutely aware there is more to the immediate situation than the ongoing physical event. In fact, the physical event itself may be unimportant. What is important is that you sense that there is more going on than what meets your eye. Judy Haims recalls a daydream in which she was standing on the steps of a school giving a speech. "It was a very strong vision, and I knew that there was more to it than just daydreaming," she notes. Years later, she delivered a speech standing on the school steps that she had envisioned intuitively as a child.

THE COLOR GREEN

As you read these case histories, we hope that you have begun to remember some experiences of your own that may have slipped from memory over the years. As you remember each one, you will be identifying your intuition.

When you do find an example of an intuitive experience, you may find it helpful to consider that simply recognizing that it occurred can give you a lot of information. Identifying an intuitive experience shows you that:

1. You have experienced intuition.
2. Intuition exists.
3. You can access it.
4. You experienced it once and you can experience it again.

These presuppositions may seem so obvious and basic that you never even thought about them. But by becoming conscious of your experiences, you are strengthening your belief that intuition is possible. You can also compare strengthening your intuition to the artistic process. For example, as you learn to paint, you don't become aware of less, you become aware of more. Suddenly, it's not just the primary colors you see. Now there are tints and shades. Your palette expands, offering you a greater range. You're using the same eye you have had all these years, but you have learned to discriminate. You have learned to see minute differences. Likewise, when you begin to observe your intuitive states, you are, in effect, saying to yourself, "I don't want a fuzzy picture with my intuition. I want to have a real, clear, sharp picture." You are beginning to become more responsible for what goes on inside you. Opening up to your intuition represents a commitment to pay closer attention to how you think and feel.

Once you open up, it is difficult to go back. And you probably won't want to. Once you have seen the color green and you fully understand green, it is very difficult *not* to see green any more.

CHAPTER 4

Your Intuitive Process

The previous two chapters gave you examples of different types of intuitive experience so that you could define and identify similar intuitive states of your own. Now, we would like you to focus more attention on your own intuitive process, that is, how *you* think intuitively.

In order to help you acknowledge, nurture, and value your intuition, we will show you how to develop a data bank of intuitive characteristics that can serve as a readily available personal resource for you. Barbara Pretto, a student in one of Robert Stempson's intuition development seminars at Programs for Human Development, has found that cultivating these inner characteristics "creates a heightened sense of awareness of your own feelings and an atmosphere that is conducive to creativity. The sensation of intuitive knowing makes you more confident. When you follow your intuition, a calming effect takes over your mind and body." Pretto notes that cultivating the characteristics of intuition can also boost your self-confidence, decrease fear and anxiety, and lead you in the direction that is right for you.

Certain activities can help you relax and think intuitively when you are feeling tense, overwhelmed, or stuck. To induce an intuitive frame of mind, you may want to try one of the following exercises:

- Relaxation exercises: Yoga, deep breathing, t'ai chi ch'uan
- Walking, running, swimming
- Daydreaming

- Listening to music
- Going to a soothing environment, outdoors or indoors
- Moving to a room decorated in soft, pastel colors with comfortable couches, chairs, and pillows
- Meditating or praying
- Listening to a psychotechnology tape
  (see the Bibliography)

When you are relaxed, visualize yourself thinking intuitively and answer the following questions: How do you know when you are thinking intuitively? What do you look like? What do you sound like? How do you feel? What physical sensations do you notice in your body?

VISUAL, AUDITORY, AND KINESTHETIC

We ask you to think about how you look, sound, and feel when you are in an intuitive state so that you can start to observe your own mental processes. As we indicated in the beginning of chapter 2, you process information from your intuition much the same way you process other forms of information. You may see a visual image or flash, hear an inner voice, or get a physical or emotional feeling. These three main representational systems—visual, auditory, and kinesthetic—serve as the screens (or filters) through which you sort information. Smell and taste, called olfactory and gustatory, are your other two representational systems. Although you may not have noticed, you tend to use one of the three primary systems more than the others. In fact, you use all of them at different times and your preferences can shift without your notice. You can develop more flexibility and expand the range of your representational systems simply by becoming aware of how you use them. As you become aware of your preferences, you will find it easier to pay attention to your intuition because you will be better able to recognize it. Whereas you process intuitive information through your representational systems, your *response* to intuition—whether to ignore it, fear it, trust it, or act on it—is a behavioral decision.

One of the most common questions that people ask us is, How do I know when I have intuition?

CHARACTERISTICS OF AN INTUITIVE PERSON

One way to know when you have intuition is to identify the characteristics of an intuitive person. After asking his seminar participants to define and identify intuition, Robert Stempson often poses the following question: What qualities or characteristics does an intuitive person have? Workshop student Julian Rowe lists "good self-image, curiosity, and independence" as his main characteristics. Andrew Moddafferi says, "An intuitive person is open to new experiences, willing to experiment, and willing to learn new things. He is adventurous and is able to change old patterns. An intuitive person is decisive and acts on what he knows." Barbara Pretto describes the characteristics of an intuitive person as "unique, self-confident, and calm."

CREATING YOUR INTUITIVE DATA BANK

We're confident that you can come up with a few negative uses for intuition if you think about it, but we believe that you will find it more useful to make a list of some positive, helpful characteristics of an intuitive person, such as those included on the list below. This list will become the basis of your intuitive data bank. You will be able to retrieve these characteristics from your data bank and use them as resources for developing your intuition. Later in this chapter, we will show you how cultivating these characteristics can move you into an intuitive state.

Here are some tips for making your list of characteristics:

- Think of a time when you experienced intuition. What qualities did you have when you were in that intuitive state?
- Think of someone whom you consider intuitive. What qualities does that person have?
- Imagine yourself as an intuitive person. What qualities do you think you would have as an intuitive type?
- Are there certain combinations of characteristics that are always present when you have intuition?
- Which characteristics are present during some intuitive states but not others?

- What does each particular characteristic look, sound, and feel like? What sensations do you get in your body in connection with each characteristic?

CHARACTERISTICS OF AN INTUITIVE PERSON

Ability to be childlike

Ability to follow impulses

Ability to let go

Ability to listen to herself

Ability to make correct choices
    without a body of logical facts

Acceptance

Acceptance of others

Assertiveness

Awareness

Autonomy

Balance

Boldness

Centered

Clarity

Comfort

Commitment

Compassion

Courage

Creativity

Curiosity

Detachment

Effortlessness

Empathy

Encouragement

Energy

Faith

Flexibility

Freedom

Interest

Joy

Lightness

Motivation

Nurturing

Oneness

Overall sensitivity

Peace

Perception

Pleasure

Problem solver

Quick thinker

Relaxation

Reliability

Risk taker

Satisfaction

Self-acceptance

Self-assurance

Self-awareness

Self-confidence

Self-esteem

Self-love

Self-trust

Spirituality

Spontaneity

Strong beliefs

Transformation

Understanding

Vision

Fun	Wisdom
Independence	Wonder
Inner strength	Add your own characteristics
Inspiration	

The following exercises work with your brain's visual, auditory, and kinesthetic systems and use neurolinguistic programming (NLP) as a base. Developed in 1975, NLP is a personal growth technology that combines brain research (neuropsychology) and linguistics. These NLP techniques are designed to help you to access your intuitive, unconscious mind.

THE INNER RESOURCE EXERCISE

Set aside twenty minutes to do this exercise.

First, spend a couple of minutes reviewing your list. Choose three characteristics. If you choose three characteristics you feel are already developed, you will be able to strengthen them. You will become more aware of how they are part of your intuition. If you choose three characteristics that you would like to develop, you will be able to build new resources. To get the most out of this exercise, we suggest that you choose three characteristics that you would like to strengthen, rather than three you feel are already developed.

We have chosen spontaneity, independence, and curiosity for this exercise. After you have chosen your three characteristics, visualize them as a sum total. For example:

Spontaneity + Independence + Curiosity = Intuition

As you think about each characteristic, we would like you to remember a time in your life when you experienced it.

Now, with your eyes open or closed—whichever is more comfortable—take several deep breaths. Relax. As you listen to the sound of your breathing and feel the rise and fall of your chest you can begin to remember a time in your life when spontaneity (or the characteristic of your choice) was present. Go inside that experience of spontaneity. See what you were seeing, hear what you were hearing, and feel what you were feeling as you were moving through it. See yourself acting and responding in a spontaneous way, and listen to any dialogue or background sounds that you associate with this experience. Think about the circumstances surrounding that time. Notice how you feel being spontaneous and be aware of any physical sensations in your body that you associate with spontaneity. Enhance your experience of spontaneity by enlarging and brightening the image and moving it closer to you. You may also wish to increase the volume of any sounds that you hear. When you feel that you have reached the peak of this experience of spontaneity, say that word three times. Hear yourself repeating: *spontaneity, spontaneity, spontaneity.*

As the experience of spontaneity subsides, allow your point of focus to return to the present. Repeat this exercise for independence and curiosity (or the characteristics of your choice), making sure you state the characteristic three times when your sense of that quality is at its peak. Saying the word for each state three times will anchor that experience in your mind. It will make an association between the word and that particular state. When you want to access the qualities of that state, you will be able to easily by saying that word. Be sure to do this exercise for intuition again after you have combined three more resource states.

AN INTUITIVE ACTIVITY EXERCISE

Another way to cultivate your intuition is to generate a behavior that stimulates intuitive activity. By generating behavior, we mean doing some activity that helps you get into that state of mind. For example, Lou Krouse, president and chief executive officer of National Payments Network, finds that talking to someone else stimulates new creative ideas and activates his intuition. "As soon as I talk to someone else about a new project or idea, I find it triggers other ideas. It's as if by talking I am listening to what I say with some other intuitive process. It seems to cross some other synapses and, lo and behold! I get a tremendous rush and go in another direction." Krouse says he could not have developed his multimillion-dollar financial services business without repeating this process over and over.

To do this intuitive activity exercise, choose three characteristics of intuition that you want to cultivate, such as self-esteem, curiosity, and independence. Next, write out a sum. For example:

Self-esteem + Curiosity + Independence = Intuition

Having identified the characteristics that you want to develop, you can then choose one activity for each and perform it regularly for a week.

- *Self-esteem.* To promote higher self-esteem, you can choose such activities as exercising, finishing up old projects, or getting to work on time. Any activity that gives you a sense of self-esteem is worthwhile.
- *Curiosity.* To cultivate curiosity, you can select a subject in which you are interested (such as developing your intuition). Find out more about it by reading, watching instructional videos, or by attending workshops and lectures on the subject.
- *Independence.* To develop independence, you can take action in some area where ordinarily you say, "I can't." You can write down what you believe you can't do, then say, "If I did this differently, this is what I would do." Then, do it.

NONHABITUAL PROGRAMMING EXERCISE

Here is another good combination for an intuitive activity:

$$\text{Spontaneity} + \text{Flexibility} + \text{Fun} = \text{Intuition}$$

You may well ask, "How can I plan a spontaneous activity? That's a contradiction in terms." That's true. But you can change your habits and routines, leaving yourself more open for the spontaneous. You can walk down a different street on your way home or take a different bus or train. Psychotherapist Gay Larned, who gives seminars at Programs for Human Development, suggests that you try her technique to cultivate nonhabitual programming. Nonhabitual programs or patterns free up the creative, intuitive part of your brain.

First, list all the habitual patterns you can remember. Habitual patterns are repetitious ways you do things, from the smallest, most routine habits and patterns of behavior to the largest. Habitual patterns often become unconscious. They include how you dress each morning, the route you take to work, how you greet people, and how you spend the holidays. When you have developed your primary list, observe yourself for a few days and see what you can add. Then note if there is a pattern to your habits.

When you are served a wedge of pie, do you automatically turn it so that it points at you? Anthropologists say that this is a North American habit, one that is so ingrained we don't even notice it. The next time you get a slice of pie, try eating it without turning the point toward you and see how you feel. Many people find that they become uncomfortable with eating the pie from a different side. This is one example of how ingrained, habitual patterns can be connected to your sense of territory and safety. Although you recognize that turning a piece of pie so that it points away from you is not going to affect your physical safety, you create many of these routines and habits out of an instinctive need to feel comfortable and secure. Your patterns exist to subtly reassure you that your world moves along as much as possible in the order that you have unconsciously chosen. If you find that changing some of your habitual patterns makes you uncomfortable, then stop and resume your regular routines.

If you find that you are comfortable with this experiment, you may want to follow some of Larned's suggestions for changing nonhabitual programming. Larned gives her clients—corporate executives and professionals—assignments to do the opposite of their habitual patterns. "Put the telephone against your other ear," she advises. "Sleep on the opposite side from the one to which you are accustomed. Chew on the other side. Cross your legs differently. Wave hello and good-bye with your other hand." These apparently minor changes in routine break up the patterns in your reptilian brain and open up spontaneity. They are also fun.

VISUALIZE A FUTURE SITUATION EXERCISE

When you have selected and cultivated your three components of intuition, set aside ten minutes to do an exercise in which you visualize yourself in the future. It will show you how cultivating the characteristics of intuition can actually work. It will also give you a sense of how you will look, sound, and feel when you are activating those characteristics in a specific future situation.

Visualize yourself in a situation sometime in the future when you would like to call on your intuition. With your eyes open or closed, take a few deep breaths. As you see what you are seeing and hear what you are hearing, and feel what you are feeling, visualize yourself being in an intuitive state that contains the characteristics you previously anchored. Allow your intuition to come through for you as you see yourself in this future situation. Notice how you look, sound, and feel when you are in this intuitive state. You can enhance and strengthen this intuitive state by enlarging and brightening your mental image. Bringing it closer to you can also make it more intense.

COPPOLA'S TAPE RECORDER

The ability to create, sustain, and manipulate visual and auditory information is part of your whole-brain intelligence system. As you would expect from a film director, Francis Ford Coppola shows a strong preference for his visual system and knows intuitively how to use it. One time he was in his car and wanted to dictate some notes. "I was angry," he recalls, "because I didn't have a little tape recorder. So I took an imaginary tape recorder and went through the process of loading it with fresh tape. Then I began to push the button and speak. I said, 'Item one, item two, and so on.' I found that later I could sit down and type the whole list just by activating that system."

MANIPULATING IMAGES

You, too, are activating your representational systems all the time. How many times have you said that you needed to take another look at a situation and you replay it in your mind? Perhaps it's an argument with your husband or wife, or a confrontation with your boss. You may want to take another look at getting fired, or getting divorced, or breaking up with your boyfriend or girlfriend. "Think about an unpleasant experience," Steve Leeds, director of Advanced Communication Training, suggests. "What happens when you abstract it like a Picasso, put a frame around it and put it on the wall? Then stand back and walk over to one side of it. Now look at it from a different perspective. What happens? How many times have you said, 'This thing is hanging over my head'? What happens if you move to the left of it, or to the right? Move your position. How does this change what you feel about it?"

Filmmakers select and assemble images to create an emotional impact. You, too, can manipulate images and by doing so, change what you feel and believe about them. Let's take another look at one of those painful situations we mentioned, like getting fired. If you have ever been fired, then you won't have any trouble calling up your personal image of it. If you have not been fired, then try something else that usually makes you feel sad, angry, or in some way uncomfortable. As you look at the image of being fired, notice whether it is a moving shot as in a film or video sequence, or whether it is a still. Zoom into a close-up and observe how you feel. You will probably find that your uncomfortable emotions intensify. Zoom out, so that the image becomes smaller and is farther away from you and you will probably notice your discomfort lessening.

Change the image from color to black and white. Is it more or less intense? Change it back to color. What happens now? When you speed up the action in your image to double speed, notice how it affects your mental soundtrack. When the audio becomes a high-pitched, Donald Duck-like blur, how does the sound affect your response? Are your feelings of sadness, anger, or discomfort more or less intense?

Now remember something pleasant, like falling in love, getting a great job, or winning a contest. Notice whether your image is in black and white or color. Is it moving or still? How do you feel when you change the color to black and white? What happens when you freeze-frame the action and change the moving image to a still? Zoom in, brighten the colors, and enlarge the image. How does that affect your responses?

Shifting to an auditory system, have you ever talked to yourself? Most of us have one or more inner voices that advise, criticize, and encourage us, and many people process intuition auditorily. Listen to a critical inner voice, a voice that says, "You'll never do it." Notice how you feel when you hear that voice and observe where the voice is located. Now move the voice to another part of your body. If it's in your head, move it to your left thumb. Now move it to another part of the room. How do you respond to the voice when it is in another location farther away from you?

Working with a kinesthetic system can have similar results. Butterflies in your stomach? Move them to your left shoulder. Now how do you feel?

Varying these different qualities or submodalities enables you to fine-tune your perceptions and change the way you feel in response to a particular experience. In general, you will probably find that when you enlarge, brighten, and get closer to an image, your feelings about it become more intense. When you reduce, dim, and move away from it, the intensity of your feelings decreases. To change how you feel, you can manipulate and play with a range of submodalities until you achieve the state that you want. This allows you to see you have choices in connection with any situation.

TAKE A PICTURE OF YOUR INTUITION EXERCISE

Set aside fifteen minutes for this exercise.

Experiment with submodalities on your own by taking an imaginary picture of your intuition. Giving your intuition a form serves as another way for you to identify it. This picture will also help you to take a new look at your intuition. And it will give you another tool for getting into an intuitive state.

Because intuition is not physical, you must give it a form in order to take an imaginary picture of it. You can use the inner resource exercise or one of the intuitive activity exercises as the basis for this exercise. Then, you can take a picture of yourself in an intuitive state. Looking at the picture will give you a new perspective on the qualities of your intuition.

Remember Francis Ford Coppola's tape recorder? Just as he took the time to visualize loading his tape, be sure that you put film in the camera. When you are finished taking your picture, you can see that it is developed, either in your own darkroom or at a photo lab.

Now, look at the picture.

Is it color or black and white? What size is it? 8 × 10? 5 × 7? Wallet size?

Is there a frame around it or is the picture unframed?

Now, you can play with some perspectives. As you do, observe how each change enhances your response. Find out what you need to do to the picture to strengthen its impact. Try the following:

Blow up the picture. Then reduce it. Blow it up again.

Make a giant poster of it.

Put a frame around it. Take the frame away.

Make the still photo into a movie. Freeze-frame the action.

If your image is in color, make it black and white, or vice versa.

Brighten the colors, then dim them.

Make a contact sheet with thirty-six identical images.

Change the contact images to black and white. Then silk-screen pastel colors across the whole sheet, like an Andy Warhol.

When you have adjusted the submodalities so that you get a strong feeling from this picture, visualize yourself putting it someplace where you will be able to look at it when you want to. When you want to get into an intuitive state, you can look at it and bring back the feelings that you associate with your intuition. Just as you can look at a photo of some special event in your life and evoke the same feelings as when you were there, this picture of your intuition will trigger your intuitive feelings. When you look at your picture, you will be able to see and identify its essential components, as well. You can select any of these components and strengthen it further using the inner resource exercise.

THE ROOM OF YOUR MIND EXERCISE

Another way to become familiar with your intuition is to take a walk through a room that represents your mind. As you stand in the room, you can see that it contains all of your mental abilities because in this room you have placed all of your multiple intelligences, including intuition. (You may want to take another look at The Triune Brain chart and Elaine de Beauport's Multiple Intelligences as you start to do this exercise [see p. 10].) Also in this room are dreaming, memory, will, and imagination. In fact, you can put any mental attribute in this room that you choose. It is your room.

As you look around the room, you can see that some of these attributes are large. Others are small. Some are closer to where you are standing. Others are hidden away or stacked up in corners, on shelves, or along the walls. Each one is a different shape and color. As your eyes move around the room, notice where you have placed memory. Where is logic? Where is dreaming? Where have you put your moods and motivation?

Notice the differences in size. Is logic larger than mood? Does it take up more space than imagination or visual intelligence? Where have you placed your sense of territory? Is it closer to, or farther away from, dreaming and language?

Now take a walk through your room. Give yourself time to get a clear sense of what each mental ability looks like. Notice its size, color, shape, and relationship to the other attributes around it. When you feel comfortable here, begin to look for your intuition. What color and shape is it? Is it close to you or far away? Is it visible or hidden? Is it large or small?

Do you feel like moving toward it or away from it? You can think of moving toward intuition as an indication that you want to know more about it. Moving away from your intuition indicates you don't want to know. If you find yourself pulling away from your intuition, notice what you do move toward.

As you move closer to your intuition, notice how you respond. If you feel anxious or uncomfortable as you approach it, move back and see your intuition become smaller. How does that affect your feelings about it?

You can walk over to it, pick it up, and examine it closely. Feel its texture. Make it larger and brighter, noticing any physical and emotional reactions that you have as you do so. If you find that this increase in size and intensity disturbs you, dim the brightness and reduce its size. Notice how your feelings change as you do this. Find a place where you feel comfortable and talk to your intuition. Find out what it wants and tell it how you would like it to help you. Ask if it will help you and when it responds, pay attention to its voice. Note the volume, tempo, and pitch. Have you heard this inner voice before? How do you feel when you hear it? Where are those feelings located in your body? Accelerate the tempo and increase the volume of your intuitive voice and notice how you feel. Select the audio quality that produces a strong, confident feeling in you about your intuition.

You can change any quality of any of these mental attributes at any time. By doing so, you can enhance or decrease the strength of your response to them. Spend some time and experiment with grades of color, brightness, size, location, shape, volume, and tone. Remember that this is your room. You have selected and arranged everything in it. You can rearrange and redecorate it so that you feel great when you are here. Spend as much time as you like in this room getting to know your intuition and your other mental abilities. Come back here whenever you need to find your intuition.

CHAPTER 5

Modeling Intuitive Behavior

As we indicated in the last chapter, some people find it easier to learn by modeling or reproducing some kind of behavior they've observed rather than by going inside themselves to access their inner resources. If you do not enjoy the more introspective exercises that involve examining your own thoughts and feelings, modeling an intuitive person's behavior may be a particularly effective way for you to begin learning about the intuitive process. Observing how an intuitive person speaks and acts when he is being intuitive gives you information about the components of intuition. You can then apply these components yourself. In addition, you may find it easier to "back into" your intuition by first recognizing it in someone else. Then you can come up with strategies for developing similar behaviors of your own.

To do this, however, you must believe that it is possible to learn intuitive behavior from someone else. One way to begin to instill that belief is simply to say, "If he can do it, so can I!" It is also helpful to know what he believes about his own intuition. Belief is the basis of intuitive behavior.

Believing is essential when changing any behavior. If you don't believe that it is possible for you to become an intuitive person, then you will find that you sabotage your own attempts to learn.

One of the best places to observe intuitive behavior is in the workplace where people use it for decision making, coming up with new ideas, and developing strategies. In the course of doing research for this book, we have found that an overwhelming number of people who rely on their hunches and gut feelings in their fields of work do so consistently. They have made a conscious decision to trust their intuition. This does not mean that they don't rely on logic and feelings, as well, but it shows how intuitive thinking can become a pattern of behavior. As you read through this section, you will find many ways in which people use their intuition on the job. When you find a description that appeals to you, you can use it to develop your own strategy for modeling intuitive behavior. To do this, you may find it helpful to keep these questions in mind:

- How does an intuitive person work? What does he do? What does he say?
- How does he act when he is relying on his intuition on the job?
- What can I do to start behaving intuitively?

Read this chapter with a view toward identifying characteristics of intuitive behavior that you use or can use in your own work. We hope that reading about people in different professions will stimulate you to ask: Under what circumstances would a (doctor, police officer, corporate executive, etc.) use his intuition? How does a (doctor, police officer, corporate executive, etc.) look, sound, or behave when he is being intuitive? The following are examples of how people act, talk, and make decisions when they are using intuition in their work.

ENTREPRENEURIAL INTUITION

Intuitive behavior comes naturally to Jeff Stein, the president and chief executive officer of the successful sportswear company Camp Beverly Hills. Jeff Stein was a young producer at Columbia Pictures when, one day, out of the blue, he got an idea to create an Army-Navy store in Beverly Hills. "In Beverly Hills in the mid-1970s, sportswear meant European designers," Stein says. "From the moment that I got my idea, it felt right to me. It was an overall feeling in my body but was centered in my gut." In addition to Army-Navy surplus clothing, the concept included vintage clothing and classic American athletic wear—people clothing, rather than designer clothing. As Stein began to research his idea, he recalls, "People told me I was crazy so I stopped asking for advice." In 1977, Camp Beverly Hills opened for business. Ten years later, the company grossed $100 million.

To access his intuition, Stein segregates himself and quiets down so that he can hear his inner voice. "Sometimes there's so much noise going on that I will not get the signal clearly and it will confuse me," says Stein. He finds it helpful when preparing a speech or presentation to go someplace with vast open spaces like the desert or the ocean. In a peaceful setting, Stein trusts that "ideas will come to me if they're given the opportunity and if I'm not acting in a defensive posture."

He regrets the times he has ignored his gut reaction, such as the day Camp Beverly Hills entered into a licensing agreement with a catalog company. "I knew from day one that they were the wrong people for it," he says. "They didn't have the level of taste or sophistication that I was looking for, but they gave me some concrete information and showed me how they could arrange the financing. I hoped that it would work out and when it didn't, I knew I should have trusted my intuition."

When you are under pressure to make a move and would like to be sure of your gut feel of a situation, give yourself four or five minutes of quiet time. Make a point of telling yourself that you want to access your intuition. Go somewhere by yourself and let the problem or pending decision be present in your mind. Don't think about it. Just be aware of it and notice what sensations, emotions, images, or subtle sounds come up for you. As you become more familiar with your own intuition, you will refine your sensitivity to your own inner messages so that they will come to you more clearly. Be sure to acknowledge them and again, be thankful that your unconscious can give you this information. At other times, you may be aware of a murmur or a slight feeling about which you are not certain enough to use as the basis for a decision. You can then decide whether to act, to wait for greater clarity, or to say no when your intuition is not really clear.

TIMING AND INTUITION

When you do get a clear signal, however, you will want to move on it right away. Intuitive people act quickly. They don't question themselves or second-guess their gut reactions. Linda Armstrong, a real-life Los Angeles lawyer whose clients run the gamut from accused drug dealers to alleged child molesters, says, "I always know right away if I can trust someone. All I have to do is look the person in the eye. It takes seconds." For Armstrong, "practicing law involves doing your homework, of course. But your initial gut impressions have to guide you." Publishing executive Helen Bowles always tries to acquire or decline a book the same day that she gets it. "First impressions are the most important," she says. "You can research the market and you try to bring in as much as you can from the factual world, but in book publishing there is nothing tangible. The reason you respond to one book and not another is intuitive." Bowles insists that "all publishers work that way. If they want to buy a book, they will play with the numbers on the profit and loss projections to justify their decision."

INTUITION AND INTERVIEWS

Whatever your occupation, you have probably used your intuition in connection with it at least once. Maybe it helped you choose one job over another, or maybe it steered you toward one department and away from another. Think back to a time when you were looking for a job or were offered a choice. How did you make your decision? What did you look like? How did you sound? What feelings did you have? Which of those sights, sounds, and emotions do you associate with intuitive behavior?

Many people who do not call themselves intuitive can come up with at least one job-related decision in which they followed their gut feeling despite rational reasons to do otherwise. Louis Barboza was about to accept a senior editor's job at a national weekly news magazine when he got an offer for another position that had less prestige and less money. "I had a very strong feeling that if I took the news magazine job, I would be miserable in three months," he says, "even though it looked better up front. I turned it down and took the other job." Barboza says that he knows he made the right move. The job he took turned out to offer more creative responsibility.

Learning the ropes on a new job means getting used to a new routine and meeting new people. If your intuition is sharp, it can signal you to stay away from troublesome people before you have a confrontation. Sheila McConnors had started a new job as an administrative assistant in a university when she was offered a choice of two supervisors. "They had just hired another assistant and so I was asked which professor I wanted to work for. I had been there all of two days and I hadn't met either of them. But I knew intuitively that working for one of them would make me miserable. It turned out that the man I chose was delightful and taught me a lot. The other assistant got stuck working for a supervisor with a mean temper."

A job interview can stimulate your intuitive responses whether you are sitting in the interviewee's chair or the prospective employer's. "I always know whether I'm going to get the job as soon as I start to talk to someone," says Marjorie Johannsen. "I get this feeling in my stomach right away." Personnel director Denise Goldenson observes, "I do a lot of hiring. Every time I haven't trusted my intuition because I learned something that overrode it, like seeing a strong résumé with good credentials, it has always turned out that I made a big mistake. I should always trust what I feel instinctively." If anything, Goldenson, along with many other managers, would like to depend on intuition more.

One well-known job applicant, Karol Wojtyla, was sequestered while waiting for the results of a secret election in which he was considered a dark horse whom no one favored to win. Between ballots, black smoke churned through a chimney to signal that thus far the electoral results had been inconclusive. Wojtyla told Wilton Wynn, *Time* magazine's Vatican correspondent and author of *Keeper of the Keys,* that "by the beginning of the second day it all had become clear. I could feel that the Holy Spirit was working among the cardinals and I could sense the outcome." Later, when white smoke billowed through the chimney, the final results of that election became known. Karol Wojtyla was the new Pontiff, Pope John Paul II.

INTUITION IN THE DUGOUT

Whether you are at play in the fields of the Lord or standing next to home plate squinting at the opposing pitcher, that sudden, immediate knowing can also help you envision the outcome.

Tom Trebelhorn, manager of the Milwaukee Brewers baseball team, has developed a reputation for playing his hunches in the heat of the game. On September 9, 1987, Trebelhorn "had a vision" that he should play Bill Schroeder against the California Angels' left-handed pitcher Chuck Finley. Says Trebelhorn, "Bill had a tough year. He had not swung the bat very well or consistently. He had been working really hard and things had been going so tough for him that I felt it was about time for something good to happen. I had a feeling that he could light one up for us, and he picked the right time, off Chuck Finley for a three-run homer."

Trebelhorn believes that "if you feel something is right, and not necessarily in line with the statistical information you have, then do it. That's how I manage and there have been times when I have had a gut feeling and I didn't follow it and I wish I had done something." In one game, he knew he had to make a move. "I said, son of a gun, I don't care if it is my ace pitcher. This guy is going to hit. Then, bang! He did."

Most of the time, Trebelhorn says, "There's no magical secret to managing. If you have good players and they play well, your hunches are brilliant and your statistical analysis is brilliant, too. In my business, you're only as good as the people who perform for you. I don't think you can be close minded and say that statistics don't mean anything or that hunches are meaningless. I don't think you can want it to be all hunch. I think it's a combination of the two, plus fly by the seat of your pants, a few Hail Marys and let's see what happens." He's confident that the "exciting internal rush, like a stage-fright feeling," is a clear signal that something will work out. "That's when my total self-image is at its peak and I am my most receptive. That's when I have the most hunches and go with them better, too," says Trebelhorn, who psyches himself into a receptive state during the playing of the national anthem. When the Brewers play the Toronto Blue Jays, he gets two anthems in which to "zero in and put the antennae out." He tells himself he's going to be the best manager ever and everything that comes to him that he thinks is right he's going to do.

Trebelhorn's confidence extends even to the time that he had "a vision" that the Brewers were going to get a runner on first to lead off the inning. "Then we were going to steal him and bunt him to third on the next pitch. The next guy was going to squeeze. What happened?

"The first guy got on and stole. We bunted him to third and the batter was safe at first. The next guy bunted a pop fly into a triple play." Was his hunch, then, incorrect? No way. "My hunch was 100 percent right," says Trebelhorn. "We didn't execute. You have to do that, too."

INTUITION AND MEDICINE

A recent survey of radiologists reveals that the most accurate diagnoses are not the result of linear diagnostic techniques. In fact, the best doctors ignore the established, sequential procedure that they themselves teach to medical students. A camera trained on the radiologists' eye movements shows that they do not scan the four quadrants of a lung X-ray. Rather, each doctor has a completely different scanning technique. When asked how they arrived at their diagnoses, the radiologists often say they have no idea.

Many medical students who are taught the four-step scanning procedure also find that following it does not produce very accurate results. In some instances, when the students ask their professors to show them how to improve their diagnostic methods, they find that their teachers are unable to do so. And over time, many medical students abandon the quadrant scanning technique and thereby start earning higher grades with their increasing intuitive accuracy. It appears that in the case of expert diagnosticians, their external knowledge base (the established procedure) is different from their implicit knowledge base. Dr. Oliver Sacks, author of *The Man Who Mistook His Wife for a Hat,* believes that, if studied, many other professions would yield identical findings to those of the radiologists. "Alphabetic methods have to be replaced with more intuitive methods. Intuition is behind every diagnosis, formulation, patient contact. If it weren't I'd be an analytic machine."

Dr. Sacks, who likes to read electromagnetic wave output, or EEG, reports in the privacy of his garden, says that here, too, the process could be seen as mechanical and could be done by a machine. "I like to take an EEG, look at it rapidly the first time and form a general impression of style and character. Then I analyze it. New EEG readers are laborious, slow, and conscious. As they become more experienced, it becomes a faster, unconscious process." In every field, he believes that specific intuitions need to be analytically checked. "There is a method involved in intuition. I don't believe it's beyond explanation," he says.

One Connecticut surgeon, who has developed his own method for working intuitively, says that meditating helps him set up the procedure he plans to use before he even sets foot in the hospital. "The night before an operation I review it in my mind's eye and visually project what I will need to do. When I go into the operating room the next day, it's just my eyes and my hands. My rational mind is somewhere else and I operate intuitively, having prepared the night before," he says.

INTUITIVE NEGOTIATING

Whereas doctors need to be sensitive to subtle impressions about hidden symptoms, brokers who finesse deals have to depend on their mental radar.

A client may bring his hidden agenda, or another broker may be negotiating with the intent to deceive. Or a deal that looked solid may be getting ready to fall through. The most obvious example of an intuitive realtor is megadeveloper Donald Trump. In his autobiography, *Trump: The Art of the Deal,* Trump describes how he investigates properties that he plans to buy by talking to residents of the area, especially cab drivers, until he gets a gut feeling. Then he decides whether to proceed with the deal.

Tim Wernet, a realtor in Akron, Ohio, pays as much attention to what he calls "the feel of the deal" as to the numbers. "I try to keep my eye on what's positive," he says. "But sometimes I get a feeling that something is wrong. I don't really know how I feel it, but I know right away. No two deals are the same." When packaging a deal between the owner of an apartment house and a buyer, Wernet recalls, "We put together a contract and I was excited about it, but right at the beginning it didn't feel right. Something strange was going on and I couldn't figure it out logically." The contract was executed, and Wernet thought the paperwork had been mailed to the seller. But because of a clerical mistake, the contract had been mislaid on somebody's desk and did not get mailed when he thought it did. "Out of the blue, the seller brought me up on charges of unethical conduct because he didn't get his contract," Wernet says. "The whole deal turned fishy. My first gut feeling turned out to be correct."

EXECUTIVE INTUITION

Tales of intuitive CEOs are becoming part of American business lore. *The Intuitive Manager,* a book by Roy Rowan, contains dozens of examples of how business leaders rely on their intuition. Hunches, flashes, and gut feelings are often cited as the reasons executives decide to raise a bid, develop a concept, or start a new business. For example, Amerada Hess Chief Executive Officer Joel Youell had a hunch he should raise his bid to the precise figure of $72.3 million in order to win a lucrative contract in Alaska. In his manuscript *The Survivor Personality,* Al Siebert quotes one of the executives who lost out to Youell in the bidding war as saying, "We got beat by a group who didn't have the information we had." Brandon Tartikoff, the president of NBC Entertainment, is renowned for his intuitive thinking. Perhaps the best-known example is the time Tartikoff had a flash and scribbled a memo: "MTV cops." The result became "Miami

Vice." Tartikoff sprouted the idea for "The Bill Cosby Show" when Cosby made a guest appearance on "The Tonight Show."

Lou Krouse, the founder, president, and chief executive officer of National Payments Network, a financial services company for low-income people, agrees that intuition is an essential skill. "I don't remember any ideas that I've had, especially for this business, that came from methodical reasoning. It's definitely a quantum jump from what you see and what you experience and what you know to something new." The idea for National Payments Network came to him in the form of "a very intangible concept that I knew intuitively would work out," he says. Although Krouse relies on his intuitive abilities, he does not believe that all CEOs do the same, pointing out that many of the chief executive officers who rise through the ranks of major corporations are diligent, data-oriented, methodical thinkers. When talking about a chief executive officer's intuition, Krouse points out that it is important to ask about his background. An entrepreneur such as Krouse, who describes himself as a "renegade," is likely to make decisions intuitively, whereas someone who came up through the ranks is more likely to rely on analytical decision-making approaches. The bestselling author of twelve books, including *Government Giveaways for Entrepreneurs* and *Information USA,* Matthew Lesko notices that more and more people in business are relying on their intuition for business information. "In the 1960s and 1970s we paid more attention to quantitative decision making, but the real impact on society is nonnumeric and nonanalytic," says Lesko, who has an M.B.A. and was trained to think analytically. "The older I get the more I believe that intuition is more important than we think."

Lesko, who "never read a book in college and barely passed in school," started trusting his intuition after his first two businesses went bankrupt and he felt he had nothing left to lose. The first business was an information service for people overseas that he started with two fellow Vietnam veterans. The second company developed marketing services for management systems. Lesko now specializes in helping people find free information about any subject through the federal government. "I found that there was more money in showing people how to get information than in actually providing it," he says. "When my computer company went down the tubes I decided that instead of trying to use everything I had learned, at least I would have fun this time and follow my gut. I threw away what I had learned and just started feeling and being more natural." Lesko's key to success: "Learning to feel. You have to listen to your gut. If you don't, you're trying to be someone else and it won't work."

One of the early examples of executive intuition can be found in the story of Conrad Hilton. As a poor young man, Hilton was advised by a family friend that he would make his fortune if he went to Texas. In his autobiography, *Be My Guest,* Hilton writes, "I didn't believe in oracles or crystal balls. I had a hunch these were my new marching orders. . . . I went to Texas on the next train."

When he got there, Hilton found a flophouse where miners slept and ate. The building was in such poor shape and had such a disreputable air about it that the "good folk" didn't go near it. But Hilton saw it as an opportunity. Although he had a hard time convincing the banks and friends to invest in the seedy, run-down establishment, he managed to get the financing he needed and soon opened his first Hilton hotel. "I hadn't been in the hotel business five minutes when I knew this was it. I dreamed of Texas wearing a chain of Hilton hotels," he wrote.

He also had a dream about guests sleeping on the tables, and although Hilton awoke from this nightmare feeling anxious, he used his dream as the basis of a remodeling scheme in which he closed down the dining room and converted the space into small, sleeping cubicles. His partner thought Hilton was crazy when he closed down the dining room and began building cubicles, but the born-again hotelier reasoned that more people checked into a hotel to sleep rather than to eat. Hilton reasoned that if push came to shove, his guests needed somewhere to sleep first and could eat someplace else. He was right. The hotel became more popular than before.

"Connie's hunches" became his hallmark after Hilton played one by buying Waldorf shares at $4\frac{1}{2}$ and selling them at 85. After submitting a sealed bid of $165,000 for the Stevens House, a Chicago hotel, Hilton awoke with a hunch that he should make that $180,000. He did, and the second highest bid turned out to be $179,800. The Stevens House is now the Chicago Hilton.

Even when he was on the verge of bankruptcy, Hilton insisted on keeping his mind clear so that new ideas and hunches could flow through. He liked to take long walks and to doodle at his desk, a pastime he called "putting his dreams on paper." It was a doodle that first gave form to his dream of the first million-dollar Hilton hotel. Writes Hilton, "I think the other name for hunch is intuition and I think intuition can be a form of answered prayer. . . . But the key to intuition is not in the prayer but in listening for a response."

DISCIPLINED INTUITION

Carol Colman, a partner at an investment consulting firm in New York City, agrees with Matthew Lesko. "You have to be willing to grit your teeth and have conviction in your own investments instead of depending on conflicting media advice," she says. Inferential Focus, Colman's firm, provides corporate clients with early information about changing trends before statistical analyses are available. "Any investing is hard work. You have to know the business and really know what you're buying. It also helps to have an added gut feel. Left brainers are not good money managers."

Founded in 1980, Inferential Focus calls itself the first "whole-brained investment consulting group." Its partners carefully review material from many disparate sources with an eye toward integrating seemingly random, unrelated pieces of information into an intelligible whole. They call on their analytical and organizational abilities as well as associational, empathetic, and intuitive qualities to provide their clients with early intelligence. "If we provide the information late, our clients can't make a decision," says Colman, who is equally strict about the need for analysis and hard data. "You can take intuition too far. There's a fine line between not knowing what you're talking about and intuition." Colman believes that saying something like "This feels right to me" can be gunslinging in the field of money management. "It may just be a lazy way to make a decision," she says, adding that Inferential Focus "does not provide off-the-cuff decisions." Colman describes her firm's research and counseling process as "disciplined intuition." When the four partners of Inferential Focus talk about having a feel for a particular situation, they are calling on a knowledge that spans a combined eighty years of experience. Aware of how the whole brain operates, Inferential Focus partners describe their work process as taking in a quantity of information through the left neocortex and allowing "the juices of the right half" to synthesize it.

One example of how Inferential Focus advises clients is its report on walking. Have you noticed that more and more people have switched from jogging to walking? Inferential Focus spotted that trend in 1985, and hypothesized that the switch in physical activities was a reflection of changing attitudes. In their search for clues to support that hypothesis, they studied reports on shopping, home, work, entertainment, and the environment. As part of this trend, they noticed that in California, BMWs and Mercedes were being sold at reduced interest rates and concluded that "we are moving away from the uniform of the BMW/Mercedes and designer clothes and that yuppies are becoming more individualistic." Added to that were reports that volunteerism was now at an all-time high on college campuses and in cities. What did all this show? "A shift to concern about other people and a moving away from power images," says Colman. "We noticed that people were now paying for clean air, clean water, education, housing, and sewer systems. Things that you need but can't see." The inferred forecast: a slower economic growth rate as consumer spending winds down.

On determining the larger perspective, Inferential Focus advised its clients how to advertise, communicate, develop, and sell the right product for this particular market shift. Their hypotheses were shown to be true three years later when computerized statistics became available. In February 1988, the *Wall Street Journal* and *Esquire* reported on the death of yuppie consumerism. But Colman points out that anyone seeking to invest in the changes taking place would have lost out by waiting three years for the computerized statistics on which the *Wall Street Journal* and *Esquire* based their reports.

INTUITION IN BUSINESS SCHOOL

One dozen kinds of meditation, dream analyses, aikido, *I Ching,* tarot cards, trance dancing, and shadow masks are now part of the curriculum at the Stanford University Graduate School of Business. Michael Ray and Rochelle Myers, who teach a popular course called "Creativity in Business," want their students to experiment with different techniques to help release intuitive and creative insights. They don't expect everyone to like each of the techniques they introduce. In fact, as many as 90 percent of the students respond negatively at times to a particular approach! But for the other 10 or 5 or 2 percent, experimenting can lead to a breakthrough.

The following are some of the techniques used by Ray and Myers in their course.

The Starter Set

Ray and Myers give their students the chance to experiment with the Sufi concept of intuition. According to Sufi tradition, the essence of the creative process consists of five basic qualities: intuition, will, joy, strength, and compassion. "We call it the starter set," Ray says. Like the ancient Hindu tradition that says you have seven energy centers, or *chakras,* aligned from the base of your spine to the crown of your head, each of these Sufi qualities corresponds to a part of your body and has its own color and slogan. The Sufi qualities also correspond to several of your whole-brain intelligences:

1. Intuition is in the head. Its color is black. Its slogan: "I know." (It corresponds to the right neocortex.)
2. Will is in the solar plexus. Its color is white. Its slogan: "I will." Will is your personal vision. It is the foundation of everything you do. (It corresponds to the left neocortex.)
3. Joy is on the left side of the body. Its color is yellow. Its slogan: "I wish." It is the motivating aspect. (It corresponds to the limbic brain.)
4. Strength is on the right side of the body. Its color is red. Its slogan: "I can." Strength is what enables you to overcome fear. (It corresponds to the limbic system and reptilian brain.)
5. Compassion is in the heart. Its color is green. Its slogan: "I am." Compassion, which recognizes the other qualities, is really loving kindness for yourself and others. (It corresponds to the limbic system and reptilian brain.)

Ray says, "Compassion is the most important quality of these five. Without it, you can't bring out the intuition. You can see little blinks of it every once in a while, but without compassion it won't go on for very long."

The Heuristics

Ray and Myers agree with author Lesko, who says, "We are all artists at something. You have to find out what your art is. Then you will use your intuition." They also believe that creativity cannot be taught; you need to experience it. It can, however, be nurtured.

Ray says that the main issues that businesspeople face are purpose, time, and stress. They also have to come up with a balance between their personal and professional lives, and to find a way to meet their financial goals without sacrificing self-esteem. Someone with a highly individual creative style also needs to find a manner to express that style in a way that fits into a corporate structure. Ray calls these issues the five challenges.

Ray and Myers believe that everybody is creative and that creativity is essential for health, happiness, and success in a business career. To express creativity, you need to experience it in your own unique way. To help students understand what that means, Ray and Myers invite speakers to share their experiences with the class so that students can model their behavior and learn how to be creative and intuitive. More than one hundred speakers have visited the Stanford classrooms. "When students are exposed to the speakers, they see that these people have done wonderful things. They may identify with one and say, 'That person is just like me and look what she's done.' It brings out their own inner resources," says Ray, who also gives his classes assignments in what he calls heuristics, or "live-withs." Every week Ray and Myers ask students to live with a certain credo, such as, If at first you don't succeed, surrender; Destroy judgment, create curiosity; Ask dumb questions; or Do only what is easy, effortless, and enjoyable. The heuristics, which form the subject of the chapters in Rays and Myer's book *Creativity in Business,* allow people to become aware of how these slogans affect thinking and behavior. The heuristics also give people new ideas on how to make their lives a work of art.

The Coin-Flipping Technique

In teaching his business students how to use their intuition, Ray often turns to an age-old technique: flipping a coin. That's right. When you have to make a decision and want a "yes" or "no" answer from your intuition, you can simply flip a coin. Of course, the coin won't make the decision for you. That decision lies within you. Intuitively you know before you flip the coin which way you want the coin to fall. "When we have to make a decision, we tend to think we don't really know what we're supposed to do," says Michael Ray. "We thrash back and forth. The big decisions in life we usually can make fairly easily. We know when we're in love. We know whom we're going to marry. We know when we're going to buy a house or take a job. But the little things drive us nuts. Which flavor of ice cream are you going to eat? Are you going to stay home and cook or eat out?"

Try it yourself. You can take any decision that's troubling you and frame it as a yes or no alternative. Yes, you should do it. No, you shouldn't. Make one alternative heads; the other, tails. Then flip the coin. Your instant, gut reaction to what the coin comes up with will reveal your intuitive call.

INTUITION AND RESEARCH

"The part intuition plays in writing a biography is as important as scholarship," says author Arianna Stassinopoulos Huffington, who also notes, "When we let go of our filters through which we perceive reality, we open up to the whole truth. Intuition does not negate reason. It takes it further." Huffington meditates every day, even when on a promotional book tour. "It's the most important part of my day," she says. "The silence in my mind helps me to access that natural knowing. Sometimes the results are deep, spiritual experiences and sometimes I just get a good rest."

When doing research for her Picasso biography, Huffington found that her intuition helped her to approach people who were reluctant to talk. In the introduction to her book, she describes how Picasso's mistress, Fran-çoise Gilot, at first refused Huffington's requests for an interview, even though the two women knew each other socially. "My intuition told me not to ask her again," Huffington says. "Even though my rational mind said, 'You have to persuade her.' I trusted that inner knowing and spoke to my rational mind so as not to succumb to the temptation." Two years later, Gilot agreed to discuss Picasso with Huffington, saying that her own "inner guidance" was directing her to do so.

Gilot, who had years earlier written her own book, *Life with Picasso,* became the most forthcoming of Huffington's subjects. Because of her own spiritual orientation, which included years of yoga and meditation, Gilot provided intricate, compelling insights into Picasso's tormented, enraged psyche. It is through Gilot's testimony that the reader comes to understand why women were attracted to him and stayed with him despite his abusive behavior.

STICKING TO INTUITIVE INSIGHTS

Eric Bergren, whose screenwriting credits include *Frances* and *The Elephant Man,* regrets the time when he failed to listen to "that nagging little voice." He had been offered a rewrite project that looked like a good career move. "I was going to work for a producer and a company that was very hot. It would be a good credit. But something was telling me that the movie was not going to be made, that the producer would be in trouble, and it would take a longer time to do than they were telling me. I got a queasy feeling and heard my inner voice screaming. It turned out to be the worst experience of my career. The producer was an idiot and the film never got made."

When working on a screenplay, Bergren first gets an intuitive flash of what the scene should look like. "When I come across something that I know is not working in a screenplay, I can visualize what I need and another picture will appear to me which is the solution." When directing, he "sees the image as a hologram in which I see the effect of the camera moving across the focal point."

Once when he was directing a low-budget feature film, Bergren had a feeling of how he wanted a certain scene to work. But, he says, "the people who set up the scene, the camera crews, and the editors gave me different advice. I was frightened because they were looking at me with expressions that said, 'Okay, go ahead and hang yourself.' But I stood up for what I wanted. It looked as good on film as it did in my head."

Francis Ford Coppola, too, has found that sticking to his intuitive sense about a project is the most reliable way to work. When he gets stuck or has a creative problem while working on a film, Coppola often goes back to his first intuitive flash and allows his intuition to serve as a reference point. "Whenever I'm stumped, I always try to say, 'What made me want to get involved with this in the first place? What did I like about this project?' By recalling what originally attracted me, I'm able to come up with a logical solution. I use analysis and logic as a tool to support my intuition whereas most people use their intuition to supplement more logical, linear methods."

Coppola says that his first intuitive flash of a scene often takes the form of "a low-grade impression of the whole picture rather than a very sophisticated view of one aspect of it. I can really see and feel how everything fits in." Once he gets a flash of the spatial setup and remembers it, he says, "I go further and work in a more regular way. Then every so often I have another flash, except that by this point the analytical work tends to reinforce the intuitive impulse so that it becomes clearer."

INTUITION AND SURVIVAL ON THE JOB

For those whose professions involve physical risk, staying alive is a job in itself. That intuitive sense of when to duck, run, or face off can mean the difference between life and death.

U.S. Army Captain Monroe Johnson of the 101st Airborne division was leading a company of about 150 men in an attack on a North Vietnamese regiment. "We went out in the jungle beyond the range of normal artillery and air support to Firebase Maureen," Johnson recalls. Maureen was called a firebase of opportunity because it had some artillery pieces that were flown in for a particular operation rather than being set there permanently. This particular firebase was on a hilltop that was inaccessible by road. "Almost as soon as I got there the clouds came down and down until we were walking around in a fog. The entire division was dependent on its helicopters and they couldn't fly in zero visibility," he says.

Johnson, who commanded Company A, was ordered to join up with the commander of Company C and wait at the top of Firebase Maureen until the helicopters could get through when the weather broke. He and his men had three days' rations. "Along about the fifth day, around three in the morning, I got up to relieve myself," Johnson says. "I had an uneasy feeling. Then I heard a sound of wood knocking on wood. Like a digging sound. My hair stood on end. I didn't know what it was but I resolved that I was going to take me and my merry band away." At first light, Johnson told the commander of Company C that he was leaving. "He told me that I was disobeying orders. 'I have orders from higher authority, highest authority. I don't like it here any more. This is spooky,' I told him." Johnson and his men had been in the jungle about four hours when he heard on his radio that the commander of Company C and a group of ten men had walked into a machine-gun ambush. He and eight of his men had been killed. To date, Johnson says, he has no idea what made the sound of wood knocking on wood. "I heard it but to this day I'm not sure what it was. All I knew was that it meant this was an unhealthy place and even if it meant disobeying an order, I had to get out." Johnson was never reprimanded for taking his men out of Firebase Maureen.

Former New York City police officer Jane Finnegan is not surprised by Johnson's story. "The best guys that I ever worked with admitted that they had feelings about what would happen."

Finnegan, who worked undercover, recalls a case in which she and two male partners were trying to catch a man who fenced stolen property. The same man would scout neighborhoods where Eastern European refugees had resettled so that he could send his own crew of thieves to the homes of people who owned family silver and jewelry. The thieves would steal the loot and sell the goods back to the fence. "We had arrested three of his guys for possession of stolen property," she says. "My partners looked at each other and told me to sit with two of the perps [perpetrators, in police slang]. So I typed up the arrest reports while they went into a room with the third guy. They took him into interrogation, then back to the cell, then back to interrogation." When Finnegan asked what they were doing, they said they had turned him, that is, persuaded him to be an informant. "Those three guys looked alike to me. How did you pick that one?" she asked. They said they just had a feeling about him.

Identifying what that feeling is and learning to trust it saved her life on at least one occasion, Finnegan insists. "We were called to help someone who was sick in a housing project. I got out of the car and told my partner, 'Something's wrong. There's something really wrong.' We walked into the lobby and it looked just like a million other lobbies but I said, 'Take out your gun' and we headed up the stairs instead of taking the elevator as we normally would. By this time, all my other senses, my eyesight, hearing, smell were totally heightened. I took out my gun as we walked up the stairs and I had my back against the wall so that I would have a full range of vision and still protect my back. I kept telling myself that I was there to help someone who was sick and that it was absurd of me to act as if there was a man with a machine gun. We turned the corner and sure enough, there was a group of kids with drugs and a 9-millimeter weapon."

Another time, Finnegan's intuition tracked down a hit-and-run driver who had killed two police officers. "I heard on the radio that the car was in a completely different vicinity. Suddenly, I said, 'Make a right on Catherine Street' even though there was no way the driver could be there according to the radio. But he had made a couple of wrong turns down one-way streets in his efforts to escape and now he was heading right toward us. He jumped out of the car and started running and I caught him."

For Jane Finnegan and Monroe Johnson, intuition is keyed into staying alive and may even be part of their biological instincts. But unlike an instinct that is ingrained in every member of a species, survival intuition comes to certain individuals whereas others don't have it. Psychologist Al Siebert, who publishes "The Survivor Personality" newsletter, says that paying attention to hunches and intuition is one of the most important characteristics of those whom he calls "life's best survivors." Says Siebert, "Good survivors have this wonderful blend of pattern empathy. They are sensitive and tough and have all these things integrated in their brains and in their lives. They are paradoxical, able to be both one way and the opposite. They can take care of themselves and not be too vulnerable to other people's emotions and hostile projections. They have a mixture of being sensitive and intuitive and empathetic."

Street smart, if you will. We see it as an optimal state in which you process information using all of your resources to synthesize data and experience. But you don't need to be facing death in order to call on your own intuitive abilities. Whether your job involves chasing criminals, crunching numbers, or wrestling with paperwork, learning how to recognize and rely on those hunches and gut feelings can dramatically improve your job performance. Next time you have a gut feeling on a job interview, pay attention to it. When you get a hunch, play it. And when your intuition is right, thank the part of you that knows how to do that truly remarkable job.

PART II

TRUSTING AND VALUING YOUR INTUITION

*"Intuition is like listening to a song
that is played only once."*

—ROBERT STEMPSON

INTRODUCTION

Having defined and identified your intuition, you may still find that you are unwilling or unable to use it because you doubt its importance. Your underlying values and beliefs about the intuitive process can help or hinder your efforts to develop those abilities. In essence, if you do not believe that your intuition is important and valid, you will not be able to trust it. Conversely, if you do value your intuition, you will find that your trust in it comes naturally. In this section, we will give you information that will make it easier for you to value and trust your intuition.

As you read this section, reexamine your beliefs and consider changing those that do not help you to trust your intuition. In chapter 6, we will discuss new research into how your whole brain works that shows intuition is a mental ability that can be nurtured and cultivated. These findings validate the importance of intuitive thinking. In chapter 7, we will discuss how traditional education sabotages intuitive development. By placing a disproportionately high emphasis on measurable thinking skills, most educational systems fail to recognize, value, or nurture children's natural intuitive intelligence. We will also take a look at how one school encourages its students to use their intuition in the classroom. And we will offer suggestions to parents who want to nurture their children's intuition.

In chapter 8, we will discuss how being afraid of your intuition can prevent you from trusting it. We will also take a look at some innovative counseling approaches that can give you a new framework for accepting, valuing, and trusting your intuitive awareness. If you are afraid of your intuition and want to learn to trust it, you can use the exercise at the end of chapter 8 to build that trust.

Because intuition is ephemeral, momentary, and mental, it is not an easy subject to grasp. As you read about these important developments in creativity training, education, and psychology, we want you to come away with both knowledge and insight. The information is valuable in itself but it will have a greater impact if it transforms your understanding of the intuitive process and gives you new insight into the intuitive part of yourself.

CHAPTER 6

Whole-Brain Creativity—The Herrmann Brain Dominance Instrument

To develop your intuition, you need to respect it as a natural intelligence. You also need to believe that you deserve to use it and that by doing so, you are developing more of your whole-brain capabilities.

Ned Herrmann, president of Applied Creative Services, Ltd., is one of the pioneers in whole-brain creativity training. Since the 1970s, he has shown thousands of people how to identify their preferred thinking styles and how to use more of their whole-brain creativity. Herrmann believes that intuition is an important element in the creative process. In this chapter, we will show you how intuition and creativity are connected and how Herrmann's new approach to whole-brain thinking can give you insight into your own intuitive thinking ability. When you know more about how your brain works and specifically understand more about its intuitive intelligence, you will find that valuing your intuition comes naturally.

UNLOCKING CREATIVITY

Herrmann's interest in studying the brain originates from his personal experience of growing up with creative abilities in two different fields of study. As a child, he excelled in music as well as science and math and felt pulled in two directions. Although he entered college as a chemical engineering student, Herrmann graduated with a double major in physics and music. "I was writing my thesis on craters on the moon while I tried out for the Metropolitan Opera," he recalls. Years later, while working full-time as a lab scientist, he began to paint and sculpt, eventually producing a body of six hundred paintings and one hundred sculptures.

As manager of management education at General Electric, Herrmann noticed that some managers seemed to get a lot out of training seminars whereas others just didn't get it at all. "I concluded that we were presenting information in a highly technical way—the General Electric norm— but that even highly technical people have different learning preferences." In 1975, he began intensive research into creativity. When he learned of Dr. Roger Sperry's discovery about the autonomous left and right cerebral hemispheres, Herrmann was delighted. "Now I could explain myself to myself," he says.

After a series of experiments using biofeedback to measure the electromagnetic wave output (EEG) in the two cerebral hemispheres, he developed the Herrmann Brain Dominance Instrument (HBDI) in 1977. The instrument is the foundation of Herrmann's Applied Creative Thinking workshops and the subject of his book *The Creative Brain.* From the Ned Herrmann Group headquarters in Lake Lure, North Carolina, Herrmann and his wife, Margy, publish and edit the *International Brain Dominance Review,* a quarterly journal containing articles on the latest applications of whole-brain research.

"MORE TO IT THAN RIGHT AND LEFT"

When discussing differences in thinking styles, Herrmann often refers to right and left hemispheres but he is quick to point out, "There's more to it than right and left." As a result of his study of the physiology and psychology of the brain during his tenure as a management and training executive at General Electric, Herrmann developed a 120-question survey to determine an individual's dominant thinking style. Based in part on Sperry's left-brain/right-brain model and Dr. Paul MacLean's triune brain model, the HBDI can define, identify, and statistically measure preferences and distinctions in the major thinking styles attributed to the four quadrants of the top two brains: the limbic system and the neocortex.

The survey asks questions about preferred work assignments, best and worst subjects in schools, decision-making styles, hobbies, and responses to a variety of business and social situations. It also asks each participant to rate herself along an extrovert/introvert scale, and to select a series of self-descriptive adjectives. More than 500,000 people, including some of this country's leading chief executive officers, have participated in the HBDI survey and have received a visual circular graph showing their preferred thinking styles (see below) as well as a more data-oriented score sheet that lists strengths in each quadrant.

As you can see, the brain profile is divided into four quadrants:

HERRMANN BRAIN DOMINANCE PROFILE

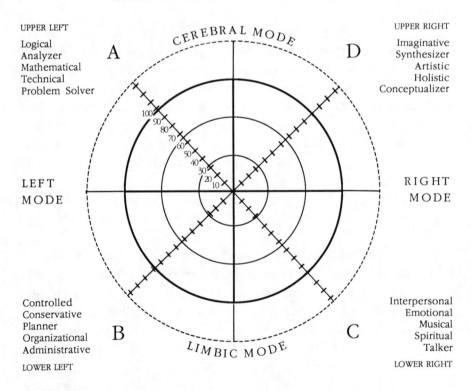

UPPER LEFT

Logical
Analyzer
Mathematical
Technical
Problem Solver

CEREBRAL MODE

UPPER RIGHT

Imaginative
Synthesizer
Artistic
Holistic
Conceptualizer

LEFT
MODE

RIGHT
MODE

Controlled
Conservative
Planner
Organizational
Administrative

LOWER LEFT

LIMBIC MODE

Interpersonal
Emotional
Musical
Spiritual
Talker

LOWER RIGHT

- *Upper Left (A)*. Logical, analyzer, mathematical, technical, problem solver.
- *Lower Left (B)*. Controlled, conservative, planner, organizational, administrative.
- *Lower Right (C)*. Interpersonal, emotional, musical, spiritual, talker.
- *Upper Right (D)*. Imaginative, synthesizer, artistic, holistic, conceptualizer.

The upper left corresponds metaphorically to the left neocortex; lower left to the left limbic system; lower right to the right limbic system; and upper right to the right neocortex. Herrmann does not include the reptilian brain in his survey because it does not have two hemispheres and does not process information in neural, synaptic responses. While the entire left side of the limbic system and neocortex is primarily verbal and structured, the upper left quadrant (neocortex) deals with facts and tends to be quantitative. The lower left (limbic) is sequential and tends to deal with structure, control, and putting things in order.

The entire right side of the limbic system and neocortex is experiential and nonverbal with a kinesthetic component in both right quadrants. The upper right quadrant (neocortex) is visual and perceives things simultaneously. The lower right (limbic) is emotional and expressive.

In this chapter, we will show you the brain profiles of Milwaukee Brewers' manager Tom Trebelhorn, National Payments Network Chief Executive Officer Louis Krouse, and Laurie Nadel, one of the authors, all three of whom filled out the 120-question Herrmann Brain Dominance survey form. The sample chart (see p. 82), showing the author's (L.N.'s) brain profile indicates fairly equal strength in both upper and lower right quadrants, and shows nearly equal preferences for visual, intuitive thinking and feeling. While the brain profile shows some preference for the lower left quadrant, indicating sequential, orderly thinking, the upper left quadrant is weak. Herrmann says this shows an avoidance of logical, numerical thinking.

THREE BRAINS, FOUR QUADRANTS?

When Herrmann's Brain Dominance Instrument began providing him with data about the brain that showed four categories of mental prefer-

LAURIE NADEL BRAIN DOMINANCE PROFILE

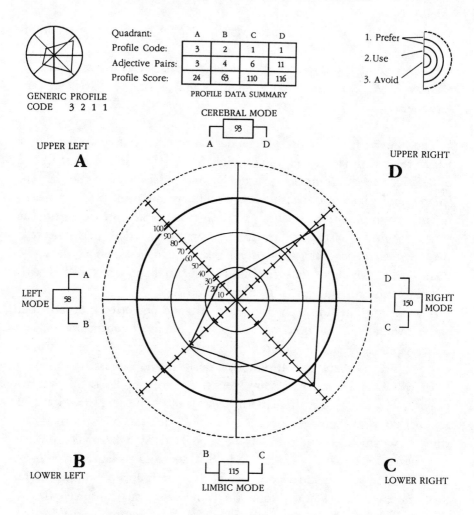

Quadrant:	A	B	C	D
Profile Code:	3	2	1	1
Adjective Pairs:	3	4	6	11
Profile Score:	24	63	110	116

GENERIC PROFILE
CODE   3 2 1 1

PROFILE DATA SUMMARY

1. Prefer
2. Use
3. Avoid

CEREBRAL MODE
93
A   D

UPPER LEFT
A

UPPER RIGHT
D

LEFT MODE   58   A / B

RIGHT MODE   150   D / C

B
LOWER LEFT

C
LOWER RIGHT

LIMBIC MODE
115
B   C

ences, he was puzzled because standard diagrams of the triune brain show only the three sections (see p. 84). The neocortex, he knew, consists of the left and right hemispheres, but nowhere in the body of whole-brain literature had he seen similar distinctions noted in connection with the limbic system. As he was driving one day, Herrmann visualized the triune brain diagram rotated and when he checked his mental image with an anatomy book, he could see that indeed, the limbic system, too, has two halves. This anchored his data more securely in brain physiology (see p. 84). "It's amazing to me that people haven't picked up on this," Herrmann says. "The limbic system, located deep in the triune brain, has a cortex. It is neural, it is synaptic, it is interconnected. It is similar in its processing to the cerebral hemispheres." That means when you get a gut feeling, an emotional rush, goose bumps, or an intuitive flash, it, too, has the same neural, synaptic base as a fact would have. While a rational thought can be affirmed in numbers, a feeling or sensing is not considered to be part of the thinking process because people believe it is not mental. But that is not true. Feeling and sensing are whole-brain abilities, too.

INTUITIVE THINKING AND FEELING

Herrmann notices distinctions between intuitive solutions (upper right) and intuitive feelings (lower right). There are some people who are very intuitive in interpersonal relationships and who feel and sense things about other people but may not be conceptually intuitive like perhaps a scientist or inventor might be. "I can make a case physiologically because these are connected. The intuition gives you direction for your creativity," Herrmann says, noting that most people who don't use their intuition tend to score high in the upper left quadrant. Learning to recognize and accept their intuition requires that they shift values to include a respect for this other dimension of their own capabilities. Many people who score high in the upper right quadrant, on the other hand, don't require a value shift in order to make better use of their upper left quadrant. Rather, they need to practice their analytical skills and to develop confidence in them.

WOMEN'S INTUITION

Women's intuition gets a boost from Herrmann, whose statistics show that women tend to score higher in the upper and lower right quadrants than do men. Backing up his findings with physiological data, Herrmann says that

THE TRIUNE BRAIN and THE ROTATED TRIUNE BRAIN

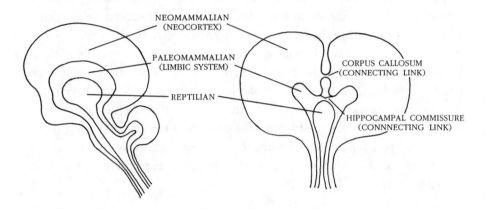

Copyright © 1988 Ned Herrmann

this occurs because the multiple axon fiber connections in the cerebral cortex and limbic system are more numerous in the female brain. "There is irrefutable postmortem evidence that when you compare the cross section of the corpus callosum, which connects the left and right neocortex, the female brain has a larger cross section of all fibers," he says. That speeds up the interactive response time between the two hemispheres, making it easier for women to blend intuition and logic. In addition, these connecting neural fibers mature up to three years earlier in girls than boys, which gives them a head start in interconnected, whole-brain thinking. In *The Creative Brain,* Herrmann wrote, "Women are, on average, more whole-brain oriented, more intuitive, and less fact-based, more open to new ideas than to the status quo, more people-oriented than thing-oriented. Therefore, they perceive their surroundings more sensitively, manage the innovative process more comfortably, and respond more rapidly to changing environmental circumstances." However, both men and women can develop and strengthen their natural intuitive and creative abilities.

BRAIN DOMINANCE AND PROFESSIONAL CHOICES

By and large, men and women tend to gravitate toward professions where they can use their natural strengths, and people in similar professions tend to have similar brain profiles (see p. 86). Thus engineers in one company will have profiles comparable to engineers in another company. While some occupations attract people who are clearly dominant in one quadrant, others, such as secretaries, attract people with multiple dominances. That's because secretarial jobs require a combination of organizational and inter-personal skills.

These patterns are not limited to the United States but occur world-wide. A group of airline pilots from India, Sweden, Japan, and the United States will have similar brain profiles even though they are from different cultures. Because their work is similar, they must excel in the same skills and therefore they will tend to think alike. Herrmann notes that their mental preferences led them to develop the competencies for that particu-lar work in the first place because we tend to gravitate toward work that allows us to be effective mentally.

Conversely, when people are in jobs that restrict or prevent them from using their natural preference, they become frustrated and depressed. Stephanie Abarbanel, now an editor at *Family Circle* magazine, spent several years as an assistant producer for a major broadcast news organiza-tion. Although her job required her to be task-oriented and involved communications skills, her real creative strength as a writer and editor was unrecognized and unused. (In terms of Herrmann's model, a television news producer would show preferences for the upper right [visual] quad-rant, the lower right [interpersonal] quadrant, and the lower left [organi-zational] quadrant. It would not require strong editorial or writing skills [upper left].) In her new job, Abarbanel relies on her writing and editing abilities, and has a chance to use all of her creative abilities. She has editorial responsibility for developing story ideas and assigning them to writers. Abarbanel's editing style is an intriguing mix of all four quad-rants: intuitive, empathetic, organizational, and analytical. "When I first read a manuscript, my major decisions are made in the first five minutes because I go with my gut feeling. I'm almost not conscious of where my ideas are coming from. Then I can feel an absolute empathy and alignment with the writer. During the second reading, I pay attention to the details." Many chief executive officers show fairly balanced dominance in all four quadrants, says Herrmann, who has obtained several CEOs' schedules and correlated their actual work with his statistical data. Over a period of two to three weeks, he says you will see a CEO's activity spread across the four

BRAIN DOMINANCE PROFILES: A Comparison by Profession

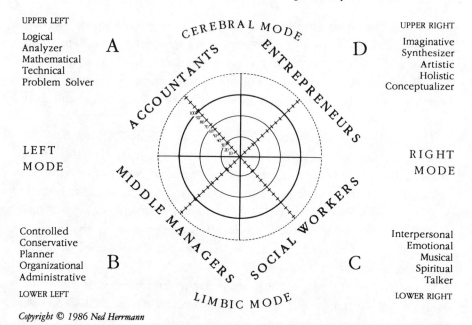

UPPER LEFT

Logical
Analyzer
Mathematical
Technical
Problem Solver

A

CEREBRAL MODE

ACCOUNTANTS

ENTREPRENEURS

D

UPPER RIGHT

Imaginative
Synthesizer
Artistic
Holistic
Conceptualizer

LEFT
MODE

RIGHT
MODE

Controlled
Conservative
Planner
Organizational
Administrative

LOWER LEFT

B

MIDDLE MANAGERS

SOCIAL WORKERS

LIMBIC MODE

C

Interpersonal
Emotional
Musical
Spiritual
Talker

LOWER RIGHT

BRAIN DOMINANCE PROFILES IN SELECTED OCCUPATIONS

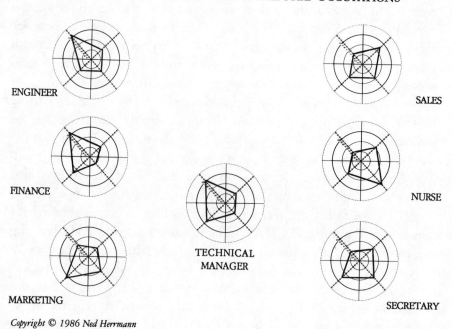

ENGINEER

FINANCE

MARKETING

TECHNICAL
MANAGER

SALES

NURSE

SECRETARY

quadrants. Herrmann finds that while both men and women CEOs score equally high in the lower left (organizational) and upper right (intuitive) quadrants, women show a stronger preference for the lower right (interpersonal) than do men, for whom it is the least-preferred quadrant. This shows that although the predominant thinking patterns are the same for men and women CEOs, women tend to be stronger in interpersonal, emotional, and expressive thinking whereas men tend to be stronger in logical, numerical thinking.

TAKING INTUITION-BASED BUSINESS RISKS

Entrepreneurs who like risk, experimentation, and creating new market opportunities score high in the upper right quadrant. Like Conrad Hilton, who stood in the lobby of a Texas flophouse and envisioned a grand hotel, an entrepreneur has the vision to perceive a need where others don't. In terms of problem solving, entrepreneurs tend to look at a problem, see what's needed, and then gather the necessary data to support their vision. The story of Lou Krouse is a case in point. As a project manager for a major communications company, Krouse was sent to an assessment center when he was being considered for promotion. During the three days of group testing, Krouse was told to examine a series of problems, choose one of three solutions, build a case for it, and present his solution scenario to the group. "I studied the problem, looked at the three solutions, and said, 'These solutions are for the birds,' " recalls Krouse. "I came up with an original solution and presented it to the group. The people in charge said, 'You can't do that. We told you to pick from the three solutions.' " But when Krouse presented his solution, it worked like a charm.

Even though his solution was effective, Krouse flunked his assessment and was informed that he was not a candidate for promotion. "They didn't want a renegade, they wanted a team player. I went home and said, 'Enough of this.' I had been there twenty-five years and decided it was time to do something else."

Krouse quit his job and founded his own company based on another idea he had come up with as a project manager. Although he came close to bankruptcy during his first year in business, Krouse's company, National Payments Network (NPN), earned $12 million during its first year and a

LOUIS J. KROUSE BRAIN DOMINANCE PROFILE

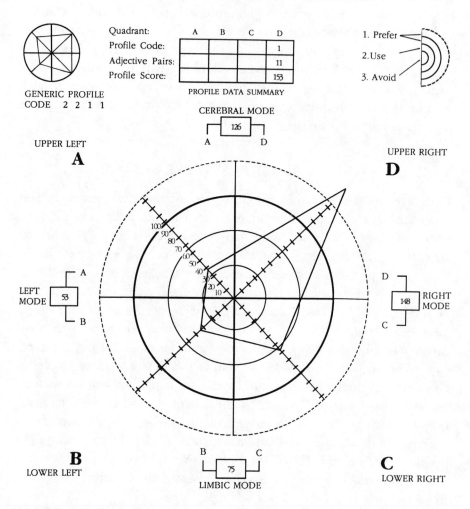

GENERIC PROFILE
CODE   2 2 1 1

Quadrant:	A	B	C	D
Profile Code:				1
Adjective Pairs:				11
Profile Score:				153

PROFILE DATA SUMMARY

1. Prefer
2. Use
3. Avoid

CEREBRAL MODE
A   126   D

UPPER LEFT
A

UPPER RIGHT
D

LEFT MODE   53

RIGHT MODE   148

B
LOWER LEFT

B   75   C
LIMBIC MODE

C
LOWER RIGHT

half. By its third year, NPN was a $22-million-a-year company. Krouse's old employer is his biggest client.

BRAIN PROFILES AND DECISION MAKING

A look at Louis Krouse's brain profile (see above) shows such a strong preference for intuitive thinking that his upper right quadrant is off the chart. An imaginative, artistic, visual thinker, his strengths are innovation, conceptualization, and integration. In his second preferred quadrant, the lower right, Krouse scores high in intuitive feeling, as well as writing, talking, self-expression, and musical ability.

The fact that entrepreneurs generally score high in the upper right quadrant reflects their overall decision-making style. Entrepreneurs tend to favor imaginative, forward-looking, risk-taking decisions and have strong conceptual intuition. When making a decision, an entrepreneur is likely to ask himself, "Have I seen all the possibilities?" He may prefer not to deal with details.

But a CEO or an executive with a preference for the upper left quadrant tends to have an abstract, data-based, theoretical decision-making style. She might ask, "Do I have all the facts?" and might overlook feelings and synergistic possibilities. Someone with a lower right preference would have an emotional, interpersonal decision-making style in which intuitive feelings would be a strong component. Such a person might ask, "How will I affect others?" and may overlook facts and planning. A manager with a strong lower left preference would tend to make decisions by asking, "Will I be in control?" She might overlook alternative solutions, novel ideas, and the big picture.

A look at the brain profile of Milwaukee Brewers' manager Tom Trebelhorn shows his preference for the lower left quadrant with its organized, conservative, and procedural decision-making style as well as an almost equal preference for the analytical, upper left quadrant (see p. 90). Trebelhorn also scores high in the upper right quadrant. The blend of discipline (lower left), analysis (upper left), and intuition (upper right) appears to reflect his balanced management style. His brain profile confirms Trebelhorn's own description of how he relies on analysis and hunches.

Conventional wisdom about executives and managers tends to attribute to them a strong preference for the lower left quadrant. But despite that stereotype, today's executives tend to be more entrepreneurial, that is they are less structured and take more risks than did executives of the past. The massive layoffs of middle managers throughout corporate America is one sign of these changing times, an indicator that conservative management styles are no longer being rewarded as they were previously. As computers take over more of the number crunching and procedural tasks, executives

THOMAS L. TREBELHORN BRAIN DOMINANCE PROFILE

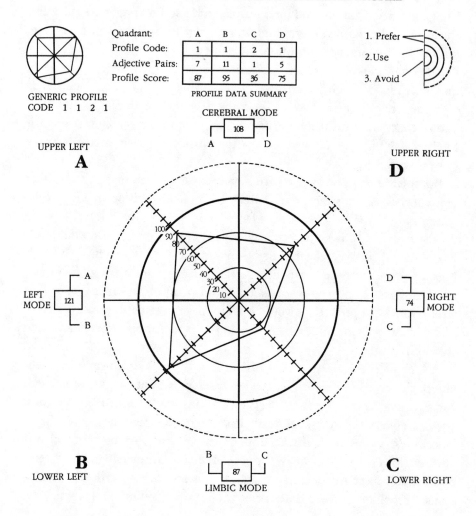

Quadrant:	A	B	C	D
Profile Code:	1	1	2	1
Adjective Pairs:	7	11	1	5
Profile Score:	87	95	36	75

PROFILE DATA SUMMARY

GENERIC PROFILE
CODE 1 1 2 1

1. Prefer
2. Use
3. Avoid

CEREBRAL MODE
108
A   D

UPPER LEFT
A

UPPER RIGHT
D

LEFT MODE 121

RIGHT MODE 74

B
LOWER LEFT

LIMBIC MODE
87
B   C

C
LOWER RIGHT

and middle managers are finding that the traditional job structures are changing. *U.S. News & World Report* projects that in the twenty-first century, successful managers will need expertise in global strategy, technological mastery, political acumen, and motivational ability—not to mention intuitive thinking.

A CORPORATE CREATIVITY SEMINAR

Such corporations as Herrmann's alma mater, General Electric (GE), Du-Pont, IBM, and Polaroid often send Herrmann top management teams in the hope that a week at his workshop will generate new ideas for particular company problems. The self-diagnostic systems on GE dishwashers, for example, came about after one of Herrmann's participants breathed "Aha!"

A group of eight Shell Oil Company executives spent four days at Herrmann's private learning center with the intention of coming up with a strategic plan involving millions of dollars. Herrmann asked them to state how they understood the plan's proposed purpose and direction. Because all eight had a different view of the problem, before turning back to it to search for potential solutions, Herrmann first had them build a model of how they perceived the structure of the problem out of wood, wire, feathers, paper, clay, and toys. Then each person described his model to the other members of the group. As the executives began coming up with some interesting elements, Herrmann took them on a boat ride to the middle of Lake Lure and told them to experience nature so as to be able to generate a metaphor related to the company's strategic problem. When they came back from the lake, the executives remodeled their problem, explained it, and looked for more potential solutions.

The next day, Herrmann escorted them to the top of Chimney Rock overlooking Lake Lure, pointed to where they had been the day before, and proposed that the executives now look at the problem from an overview perspective. When they returned to the conference room, they repeated the remodeling process and search for solutions, then listened to Herrmann conduct a guided visualization in which he asked each participant to see himself fifteen years in the future looking back at the implementation of this strategic plan.

Full of new ideas and enthused about presenting them, the executives returned to Shell Oil Company feeling that they had accomplished their mission. "What I did in that situation was try to provide a process and a climate and environment that facilitated modes of thinking that these people don't normally use but which were present at some level in each one," Herrmann explains. "I gave them permission to be playful, exploratory, and experimental. I took advantage of their differences. I orchestrated the creative process by using metaphor and intuition."

AN APPLIED CREATIVE-THINKING WORKSHOP

Herrmann likes to begin his workshops by dividing participants into groups of four, representing his composite of the whole brain. Each participant completes Herrmann's brain dominance survey prior to the workshop and is assigned to a group based on his or her preferred thinking style. Thus in any group of four, you will find one analytical thinker, one organizational and procedural thinker, one emotional or kinesthetic thinker, and one intuitive thinker. Then Herrmann presents the group with a special problem, one that can best be solved using the whole brain. "I teach people by having them experience their differences so that they can discover that there must be a value in the other person's way of thinking," Herrmann says.

In one of his favorite examples, an army colonel teamed up with a music therapist as part of a four-person team to solve a problem that required synthesizing very different sets of information. The analytical army colonel began writing down formulas while the music therapist looked out the window and seemed almost to doze off when she announced, "I've got it!"

The colonel replied, "What the hell do you mean you've got it?"

"I think I understand," she said.

"Oh yeah? Tell me."

The music therapist moved her body, demonstrating the solution kinesthetically. "You're right," the army colonel said. "You have it."

The next step was reporting back to the main group, but the music therapist could not explain in words how she had come up with her solution and asked the colonel to do it for her. When he had made his presentation, she said, "I wish I could do that!" As a result of the workshop, the colonel began to honor the instinctive, experiential, humanistic intelligences that he had been trained to reject. As a military officer, he had been told, "Don't go with that crap. Just stick with the facts." Now, he could see a place for intuition in his life. "Not all the time, though, I'd get the willies," he said. But he was willing to experiment with some of Herrmann's exercises at home. He got down on the floor with his grandchildren and began to see the world through their eyes.

The music therapist, who had avoided using her analytical and organizational abilities, decided to pay more attention to those areas. Her lack of confidence in her own analytical abilities had led her to not pay attention to some important business matters, with the result that her associates had been able to exploit her talent. When she returned from the conference, she was able to put a lawsuit together against those colleagues and moved on to produce a series of her own music tapes.

For participants like the music therapist, who have trouble with numbers and analysis, Herrmann likes to teach statistics using M&M's candies. By counting the varying numbers per bag in a playful way, people with no sense of their own mathematical strengths find they can suddenly understand terms such as mean, average, and other statistical functions such as standard deviation and central tendency. Loosening up is an integral component to the creative process, whether you are becoming more fluent in experiential, intuitive awareness or becoming proficient in organization and logic. Because many people associate creativity with proficiency in the visual arts, Herrmann spends time helping participants discover their latent talent at drawing, painting, and sculpture through a series of exercises that relax the critical inner voice that says, "You can't draw." Herrmann calls his approach "disabling language logic" and says, "For most people, it's a question of detuning the left hemisphere, the seat of language logic, through a series of exercises. When it disengages by dropping into alpha or theta brain waves, it allows drawing to take place by giving the right hemisphere subtle, mental permission."

Although he sees intuition as a valuable part of the creative process, Herrmann does not teach intuitive thinking as part of his workshops, noting, "It's accessible, confirmable, and affirmable. We provide an atmosphere in which people can become aware of it, are not punished for it, and can see that there is a reason to develop and trust it."

BRAIN PROFILES AND RELATIONSHIPS

Herrmann sees his work as a way to help people understand themselves as well as a way to enhance their creativity. The circular brain profile is also a source of data on how couples and family members communicate (see pps. 94 and 96). In a study of more than five hundred married couples,

HERRMANN BRAIN DOMINANCE PROFILE

Husband and Wife

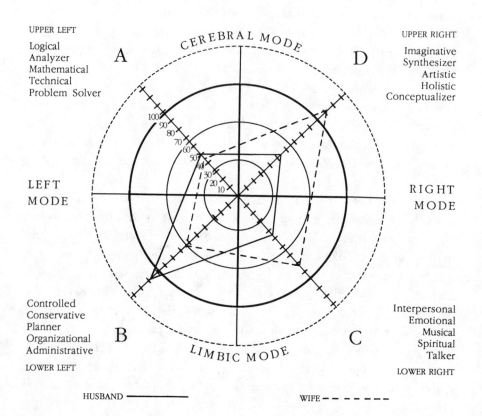

UPPER LEFT

Logical
Analyzer
Mathematical
Technical
Problem Solver

A

CEREBRAL MODE

D

UPPER RIGHT

Imaginative
Synthesizer
Artistic
Holistic
Conceptualizer

LEFT
MODE

RIGHT
MODE

Controlled
Conservative
Planner
Organizational
Administrative

LOWER LEFT

B

LIMBIC MODE

C

Interpersonal
Emotional
Musical
Spiritual
Talker

LOWER RIGHT

HUSBAND ——————   WIFE – – – – – –

Herrmann found that in 75 percent of those couples, husband and wife
had markedly different brain profiles. In less than 20 percent of the couple
profiles he studied were there any significant similarities. Generally, men
tend to favor the upper left and right cerebral hemispheres and women tend
to prefer the lower left and right limbic quadrants. (Cerebral thinking is
conceptual whereas limbic thinking is sensing and feeling.) In terms of left
and right, the majority of men surveyed showed a preference for the left
side and women, the right. In his book *The Creative Brain,* Herrmann offers
a hypothesis for this pattern: Opposites attract, he says, possibly because

each partner seeks wholeness and therefore gravitates to someone whose thinking style is complementary.

Herrmann, who has used the HBDI profile in consultation with couples, finds that when one partner looks at the other's brain profile, he or she gets new insight. Simply reviewing the chart often helps to alleviate tension. Many people have expressed relief at seeing a visual representation of their partner's thinking style, and quite a few have exclaimed, "Oh, you are different. I thought you were doing those things on purpose just to upset me."

In another case, Herrmann drew up brain profiles for a family of five, at the request of the father who was having difficulty understanding one of his sons. He and the rest of the family called this boy "Weird John." John was an artistic boy whose behavior, interests, and friendships were different from those of the rest of the family, which tended to be more pragmatic. The brain profile composite showed John's preference for the intuitive, creative, upper right quadrant whereas the other four family members were solidly in the upper and lower left. After examining the composite chart, John's father and other members of the family were able to reach out to him and accept him as someone who is different rather than weird.

FINDING A METAPHOR FOR INTUITION

A psychologist who had been working on a theory of memory recently proposed in a lecture that memory could be represented as a very large bureau with drawers in it. When a piece of information comes along, you open the drawer, put it in, and close the drawer. The critical part is getting the labels on the drawers. In the middle of his presentation, a man in the audience, who had been getting angrier and angrier, stood up to speak. With smoke curling out of his ears, he said, "I'm a neurosurgeon and goddamn it, I've opened up hundreds of skulls and I have never seen a drawer!"

The psychologist leaned down from the podium and said, "Yes, Charles, I understand your problem. But you see, they're very, very tiny."

Several prominent neuroscientists have laughed at this joke based on a collision of the left- and right-brain ways of looking at the world, but like the neurosurgeon in the anecdote, if you are predominately left brained,

HERRMANN BRAIN DOMINANCE PROFILE

General Composite of Male and Female

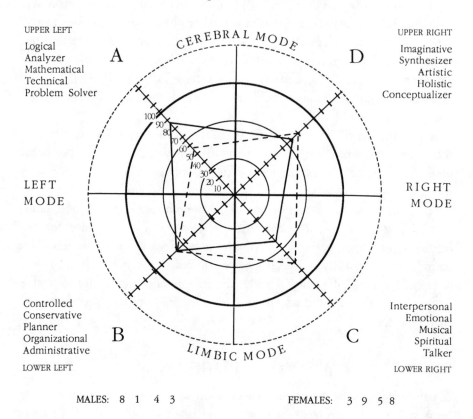

UPPER LEFT

Logical
Analyzer
Mathematical
Technical
Problem Solver

A

CEREBRAL MODE

D

UPPER RIGHT

Imaginative
Synthesizer
Artistic
Holistic
Conceptualizer

LEFT
MODE

RIGHT
MODE

Controlled
Conservative
Planner
Organizational
Administrative

B

LIMBIC MODE

C

Interpersonal
Emotional
Musical
Spiritual
Talker

LOWER LEFT

LOWER RIGHT

MALES: 8 1 4 3   FEMALES: 3 9 5 8

you may not find it funny. Literal explanations may work for you whereas
metaphors may not. The metaphor, which gives you a verbal image of a
situation, speaks directly to the holistic part of your brain. When you are
learning a subject, assembling a theory, or working with complex concepts, creating a metaphor is a good way to show that you've understood.

As we mentioned earlier, one of our favorite metaphors for intuition
describes its function as a satellite dish in the mind, able to pick up signals
from the unconscious and transpose them in the form of images, ideas, and
feelings onto the screen of conscious awareness. (A number of scientists

have called our metaphor "perfectly respectable," although Dr. Sperry laughed and said, "No one can prove you are wrong.") Robert Stempson says that intuition is like listening to a song that is only played once. For magazine editor Stephanie Abarbanel, intuition is like being at the controls of a spaceship for the first time and knowing exactly what to do. Ned Herrmann describes intuition as "a kind of sonar that searches for information that might be within. It can also be seen as a kind of braille wherein the sensitive fingertips of the mind pick up encoded information and are responsive to it." Metaphor is a powerful way of knowing and communicating what you know, especially when you are dealing with a nonverbal essence like intuition. Finding your own metaphor for intuition is one of the best ways to give it form, an essential step in developing your intuitive thinking.

Herrmann likes to ask participants in his creativity workshops to come up with their own metaphors in connection with new concepts and solutions to problems. "I use the metaphor as a way of testing for understanding. When you can translate back into a metaphoric mode, then you can demonstrate whether you understand. The translation gives you a direct hit or a clear miss because if you don't get it, you can't come up with a metaphor." Near the end of his workshops, Herrmann will ask participants to draw a picture, build a model, or write a couple of lines of poetry as a metaphor.

The Herrmann Brain Dominance Instrument is itself a metaphor for your brain and how it functions. In evaluating his own work, Herrmann believes one of his main accomplishments is presenting a model of brain function that establishes and validates the legitimacy of intuitive processing. "I feel very secure because it is validated in everyday life," he says. "When there is hard data over here and then soft, unprovable data over there, we tend to deprecate our intuition even if the hard data is false." Instead of vascillating, we need to value, acknowledge, and trust our intuition for what it is, a sense of truth.

CHAPTER 7

The Brain You Took to School

Considering how many of us have learned to trust and value our intuition as adults, doesn't it strike you as ironic that no one taught you to value it in school? Perhaps you used it and were punished, so you gave it up. Captain Monroe Johnson, the company commander who had a hunch he should get his men away from Firebase Maureen, remembers, "As a kid, I did arithmetic with intuition and allowed the answer to compute. I got the answer ten times faster that way." But in junior high school, Monroe's teachers flunked him for getting the right answers without being able to show the steps by which he arrived at them.

Perhaps you were scolded for daydreaming, doodling, or looking out the window. Or you found it hard to sit still. Maybe some of your teachers went so far as to label you lazy, inattentive, hyperactive, or even learning disabled even though you may have demonstrated unusual strengths, like taking a watch apart and putting it together without instructions. Perhaps you were ridiculed when you did not know the right answer. Most of us have had learning experiences as children that made us feel uncomfortable. Many of us were intimidated and pressured into learning how to pass tests and please teachers rather than stimulated to enjoy discovering new ideas.

In its failure to value differences in the way people learn, the educational process often suppresses intuition, creativity, and your sense of identity. Trusting your inner voice, which is one of the critical steps in developing intuition, is predicated on being truly self-confident. Learning how to trust your intuition is really learning how to trust that part of yourself that knows from within. But because traditional education does not recognize intuition as an intelligence—that is, a recognizable style of absorbing and processing information—you have to broaden the conventional definition of "intelligence" for yourself and learn how to use your full intellectual capacity again. Only then will you be able to believe in your intuitive abilities.

Each of us has more intelligence than we are trained to use and the part that we get graded on in school doesn't amount to much. Most of us were taught that only those step-by-step processes that lead to conclusions or right answers are valid mental skills. We went to school to train this kind of intelligence and when we used it well and got high marks our parents, teachers, and relatives rewarded us with A's. But how many of us can say that we got an A in intuition? In visual thinking? In kinesthetic intelligence?

MULTIPLE INTELLIGENCES: GARDNER'S MODEL

Educators are starting to realize that there is more untapped mental ability available to children than ordinary education reaches. In his 1983 book, *Frames of Mind,* Harvard educator Howard Gardner identifies seven recognizable and different ways of processing information. He calls them multiple intelligences, and defines them as:

- *Linguistic Intelligence.* Ability to use language, auditory skills.
- *Logical-Mathematical Intelligence.* Ability to think logically, sequentially, and numerically.
- *Spatial Intelligence.* Ability to visualize and manipulate images mentally.
- *Musical Intelligence.* Ability to hear, appreciate, and play music. Sensitivity to nonverbal sounds.
- *Bodily Kinesthetic Intelligence.* Physical ability—athletic or fine-motor coordination. Ability to process information through body movement and "gut feelings."
- *Interpersonal Intelligence.* Ability to get along with people.
- *Intrapersonal Intelligence.* Ability to be self-motivated and inner directed.

A teacher who recognizes that a child's particular strengths may lie in a nontraditional intelligence rather than in the established, academically accepted intelligences can help him to learn by building on those strengths. According to Gardner's model, for example, a child who could not sit still might be strong in bodily kinesthetic intelligence and would probably benefit from a program that incorporated physical movement. He might need to take frequent breaks so that he could run off some energy and would benefit from exercises that bring the left and right sides of his body together, such as calisthenics or stretching. Exercises like these create connections between different parts of the brain and make it easier for someone with kinesthetic intelligence to learn.

There is clearly a gap in the education system that completely overlooks the importance of intelligences that are not rational, sequential, and measurable. By not seeing that each of us has several intelligences and different strengths that function simultaneously, and by not teaching in a way that allows us to make best use of those resources, the educational process restricts and even cripples some of its brightest students. "School is set up to be a paradigm for reality and that paradigm limits us. It gives us a handle on how to live in the world and it also keeps us confined within that paradigm. That's the double-edged sword of education," says psychologist Dan Miller. An intuitive student, for example, will only have the confidence to tackle a variety of subjects when his particular strength is considered a mental skill.

NEUROEDUCATION

In France, some educators are starting to take this into account by promoting neuroeducation, a process that integrates new information about the brain and thinking styles into the curriculum. A music teacher would instruct a student with left-brain dominance differently than he would a student with right-brain dominance. The teacher would recognize that the former would understand music as a series of sequential notes heard and played one by one and the latter would hear and play melodies. In other subjects, a left-brain dominant student would be strong on factual, objective information and would respond to unemotional presentation whereas a right-brain dominant student would enjoy doing several things at once and would be able to draw associations and comparisons. A left-brain student might see a subject as the sum of its parts whereas a right-brain student would start by getting the whole picture. French educators have also noted some patterns in writing styles. Left-brain dominant students tend to be criticized for repetitive writing, dry style, and a lack of creative ideas, whereas right-brain dominant students are often told that they have interesting ideas presented in a disorganized fashion.

Ned Herrmann believes that differences in learning styles can be explained in part as reflections of natural thinking style preferences as seen in the four quadrants surveyed in the Herrmann Brain Dominance Instrument. He advocates developing different design and delivery styles to reach students with different thinking and learning preferences (see p. 102).

Dr. Mary Schmitt, a neurophysiologist and whole-brain learning specialist, is finding that many North American teachers are now aware that education as we know it is undergoing a transition marked by "a shift in thinking as all-encompassing as that of the Copernican revolution three hundred years ago." Says Dr. Schmitt, "Today the very foundations of our understanding the role of our consciousness are being reevaluated. It is time to integrate right-brain knowing with left-brain thinking and to use the many cognitive, affective, physical, and intuitive techniques for whole-brain learning."

THE MEAD SCHOOL

Dr. Schmitt has been applying scientific research on the brain in the field of education since the mid-1970s when she conducted the first biofeedback experiments for fifth-, sixth-, and seventh-grade students at the Mead School for Human Development in Greenwich, Connecticut. Founded in 1969 by educator Elaine de Beauport, Mead was the first school in the United States to encourage children to use all their mental abilities—including intuition—as part of the learning process. "Long before people knew about the right brain/left brain, Elaine had an intuitive sense that this is the way education had to be," says Dr. Schmitt. Alarmed by what they perceived as their own children shutting down creatively, several parents joined forces with de Beauport to create a place where kids who had learned how to conform to traditional school rules by not thinking for themselves could learn in their own way. If a child hated language but loved animals or the environment, Mead teachers would try to find a way to utilize that love of learning to give the child some needed language skills.

WHOLE-BRAIN LEARNING AND DESIGN CONSIDERATIONS

UPPER LEFT A

LEARNS BY:

Acquiring and Quantifying Facts
Applying Analysis and Logic
Thinking Through Ideas
Building Cases
Forming Theories

LEARNERS RESPOND TO:

Formalized Lecture
Data Based Content
Financial/Technical Case Discussions
Text Books and Bibliographies
Program Learning
Behavior Modification

UPPER RIGHT D

LEARNS BY:

Taking Initiative
Exploring Hidden Possibilities
Relying on Intuition
Self Discovery
Constructing Concepts
Synthesizing Content

LEARNERS RESPOND TO:

Spontaneity....Free Flow
Experiential Opportunities
Experimentation...
Playfulness
Future Oriented Case Discussions
Visual Displays...
Aesthetics
Individuality...
Being Involved

LOWER LEFT B

LEARNS BY:

Organizing and Structuring Content
Sequencing Content
Evaluating and Testing Theories
Acquiring Skills Through Practice
Implementing Course Content

LEARNERS RESPOND TO:

Thorough Planning
Sequential Order
Organizational Case Discussion
Text Books
Behavior Modification
Program Learning
Structure
Lectures

LOWER RIGHT C

LEARNS BY:

Listening and Sharing Ideas
Integrating Experiences with Self
Moving and Feeling
Harmonizing with the Content
Emotional Involvement

LEARNERS RESPOND TO:

Experiential Opportunities
Sensory Movement
Music
People Oriented Case Discussions
Group Interaction

"Ninety percent of what we did that very first year was to turn children from passive learners to active learners," says Joan Pankosky, one of the Mead School's founding teachers. "I think we had no absenteeism for three months. My own child used to cry and say that he would never talk to me again if he had to stay home." Going to Mead was a lot like being turned loose in a candy store because when the students arrived for the day the teachers would ask them, "What do you want to do today? Where do you want to go?"

Although the school has grown from 40 to approximately 170 students and the school day is now more structured than it was at the beginning, Mead students still plan their own programs and do not receive formal grades. In those respects, and in its strong arts program, Mead could be called an elementary-school level equivalent to such progressive colleges as Sarah Lawrence and Bennington. Founded on a set of principles called The Seven Skills, the Mead School defines the learning process as thinking, intuiting, imagining, expressing, receiving, respecting, and acting. The most important and, at the same time, most elusive skill is respect. Defined as meaning "to look again," respect does not have the old-fashioned connotation of deferring to teachers as authorities. Here, respect means truly caring for yourself, appreciating your own self-worth, respecting and caring for others, and appreciating and caring for materials and for each person's physical space. Another credo concerns intuition, which the Mead School believes is a skill that exists in some form in everyone and that can be developed. "This skill can be used successfully along with the more traditional and accepted ways of thinking: strategic, logical, visual, and cognitive," states another Mead School pamphlet.

With an overall teacher-student ratio of 1:7, classes at Mead are divided into home centers, made up of students who are the same age, and curriculum centers where students of any age can learn about a particular subject. Home-center directors help each student discover his strengths and needs, and serve as a liaison between children and parents. Visual and expressive arts make up more than 50 percent of the school's curriculum. The Mead School believes that the arts are central to the cognitive process and that together with traditional academic subjects they form the core of true education. In addition to developing an aesthetic sense, art nurtures such skills as trusting personal decisions, distinguishing parts from the whole, and converting unintended results into new concepts. Geology, biology, chemistry, oceanography, and computer classes focus primarily on hands-on experiential approaches. Although there are no internal grades, Mead students score above grade level in all SAT subjects. Children who score below grade level in the first three years tend to improve so that they score at or above grade level by the fifth and sixth year. Notes Pankosky, "A lot of the children who come to Mead are children who weren't succeeding at other schools. The reason turns out to be that some of them are so intelligent that they were bored silly elsewhere."

HEMISPHERIC LEARNING STUDIES

By the mid-1970s, educators were becoming aware of the work of Dr. Roger Sperry, the neuroscientist at the California Institute of Technology who discovered some of the fundamental differences between the left and right hemispheres of the neocortex. Elaine de Beauport was initially skeptical about the findings. "I didn't believe it very much," she says.

Dr. Schmitt borrowed a large polygraph machine from the Graphs Instrument Company in Boston and brought it to the Mead School where she connected electrodes to the heads of fifth, sixth, and seventh graders during art, math, language skills, and doodling activities. They were soon able to see the polygraph paper emerging from the machine and could tell whether their left or right brain was trying to solve a particular task. They could also see if their muscles tensed up while they were doing math or spelling and were later shown some techniques to help control those nervous responses so they could improve their learning.

Dr. Schmitt's findings showed that many children had definite tendencies to use one hemisphere more than another for every assignment, whether the task be primarily right hemispheric, such as art, or left hemispheric such as language or mathematics. Other children showed fairly equal bilateral activity. Those who had difficulty with art tasks emitted very slow brain waves coming from their right hemisphere, a sign that the right neocortex was not engaged in that particular assignment. One boy, who was having trouble doing a long-division problem, found that by looking at his EEG output he was able to see that he was trying to follow his left brain. Dr. Schmitt advised him to try another long-division problem and solve it any way he wanted to. Within seconds, he came up with the right answer to a three-digit number divided by a two-digit number. "When I asked him how to do it, he said he didn't know," Dr. Schmitt recalls. "By watching his brain-wave pattern, we could see that he was doing it in a right-brain way, rather than in sequential steps the way the left brain does it."

For teacher Pankosky, the studies provided verification for what Mead teachers were doing all along. "The studies were outward signs that you could hang your hat on and you could talk to parents about. We could tell them, 'When you're in alpha, you can absorb more and think more clearly.' We could justify ourselves to parents." De Beauport correlated the EEG results with each child's written records and was astounded by the results. "I wouldn't have believed it if it had just been the machines. But we had each child's school records to show similar learning patterns. What was beautiful was that the kids could talk about it, too."

As a result of the hemispheric learning project, de Beauport began her own research into the brain. Dr. Paul MacLean's triune brain model confirmed the validity of how Mead School teachers experienced their role in education. "The triune brain is an incredible charter for the human family and I have taken the freedom to interpret it," de Beauport says. With a new awareness of the reptilian brain, Mead School teachers came to further emphasize respect for personal space and territory. The first rule for learning became: Be comfortable. When it does not feel comfortable or secure, the reptilian brain sends out distress signals to the higher brains, effectively blocking the energy needed for focused attention. Mead students are encouraged to use their limbic intelligences by knowing their own feelings and learning to express them. Motivational intelligence is stimulated by a variety of interactive projects, like the Happy Hands Hotel for pets. One of the first experiential projects at Mead, the Happy Hands Hotel was a place where students could arrange to bring their pets in for the day by booking space in advance, as if for a hotel. Then they would introduce their poodle, goldfish, or boa constrictor to the other children. For a social studies project on Africa, Mead students created an African village in the gym and learned an African dialect. They performed dances, games, and rituals and prepared meals of yams, honey, and yogurt.

Presenting students with a menu of mental abilities that they can call on as needed increases their flexibility in all situations. Intuitive thinking, which Elaine de Beauport describes as "the ability to validate from within," is equally as important for children to learn as the ability to verify externally. "Babies are very interior, but when they get to first grade, immediately they start looking around and they have to validate what they're learning from books, from the teacher, or from each other. By the sixth or seventh grade, they often don't believe that they know anything from within." Teaching that there are things they can validate from inside themselves as well as externally is an essential component of helping children develop integrity.

With that in mind, the Mead School offers students various meditation, guided imagery, and visualization exercises. Pankosky helped her class prepare for taking the first standardized tests by asking them to close their eyes and get in touch with their wise person within. "I would do a guided imagery where they would get in touch with their teacher within who really knew how to take tests and who had been taking tests for them. I would ask them to close their eyes, to take a deep breath and that would stop the panic. By closing their eyes, they would make contact with that inner part of themselves." Pankosky would guide them through a meditation where they would go into a sunny field and relax. "By leading each child to that part of him or her that really knows, I was able to show a connection. Instead of its being strange, they could say, 'There is a part of me that really knows how to take tests.' When they made contact with that part, I asked them to turn over their question to the wise part of them that knew how to take tests and then just go with whatever response came to mind." Parents for whom a school like Mead is not an option can introduce their own children to the wise teacher as a way of helping them overcome anxiety and begin to recognize and trust their intuition.

Pankosky found that not only did her students relax and perform better during tests but that when she was away from class, her students would include the wise teacher meditation to help them with other stressful situations. Several years after introducing this guided meditation, a medical doctor contacted Pankosky to discuss one of her students. This little boy's friend had died when they were in kindergarten and he had become afraid to go to sleep. But he told the doctor, "Every night I go to sleep with the wise part of me that knows how to go to sleep and wake up in the morning. I feel safe since I know that part of me is always helping."

THE MEAD SCHOOL EXPERIMENTS

If you don't think that helping a child learn how to rely on his inner knowing is a legitimate intellectual skill, that could be the result of your own education and conditioning. As we have said, rational, sequential intelligence is only one piece of the whole brain. The left neocortex, which we call "the brain you took to school" can only perform certain functions having to do exclusively with external reality. Although the left neocortex is the center of language, the other brain systems are nonverbal and cannot measure time and space. The right neocortex is continually absorbing information from both the external and the internal worlds. It translates its perceptions into visions, glimpses, innovations, and intuition. The left neocortex then processes these perceptions as language so that we can speak about them and make them concrete. We tend to denigrate information that we sense, feel, or intuit because the process by which we obtain it cannot be reduced to a step-by-step procedure. But intuition is nonetheless an intellectual skill, one that cannot be systematically measured or graded.

IQ tests, for example, measure only two and a half intelligences—logic, language, and spatial. Some of the early IQ tests given to four- and five-year-old children, who do not yet know how to read, involve spatial and kinesthetic skills such as picture identification and drawing. Many children score higher on these preverbal IQ tests when they are younger because they are using more of their whole brain. Then, around the age of eight or nine, their IQ scores often drop simply because their language skills are limited. Traditional education emphasizes measurable brain skills to the exclusion of those such as intuitive intelligence, which cannot be quantified. However, intuition is a big help when taking IQ tests. Because it is an immediate knowing, it can help a student set priorities as well as providing answers. Many people find the spatial questions the most difficult to answer in an IQ test because it is hard for them to mentally manipulate images. Spatial and intuitive intelligences are closely linked in the right neocortex, and a strong intuition can boost spatial problem-solving abilities.

Given intuition's subtle nature, we believe teachers can nurture it even within the constraints of a traditional academic system and thereby maximize each student's potential. De Beauport points out that simply by "waiting for answers, for reflections, and for insights," students can learn how to be receptive to that still, small voice within. In fact, to do otherwise is cheating them. "When you look at the light going off in any little kid at the age of three and then you look again at eight, it's heartbreaking. They ought to teach kids to take it all in and see what comes to them. Let them say, my hunch is this, my guess is that, or maybe I could try this," de Beauport advises.

Rather than having children read to get to the end of a paragraph so that they can summarize it, a teacher can ask them to wait for glimpses of meaning, for the "aha!" In history, it can mean waiting for new ways to see old information and then validating that new insight. For example, in math, students can wait for new configurations; in geometry, for new ways of grasping wholes and seeing new arrangements of symbols. In science, it's waiting for an hypothesis. "The way you learn rational thinking is to put one foot after another. You learn to doubt, you learn to question. If you want to learn intuitive thinking, you have to learn to wait for the insight," she says. You probably remember a kindergarten exercise in which you were asked, "What's wrong with this picture?" To stimulate intuitive thinking, you might ask a child, "What would you like to add to this picture? What do you like about this picture? What does this picture tell you? What feelings do you get from this picture?"

HOMEWORK FOR PARENTS

Stepping back and waiting for a child to come up with an insight or answer is one way for parents to encourage intuitive thinking. As de Beauport explains, parents conceive their role as being directive but they need to see that standing back is equally nurturing and instructive. Parents must take responsibility for not showing a child how to put a toy together or how to climb a jungle gym. Not intruding inspires trust and lets the child know that he is a capable person. That's how you communicate respect and love.

Respecting a child's personal space also helps to build self-confidence. One of the strongest ways to be able to access intuition comes from feeling grounded in the sense of self. That means acknowledging that a child has his own territory and his own place in it, and that he deserves to be there. It is hard to risk being sure of something that is not concrete, like intuition, without that inner knowledge of wholeness.

This is the same for boys as for girls. Until very recently, the education system fostered many gender-based distinctions that have been reflected in adult society. Boys were expected to be reasonable, unemotional, levelheaded, and proficient in mathematics and science. A boy who was a talented artist or dancer was called a sissy. Girls were expected to do well in art and music. It was okay for them to have feelings. Those girls who excelled in science and math were often socially ostracized. Expectations like these reinforce the myth that women's intuition is somehow second rate compared to rational problem solving. "Men are not brought up to understand that being intuitive is an extremely valuable part of being a man," psychologist Miller says. Miller has treated women who lack intuition as well as men who are highly intuitive. He notes that "we are brought up to be scientific, rational, and with common sense. The intuitive part of ourselves has been squelched by all the various factors of our upbringing." Placing this derogatory value on intuition effectively makes it harder for boys to accept their own intuitive thinking abilities. And that, in turn, makes it more difficult for them to accept the intuitive side of themselves when they leave school and need to call on it in the adult world.

As a parent, you can approach your child's teacher and say, "I value my son's intuition and I would like you to, also." Or you can say, "I want my child to use his whole mind." If the teacher is not receptive, bring in articles and books to support your position. It is up to you, the parent, to help the teacher and the school understand that intuition is a part of a child's intellect, that it is a skill for living, and that it's important that each child be able to express himself in this individual and creative way.

By listening attentively, you let your child know that his sense about a feeling or a dream is valid. When a child knows something for which there can be no rational explanation, explain the concept of intuition. You can reassure the child by giving that way of knowing a name.

Any fear that Kelly Tyburski may have had about discussing her dreams was overshadowed by the gruesome truth that they foretold. According to an Associated Press report, Detective Richard Pomorski of Canton, Michigan, said that Kelly "had nightmares or dreams, or whatever you want to call them, that her mother was in a place where she couldn't move, either tied up or locked up." Kelly's mother had disappeared in 1985. After dreaming about her mother, Kelly remembered that a locked freezer in the house had not been used since her mother's disappearance. The key to that freezer had mysteriously disappeared but Kelly pried the lock off and found her mother's body. Then she told the police. Her father, Leonard Tyburski, confessed to the murder.

Sometimes children are so highly intuitive that parents pull back in fear, signaling that this way of knowing is unacceptable. Lisa, now sixteen, says that her parents didn't know what to make of her when she would announce that some faraway relative was sick, or that some friend of the family had just had an accident. "They thought I was weird," she says. "Like the time we were waiting for my Aunt Bertha and I told my mom that Aunt Bertha wouldn't make it because she had just been in an accident. But then they got used to it and started calling me the good witch." Her family's humor only served to increase Lisa's feelings that there was something wrong with her. She is now working with a psychotherapist who acknowledges intuitive experience as important, and she is becoming more comfortable with that part of herself.

Sometimes parents are too preoccupied with their own concerns to pay attention when their child expresses strong gut feelings about a person or place. When Abigail Ferrante decided to remarry, her ten-year-old daughter, Samantha, behaved in a distraught manner. Although Samantha had indicated that she distrusted Abigail's fiancé from the first time she had met him one year earlier, Abigail discounted her daughter's reaction as simple jealousy. When Samantha pointed out that even Abigail's first impressions of her fiancé had been negative, she was told by her mother that she was overreacting. At the wedding, Samantha clutched her mother's gown and cried off and on for several hours. Asked by friends whether Samantha may have genuine concerns, Abigail insisted that this was just a jealous ten-year-old overreacting. Two weeks after the wedding, Abigail's new husband told her that Samantha would not be allowed to bring her toys into their three-bedroom apartment because there was "no room." Charging that the little girl was unstable, he threatened to have Samantha placed in a psychiatric institution. Several days later, he started screaming at her and then punched the little girl with his fists. Abigail called the police, had him removed from the premises, and began divorce proceedings. "I guess she knew something," Abigail conceded several months later. "For that matter, I should have trusted my gut feelings about him, too."

As children, most of us learned to ignore our intuitive feelings or to be quiet about them. Because our parents probably did not speak to us about their intuition, we modeled their behavior and stopped discussing it because we sensed that it would be socially unacceptable to do otherwise. So when your child tells you that he had a strange feeling about something or someone, acknowledge his intuitive feelings and discuss what they feel like. In this way, you can do a lot to reverse many of the negative social messages that will block future intuitive perception.

You can also encourage your child to trust his gut feelings when making a decision. When Helen Alexander applied to nine colleges, she was having a hard time deciding which one to choose. She and her mother examined the list with several questions in mind. Were the courses interesting? Was the faculty interesting? Did you like the person who interviewed you? Did you like the campus? After narrowing the choice to three finalists, Helen's mom asked her, "In your gut, which is the one that seems to speak to you the most? Because even if you change your mind, that is the most honest decision and it will be the best one for you."

As a child, you may have been called weird for talking about your dreams, feelings, or premonitions, and you may have decided that it was preferable to tune intuition out rather than tune it in. Teachers, friends, and family may have subtly reinforced that self-judgment over the years. If you are naturally intuitive, then no matter how hard you tried to suppress it, nothing really worked. After several experiences in which your inner knowing was confirmed by external events, you probably breathed a sigh of relief and allowed yourself to accept and trust it. If you are not naturally intuitive, you may have had one or two experiences that made a strong impression, but you are not comfortable talking about them. Or you may have discovered naturally the value of respecting your hunches and gut feelings over the course of time, without thinking about it. Now, as a parent, when you begin to notice signs of intuition in your children, you may want to take some time to think about how you would like to respond. You can snuff it out subtly by ignoring it or attempt to squelch it outright if it makes you uncomfortable. Or you can reexamine your own education and life experience and find a way to let your child express his inner truth.

CHAPTER 8

Intuition Anxiety and Intuitive Counseling Approaches

Not only are we educated to undervalue intuitive thinking as an intellectual ability but many of us are simply frightened by the impact an intuitive experience can have. Whatever the causes, intuition anxiety can prevent you from using this powerful tool for getting information. Intuition anxiety, which we also call *the undermind factor* because it undermines your mind, seems to have a life of its own. When you allow it to scare you, not only do you undermind communication from your own intuition but you also undermind your belief in its validity, thereby preventing the necessary trust from taking hold.

In this chapter, we will discuss intuition anxiety and how it can prevent you from trusting your intuition. We will also take a look at how certain therapeutic approaches can help you value and trust your intuitive process.

Many people who begin to open up to their intuitive awareness are frightened by what they perceive as a loss of control. They say, "I'm going into a void. I'm scared of change. I don't know what this is going to look like. I don't know who I will be after this is through." Unaccustomed to being able to receive and process information in this new way, others are scared by the sense of their parameters moving out. When you embrace intuition, there are no boundaries for safety, only limitless possibilities. As in any new experience—be it a job change, new relationship, or a new home—it takes time to become comfortable with it. Focusing on your fear makes it more difficult for you to move to a state of trust.

HOW FEAR UNDERMINDS INTUITION

Because intuition is a personal dimension of knowing, your failure to trust it is also a failure to trust yourself and to love that part of yourself that recognizes truth. When you are afraid of your intuition, you are underminding yourself. Eleanor MacIntyre, an entrepreneur whose company manufactures and distributes children's clothing, found this out the hard way. MacIntyre, who attributes her long-standing resistance to discussing intuition to her Catholic upbringing, allowed other people's intuition to guide her for most of her life. When her partner in a marketing venture spoke about a hunch or gut feeling, they would both pursue it. "About a year before we folded the company, I had a gut feeling that we should stop production," MacIntyre recalls. "I told her to stop a $1,200 order for promotional materials because we had no orders for the product. But she told me, 'My intuition is always right. You don't have any.'" One year later, MacIntyre and her partner went bankrupt. "I lost all the equity in my house and six years later I have still not recovered financially."

Partly as a result of this disastrous experience, MacIntyre sought help from a psychotherapist who encouraged her to meditate and visualize to get in touch with her intuition. "I sit in front of a mirror with a candle at chest height affirming 'I love and approve of myself.' When I'm in the shower, I picture the candle getting bigger and the flame surrounding me. I say, 'I am in your hands.' This gives me time to focus and clear my head so that my intuition can show me how to get to step B. I have to step back from the situation to experience it."

Mary Alexander, the mother who encouraged her daughter to pick a college based on her gut feelings, spent years working on learning to trust her own intuition. Alexander says that as a child she was sexually molested, but her mother refused to believe her. "My earliest recollection is learning how to ignore my instincts and instead try to dope out what my mother wanted so I could give it to her," she says. "Finally I lost touch with what is right and real. I jettisoned my intuition in order to survive and part of me was simply eradicated." It took seven years of intensive psychological counseling for Alexander to learn to trust herself. "What's real for me is the gut. Now when I feel that shot of adrenaline or my stomach turns over, baby, I go with that feeling."

As we discussed in the previous chapter, most of us were not taught to accept intuitive knowing. That conditioning throws up a powerful barrier when intuition begins to surface. Museum registrar Carol O'Biso, the woman who recognized someone she had never met before, was frightened after that spontaneous incident. But with the guidance of an experienced friend who said "when you learn which pocket to reach into in order to get it, intuition can be a tool," O'Biso learned how to tap into it when she needed help. O'Biso once made a sewing mistake in a leather skirt and vest she was making, so she returned to the leather manufacturer to find a scrap that would match her unfinished garment. When she got there, she found huge bins overflowing with all kinds of different scraps. "I was rooting through these bins thinking, this is hopeless. I'm never going to find a piece of leather that will match exactly. But then I realized that there were other ways to approach this. I blanked out for a minute and stopped the intellectual process." O'Biso says she next found herself walking over to the third bin on the right where she stuck her arm all the way to the bottom and came up with the exact piece of leather.

In other instances, intuition anxiety occurs in the aftermath of a tragic event in which the intuitive process is unfairly blamed for causing the event. Charlene Harrington still finds it hard to talk about what happened when she was seventeen years old. "For about a year, I repeatedly had flashes and images of being with a group of people and learning that my brother had died. The night before he did die by falling off a roof in a freak accident, I dreamed of a giant round clock that stopped. In fact, I had a pocket watch that stopped and wouldn't start. The next day, I was sitting in a room with the same people I had been seeing in those flashes. When the phone rang, I knew what was about to occur." Harrington believed that she had caused her brother's death because of those premonitions and the dream. "I went through years of intense denial that my intuition existed. I was afraid to tell my family and had no one with whom I could comfortably discuss what had happened." Over the years Harrington has grown more able to relax and believe in her intuition.

In the past few years, as millions of people have become interested in psychic phenomena, it has become more acceptable to talk about such things as gut feelings and precognitive dreams. In some cultures, including Native American and Philippine societies, people have traditionally accepted intuitive phenomena as a real component of everyday life and incorporated such experiences without personal conflict. In *Natural History* magazine, Ralph Coe, curator of a Native American art exhibit called "Lost and Found Traditions," said, "In many of the communities I visited, the Indians never said anything but I felt they were studying me. I sensed they knew things about me that I didn't know. Sometimes they knew when I was returning, even though I had not phoned ahead to tell them. One of my colleagues arrived at an Indian home to find them setting the table for him." When Coe returned to a remote Pacific Northwest village after a long absence, an Indian woman told him, "I saved you a cake because I knew you would come." In the course of nearly a decade spent traveling through the back roads of Native American country, Coe came to rely less on verbal communication as he grew to accept the intuitive nature of Native American society. In the Philippines, people are encouraged to "talk the dream" to a person or even a plant to dispel its energy. But such acceptance is rare in Western society, and as a result many people either suppress, ignore, or hide from their intuition when it surfaces. Had Harrington been able to feel comfortable discussing her intuitive perceptions about her brother at the time of the events, she could have avoided years of feeling guilty about her inner knowing.

"I only experience intuition in connection with something bad," several people have told us. But that's not true. Every one of us has had at least one positive intuitive experience even though we may not remember it. Every one of us has met someone we liked immediately. Some of us have even fallen in love at first sight. These, too, are positive examples of intuition. But the dramatic impact of suddenly knowing that something is wrong can become such a strong memory that when you think "intuition," that's the image you recall.

Former New York City police officer Jane Finnegan, who credits gut feelings with saving her life as well as catching criminals, still finds that one of her predominant memories is the time she was driving to work and was overwhelmed by a feeling in her stomach. "Something kept telling me, 'You've got to call your mother.'" Instead of listening to it at first, Finnegan judged herself. "I wondered what was wrong with me. Then it became so intense that I stopped next to a bridge and called my mother. 'It's terrible, it's terrible,' were her first words." Finnegan's sister, hospitalized for a minor operation, was suddenly in critical condition. "I still feel afraid of that sense whenever I think about my sister," Finnegan says.

"The defenses against inner knowing are so powerful, so big, and so enormous. One of the most unfortunate things we do to ourselves is create these defenses out of fear," says psychologist Dan Miller. Miller believes that "it's perverted to think you are causing an event when in fact you have been in touch with it synchronistically."

If the thought of trusting your intuition brings up feelings of anxiety, you may find it helpful to trace that fear back to its source. Are you frightened because of a previous experience? Are you anxious because the random, spontaneous nature of your intuition thus far has led you to feel out of control? Or is it the nonrational element that causes you discomfort? Often, people confuse anxiety about an event with intuition. "Normally I like to fly but sometimes I get a bad feeling before I get on a plane. I'm afraid it's going to crash. Is that intuition or indigestion?" asks administrative law judge Patti Harris. That's a tough one to answer. One well-known actor once followed a very strong gut feeling that he should not get on a particular plane by canceling his flight plans. The plane he was supposed to take crashed after takeoff, killing everyone on board. If you feel worried every time you are about to fly and nothing happens, then you are experiencing fear, not intuition. How can you tell the difference? Learn to identify your intuition in specific detail and learn to distinguish it from wishful thinking, and imagination. In our earlier chapters, we presented several techniques for locating and identifying your intuition. You may wish to refer back to those when you experience anxiety about a coming event. You can also identify your fear. However, we recommend that you become more aware of your intuition and use that, rather than your anxiety, as your point of reference. After all, you're not trying to develop anxiety; your purpose is to develop intuition.

As you zero in on it, you will find that intuition feels, looks, and sounds a lot different than fear. By tuning in to your own inner signals and becoming sensitive to your own body language, you will learn to tell the difference. When you can locate a physical sensation in your body that corresponds to your intuition, you will be able to differentiate that feeling from anxiety and other emotions. Even with a strong gut feeling, intuition tends to make itself felt in a particular part of the body rather than spreading across a wide area as does anxiety or panic. When intuition speaks, its voice is gentle. It does not debate with you, argue, or manifest itself as a soundtrack with more than one voice. When you hear an inner dialogue, that's mental noise and it blocks your ability to sense intuitively.

Another distinction concerns specifics. If your intuition is warning you not to get on a particular plane, you will process it as a distinct, one-time communication. If you are anxious about flying, you will process it as a diffuse, all-encompassing worry about planes in general that probably stems from a belief that flying is dangerous. Intuition disregards your personal beliefs when transmitting information from your unconscious mind.

"When we ignore our intuition, tension builds up. Intuition knocks with a louder and louder hand until, finally, to get our attention, it develops frightening images," says author and psychoanalyst Ernest Rossi. If you fear your intuition, this could be a sign that you have been ignoring it or denigrating it for a long time. "For people who are afraid, my hypothesis is that you've been suppressing too much," says Rossi, who cautions that when you begin to tune in to your intuition "you might go through some rocky times."

THE TREACHERY OF TRADITIONAL PSYCHOTHERAPY

An experienced counselor, friend, teacher, or seminar leader can help you understand some of those confusing, troubling first encounters with your intuition. Workshops on intuitive development, such as the ones offered at Programs for Human Development in Greenwich, Connecticut, can be an excellent way for you to learn about your own intuition and get support from other people who have had experiences similar to yours. By sharing personal events, insights, and discoveries with an experienced seminar leader in a workshop setting, you can discuss your intuition anxiety and feel safe. Whatever course you choose, you should not underestimate the benefit of finding someone who is both sympathetic and experienced with whom you can discuss your intuitive experiences. "Throughout history, the function of a guide is to help you through the rough period," says Rossi. "It's only rough because you've ignored it so long." While many people seek some form of psychotherapy when they first begin to have intuitive or psychic experiences, they can be helped or harmed by the therapist's point of view. If you have a precognitive dream that comes true, or you suddenly find that you are picking up other people's thoughts, you may believe that you are going crazy. Some psychotherapists will be pleased to confirm that self-diagnosis, whereas others, trained to recognize and value intuition, will guide you to a better understanding. It is the role of the therapist, as it is with any guide or friend, to allow you to make your own discoveries. Anyone who imposes her own conclusions on you in an effort to prove a particular ideology is guilty of what Rossi calls "the therapeutic treachery." "There are a lot of therapists out there who can actually make you worse by trying to sell a certain point of view. They may help you through the fear period, but then they should hang back and see what your individuality wants to say," Rossi notes.

Although the root of the word *psychology,* like the root of the word psychic, is *psyche,* meaning "of the soul or of the mind," many traditional psychotherapists in this country do not validate the intuitive aspect of the psyche. For example, Herman Weinstein, a former psychotherapist, says, "I don't really believe in intuition. It's clinical judgment confirmed by everyday experience. Actually it's countertransference, your reaction to the other person. I learned by practice and training to develop logical diagnostic methods." Although he used to get a strong gut feeling when diagnosing schizophrenic patients, he refused to allow that gut feeling to be the basis of his assessment, even though it usually proved to be an accurate response.

In graduate school, psychologist Al Siebert remembers learning about a survey in which 86 percent of the psychologists polled reported that they did not believe in psychic experiences. Siebert, who dates the start of his own exploration as the day he felt compelled to walk in a certain direction where he encountered a wounded bird, now teaches seminars on parapsychology for skeptical people. When he opened his class by asking student nurses about their intuition, Siebert found "a whole world opened up with all these things that people don't talk about."

As a practicing psychiatrist, Dr. Sherman Schachter would spontaneously write his personal predictions after meeting a new patient. Later in the treatment process, he would check it to see where his intuition and judgment had been correct. As director of the New Hope Guild for Emotionally Disturbed Children, Dr. Schachter often used the same technique when he interviewed prospective job applicants. "More and more I value the unexplained, nonidentified, unsupported way of experiencing. You cannot successfully negotiate the world unless you negotiate in an intuitive way and put value on that," he observes. But most traditional schools of psychotherapy do not teach people how to do that, relying instead on the presupposition that analysis alone can bring about transformation. The word analysis describes a specific mental process that is sequential and logical. In placing exclusionary value on the analytic process, these traditional psychotherapies reflect and support the same values as our education system. "A simplistic, logical system is not a substitute for change. The idea that the question Why? is important is the elephants' graveyard of psychiatry," Dr. Schachter observes.

JUNG'S INTUITIVE FUNCTION

Swiss psychiatrist Carl Jung, who studied with and later broke ranks with Sigmund Freud, valued intuition as one of the primary ways of getting information. Jung believed that intuitive perception was natural and common and that a therapist should not denigrate a patient's intuitive awareness. He also believed that Freudian psychoanalysis had limitations. "Mere self-observation and intellectual self-analysis are entirely inadequate as a means of establishing contact with the unconscious," he wrote in *The Structure and Dynamics of the Psyche.* Jung's theory of analytic psychology focuses on how as well as why an individual perceives the world a certain way. According to Jung's theory, there are four psychological functions: thinking, feeling, sensing, and intuition. While one of those functions is dominant in each of us, the others operate simultaneously. In *The Collected Works of C.G. Jung,* Jung described the intuitive process as "neither one of sense-perception, nor of thinking, nor yet of feeling, although language shows a regrettable lack of discrimination in this respect . . . intuition as I conceive it is one of the basic functions of the psyche, namely *perception of the possibilities inherent in a situation.*" These perceptions often prove to be factually accurate. Although brain research had not yet produced the triune brain model, Jung seems to have intuitively sensed it. His four functions correspond to the predominant intellectual skills of the reptilian brain (sensing), limbic system (feeling), left neocortex (thinking), and right neocortex (intuition). Freudian theory, which does not contain a function-based typology, lacks a similar correlation to the triune brain although the subconscious corresponds to the reptilian brain, the id to the limbic system, and the ego to the left neocortex.

Jung believed that not only sensory-based intuitive functioning but psychic phenomena, too, were an important part of many people's everyday life. His concept of the unconscious mind embraced these possibilities where Freud's idea of the subconscious mind did not. "I think the reason why Jung has so much to contribute to intuition is that he saw the unconscious as more than a reservoir of repressed urges and talent, most of them negative, as did Freud," says psychologist Stanley Krippner, who notes that "Jung took a more positive attitude." Jung, who did not place as much importance on sexual feelings as Freud, criticized the father of modern psychoanalysis for his mechanical, reductionist approach, saying, "If a church steeple is a penis and a pencil is a penis, what does it mean if you dream of a penis?"

The instinct to worship, Jung said, is as important as the instincts to survive and to procreate. "There are certain human traits which exist in every community, and there is no such thing as a society that hasn't set up some kind of worship," says Jungian psychoanalyst Genevieve Geer. "Many of the images, metaphors, fairy tales, and motifs are the same in every single country of the world although each culture filters the images in a certain way." These images, or archetypes, emerge from what Jung called the collective unconscious, a universal pool of symbolic information that has evolved with the human race. Everyone in the world inherits the collective unconscious and can access it through memories, dreams, and reflections.

Memories, Dreams, Reflections, the title of Jung's autobiography, is a tale, in part, of how Jung discovered his own intuitive abilities that, in turn, led him to develop a personality theory that validated the role of intuition as a way of perceiving the world. "In the course of my life it has often happened to me that I suddenly knew something which I really could not know at all. The knowledge came to me as if it were my own idea," Jung wrote. But he, too, found it socially acceptable to suppress some of his intuitive observations: "School and city life took up my time, and my increased knowledge gradually permeated or repressed the world of intuitive phenomena." Aware that many people are frightened by their own psychic experiences, Jung sought a way of helping his patients come to terms with them. Nonetheless, he was aware that "wherever there is a reaching down into innermost experience, into the nucleus of personality, most people are overcome by fright and run away."

Jungian psychotherapy is very popular in Europe, where Prince Charles, among others, has been studying Jung's work. In a 1982 interview with the *Washington Post,* the Prince of Wales credited the works of Carl Jung with enhancing his spiritual understanding. "Surely the reason, I think, for our existence on this earth is to try and make the most of our human qualities and our human adaptability. Which leads me to the other thing which I'm beginning to feel more and more strongly about, which is the more spiritual aspect of life. It means much more to me than it did," said Prince Charles, adding that he had found Jung's work "absolutely fascinating and very much an inspiration and a help to me in trying to understand the psychology of humanity." He observed, "If we can but understand our own innermost workings, there is so much that we can then do to control, perhaps some of the worst excesses of human beings, in terms of good and evil." Prince Charles recently told CBS News that he relies on his intuition, which he calls his "sixth sense," when deciding whether to speak out in public on such subjects as the environment and architecture.

Although Jung has been attacked in this country for his mystical inclinations and for his acceptance of psychic phenomena, he wrote, "there was nothing preposterous or world-shaking in the idea that there might be events which overstepped the limited categories of space, time, and causality. Animals were known to sense beforehand storms and earthquakes. There were dreams which foresaw the death of certain persons, clocks which stopped at the moment of death, glasses which shattered at a critical moment." No wonder then that Carl Jung considered intuition to be the quality that sees around the corner.

Jungian psychotherapists, who number about four hundred nationwide, are clearly a minority in this country, although their numbers are growing. Psychologists from other disciplines say that Jung's unpopularity here can be attributed to several factors. Siebert, a member of the Friends of C.G. Jung Society in Oregon for the past fifteen years, sees the Jungian movement growing as the Freudian movement becomes less popular. "Freudian psychology dominated and suppressed Jungian psychology," notes Siebert. Another theory says that the manner in which Freud's work was translated made it appear more scientific than it actually was, giving it greater appeal to the medical community in the United States. Krippner points out that Jung's political naïveté damaged his reputation with the psychoanalytic community in the United States after he served on the advisory board of a Nazi publication. "I don't defend Jung on that point," says Krippner. "A lot of people who are introverted in Jung's sense of the word don't explore the environment properly. They don't make reasoned decisions about political and economic events."

Nonetheless, Jung's contributions are making an impact in such diverse fields as communications, the arts, personal growth, and business. Bill Moyers's television specials on the late Joseph Campbell, a Jung scholar, explored the connections between mythology and how we as individuals understand our role in the world. Symbols from Greek mythology combined with Jungian interpretations form the basis of the new mythic tarot deck, developed in 1986. Although the tarot has been used since the Middle Ages as a divination tool, each mythic symbol in the Jungian deck represents an aspect of the psyche of the person being read. A reader studies the symbols on each card and interprets them in a manner similar to Jungian dream interpretation by determining how each particular symbol is connected to a part of the person being read. The reader's intuition as well as her knowledge of mythic archetypes enables these cards to be used as a tool for personal insight and traditional divination. Another offshoot of Jungian theory, the Myers-Briggs type indicator, is used by personnel directors and recruitment officers to get a comprehensive profile of prospective employees. Developed by Katharine C. Briggs and Isabel Briggs Myers in 1943, the 166-question survey asks you to fill in each multiple-choice section according to your initial gut reaction. The survey asks about your activities, preferred hobbies, behavior in social situations, responses to conflicts, judgments about others, and self-image. When processed, the Myers-Briggs type indicator provides a profile of your four functions: thinking, feeling, sensing, and intuition. It also shows whether you tend to be extroverted or introverted, Jung's two basic personality types. Jung first came up with these typologies as the result of his clinical work with patients and they are now being validated statistically as well as culturally. The Swiss psychiatrist's theories are becoming so fashionable that in its list of "Ins and Outs" for 1989, the *Washington Post* listed Jung In, Freud Out.

INTUITION IN PSYCHOTHERAPY

Although most traditional psychotherapies overlook intuition, Jungians, too, caution against overdeveloping it or relying on it too much. "There are some people to whom you almost have to say, forget intuition. You have to help them put it in perspective," Geer says. When a patient comes to her frightened by some psychic experience, Geer may counsel her with reason, saying, "Maybe you heard something. Maybe you saw something. And maybe you don't know you did." Unlike some psychotherapists, as a Jungian, Geer will not rush to diagnose a case of schizophrenia. Rather, she will seek to help the patient integrate all four functions into a balanced whole. "Intuition is the ability to go from here to there without going through A, B, C. Sometimes with patients of mine who are very intuitive, I say, don't forget those steps."

But for most people, intuition remains the inferior function, that which is most elusive of the four and most difficult to define. Each of us has a preferred or dominant function, through which we tend to perceive the world most of the time. Then there is an auxiliary, or second function, followed by a third and then the inferior function, which Jung said you should regard as you would a mentally slow child: Train it as best you can but don't expect too much. Although someone whose thinking function dominates is often suspicious of her intuitive function, others can carry intuitive functioning to an extreme. We are all familiar with the stereotype of the absentminded professor who forgets what time it is. In Jungian terms, the professor would have a dominant intuitive function with an inferior sensate function, making it hard for him to pay attention to physical tasks such as going to the store and coming back with the correct purchases and change. Geer recalls a philosophy professor whose wife had to write down how much money he had and what everything cost. "Once we had coffee four times in the course of taking a walk because he forgot we had just had coffee. An intuitive with an inferior sensation function lives in a different world," she says.

Rossi, who switched to a Jungian framework after years of Freudian training, also advises some highly intuitive clients to think and validate their hunches rather than relying on them without checking. But he may use all his methodology to help an intellectual who is not in tune with her intuition become more comfortable with it. For others, he may nurture feeling or sensation. When someone appears to be inclined toward intuition to the exclusion of rationality, Rossi likes to point out that "the unconscious is like an experimental theater in that everything that comes up from the unconscious is not valuable. Your ego has to mediate between reality and these inner experiments." Paraphrasing Jung, Rossi notes that "we are all experiments of nature and the profound aspect of human development is how we react with nature." We can help, hinder, or blind it.

INTUITIVE THERAPEUTIC APPROACHES

There are now more than three hundred different types of psychotherapy available in the United States, according to a 1987 estimate by the Evolution of Psychotherapy Congress. While you might be inclined to laugh at such a high number, it shows how the psychotherapeutic community is diversifying its approaches to fit different needs. As you have seen in our discussion of Jungian therapy, some of us can benefit from learning how to rely on our intuition whereas others need help learning how to be more rational. Each of us is unique, with particular sensitivities and awarenesses. One approach may spark new growth, while another may only generate meandering introspection. Although one method may work for some people at some time or another, another may hold you back. When selecting a form of psychotherapy, only you can decide which approach fits your needs. You may wish to ask yourself: How can I access the intuitive door to my own capabilities, whatever they are? How can I find the person whose technique will strengthen my ability to use all of my inner resources, including intuition? Which of these approaches will best enable me to fully explore all the dimensions of myself?

Some of the new therapeutic techniques presuppose that getting in touch with your intuitive self can start the self-healing process. Not all of these approaches are strictly psychotherapeutic. Several combine visualization with hands-on methods to treat physical ailments that are interconnected with psychological distress. With the growth of the New Age movement, some practitioners now incorporate meditation, guided imagery, yoga, breathing exercises, prayer, Native American rituals, and other metaphysical approaches into their work with remarkable results. For Gay Larned, who was trained as a social psychologist, "Nontraditional therapy allows your healthy, intact, true self to emerge. It's critical for the client to tap into that intuitive vein in order to release fear and bring about positive change." For her part, she says, "My intuitive self works with the client's intuitive self. I always tell them, 'I don't know what I'm doing but I follow my intuition and I do the right thing.' " As a practitioner of rebirthing, a breathing technique that moves the client's point of focus from the left to the right brain thus producing an altered state of consciousness, Larned helps each client restructure subconscious patterns without spending years delving into her personal history. "Traditional forms of therapy do not always produce change. They push the symptoms around and the symptoms reemerge," Larned asserts. In one instance, a former Peace Corps worker came to Larned suffering from a rare bleeding disorder that doctors had told him was incurable. "I sensed intuitively that his disorder was connected to his mother," Larned says. "During the rebirthing session, I provoked his anger and he cried out, 'Mom, what do you want me to do, bleed for you?' " Although after the session, he did not remember saying this, he commented, "That sums up my experience with her." Shortly after that session, the man went into remission and is now enjoying his travels around the world.

Therapeutic touch, a hands-on healing technique, requires that the practitioner meditate and defocus her attention to develop sensitivity to the energy field, or aura, surrounding the body. Anyone can learn how to perform therapeutic touch, which consists of centering, or shifting your point of focus to an intuitive state; assessing or feeling the energy field for heat, cold, or other sensations; and treating the field with your hands. Developed by Dolores Krieger, a professor at the New York University Division of Nursing, and Dora Kunz, a spiritual healer, therapeutic touch is gaining clinical acceptance around the world and is used in many hospitals. Not only does it gently stimulate the body's natural healing response, therapeutic touch is calming both for the healer and the person being healed.

Stephen Hinkey, a chiropractor and kinesiologist who uses physical pressure points to release emotional as well as physical blocks, sees the healing process in metaphysical terms. "Disease is inhibited soul life and all healing occurs in the soul with love and forgiveness," he says. Hinkey describes himself as a physical psychotherapist whose technique combines "saying the right command at the right time plus touching the two most vulnerable places in the physical body to release sensitive and painful past memories." As a practitioner of the Bio-Energetic Synchronization Technique developed by Dr. Ted Mortar, Hinkey also uses esoteric healing,

Native American, and Japanese Reiki techniques. Having trained himself to see auras and energy patterns around and within a patient's body, he draws a picture of those patterns and interprets it for the patient before beginning treatment. Although many people have trained themselves to see auras, Hinkey's ability to perceive the energy dynamics within the body is very rare. "I learned how to see the energy patterns by first imagining that I could see their color, sound, and vibration. Over time, as my intuition kicked in, I became able to see them clearly. My intuition also lets me know which two points on a patient's body I need to press to release physiological and emotional patterns." Hinkey has his patients visualize during treatments and helps them build their own intuitive awareness. At the end of a session, he often asks a patient to give an intuitive assessment of her recovery time.

Bringing intuitive processes into conscious focus is one of the objectives of neurolinguistic programming (NLP). Although NLP uses visualization techniques, it is based on scientific findings about the brain and is not based on metaphysical material. An NLP practitioner notes a client's language, breathing, and eye movement patterns and uses them to make certain interpretations. She is also trained to notice her own hunches and gut feelings and to express them. By watching how the client responds and comparing those findings to her own intuitive assessment, an NLP practitioner can then get a clear reading about her intuitive accuracy and can thereby fine tune her own intuition. "If you're going to pay attention to all the input channels, the final check should not be internal. You have to validate from the outside," says NLP trainer and master practitioner Steven Leeds.

Such new therapies call on both the patient and therapist to work from their gut and to regard all healing as a psychophysiological process. Although many of the techniques now available are comparatively new, the term *psychophysiological,* which means "the reciprocal actions of mind and matter on each other," has been around since 1855. Certainly, meditation, guided imagery, and breathing exercises have been around a lot longer than that. What's interesting about many of these new approaches is how they synthesize theory and technique from metaphysical philosophies to form a new whole. In valuing intuitive awareness as part of the healing process these psychotherapies can help people lose some of their intuition anxiety and build a new sense of trust.

THE SWISH EXERCISE: CHANGING INTUITION ANXIETY TO TRUST

If you are afraid to trust your intuition and would like to be able to rely on it, you can change your fear into trust without having to examine why you are afraid of it. To do this, you will be using a technique in NLP called "the swish." The swish is essentially a split-screen exercise in which you quickly switch two images.

There are two steps to the swish: setting it up and swishing the images. The key to a successful swish is setting up the images carefully. You will need about ten minutes for this exercise, although you may want to spend more time setting it up.

Step 1. With your eyes open or closed, visualize yourself getting a hunch, gut feeling, or some other form of intuition and feeling anxious about it. What, specifically, is the image that you get? Now take a step back and pinpoint what you are doing just *before* you feel anxious. Hold that image. It is the picture of the trigger that sets off your intuition anxiety.

As you look at this image, notice its strongest components: color, shape, size. Locate any physical sensation that accompanies this anxiety. Identify any sounds, including an inner voice. Be sure to make your image of this trigger scene as specific as possible. Set this image aside.

Now picture yourself trusting your intuition. What, specifically, is the image that comes up for you? What resources would you need to have that trust? Now picture yourself having those resources. See how you would look, sound, and feel when you are able to trust your intuition. Hold that image.

Step 2. Take the first image of yourself in a state of intuition anxiety and see it in front of you as a *large, bright* picture. Practice enlarging and brightening the picture to be sure that this intensifies your feeling of anxiety. (If enlarging and brightening the picture does not intensify your anxiety, experiment until you find the right combination.)

In the lower left corner of this large, bright image of you experiencing intuition anxiety, place a *small, dark* image of how you will look, sound, and feel when you trust your intuition. Now, practice the swish: As you say, "One, two, three, swish," see the large bright picture *shrink and get dark* as it moves into the lower left corner. At the same time, see the small, dark picture *enlarge and brighten* as it replaces the original image. Do both procedures simultaneously. This is tricky but you will get it if you practice a few times.

When you are comfortable doing it, swish these images six times. Be sure to blink, open your eyes, or in some way clear your mental screen before you repeat the movement. As you repeat the swish movement, it will become harder for you to hold that first image of intuition anxiety in your mind. The image of you trusting your intuition will become the dominant one.

To test the swish, use the future projection technique from chapter 4. Think of some future situation that would ordinarily cause you to get intuition anxiety. Close your eyes and see yourself there. Practice the swish technique. When the swish holds, you will automatically feel trust instead of fear. That's because the visual swishing movement is a way in which you direct a movie for your brain. As it takes in both images simultaneously, your right neocortex also follows the momentum of the image shift and retains the new picture as the preferred one.

Another way to stop feeling scared by your intuition is to go directly to your reptilian brain, that part of your whole-brain system that knows how to create a sense of safety. We will explain how this works in the next chapters.

PART III

YOUR
WHOLE-BRAIN
SKILLS
EMPORIUM

"If the brain were simple enough to understand,
we wouldn't be able to understand it."

—Dr. Sherman Schachter

INTRODUCTION

This section of the book functions primarily as a workbook. As you read through it, you will probably find yourself saying, "I recognize that but I didn't know that it is the physiology of my brain that caused me to feel, think, and sense that way." Chapter 9 tells you how to recognize the physiological signs of intuition. By becoming sensitized to your body's signals, you can learn to access your intuition when your body is in a naturally intuitive phase. Chapters 10 through 12 consist primarily of direct, firsthand, information to help you discover more about your triune brain—the reptilian, the limbic, and the neocortex—so that you can experience how it works for you. Chapter 13 gives you exercises for an intuition notebook and explains how to create mind maps and treasure maps for stimulating intuitive awareness. In chapter 14, we take you back to the room of your mind that your first explored in chapter 4. Chapter 15 contains a Ten-Step Program and offers some ideas on how you can use it.

Some of the workbook exercises will stimulate your intuitive awareness, whereas others will let you develop mental abilities that you may never have perceived as intellectual skills. All these techniques will help you to move your point of focus to different intelligence centers in your triune brain—at will. The more you experiment with these workbook exercises and develop sensitivity to your own patterns, feelings, and intuition, the more familiar they will become.

Although these techniques have been created as a result of research into the triune brain and its impact on behavior, they are not the product of hard scientific data. Rather, they are interpretations of scientific research that have been validated by years of teaching and counseling experience. The triune brain is an exciting model for these applications because it shows that built into the physiology of our brains is deep knowledge of behaviors, feelings, and thinking abilities that have developed in the course of evolution along with the human body itself and its motor functions. And our brains are continuing to evolve.

As a species that is evolving in awareness as well as adapting physiologically to a changing world, we can re-vision ourselves as human beings. To do so, we need to accept that we are growing in our ability to make better use of all of our mental abilities and that we are capable of moving energy through our brains so that we can create the kinds of experiences and responses that we want to have in our lives.

When we talk about moving energy, we mean the energy that is the sum of all of the thoughts and feelings that you have in your mind, as well as all of your attitudes and belief systems. Your habits, patterns, and routines, too, are all forms of energy. These split-second synaptic sparks are firing throughout your triune brain system all the time, creating different combinations and forms. The form that your energy takes when you feel happiness is different from the form your energy takes during the intellectual exercise of computing 2×10^{10}, but it's all energy.

We now know that you can shift energy in your brain from thought to feeling to mood to attitude to belief system and back up to thought again if you want to. You don't have to be saddled with a belief or self-concept or feeling that doesn't serve you. If you don't believe that you have intuition or that you can be intuitive, you can shift your energy to that part of your brain that naturally functions intuitively and experience it firsthand for yourself. It takes practice, but with work, you can change your thoughts, feelings, and beliefs according to your needs.

We refer to the different processing systems within each brain as intelligences. While you can focus on one specifically by shifting energy, you can also be aware of several at once. The key to learning how to use your intelligences is to become aware of what each one is and how it functions. As you become better able to identify each one and shift your energy so that you experience it at will, you will become able to consciously use and change it. We believe that by becoming more conversant with your whole-brain resources, your intuition will naturally become more accessible. As you become comfortable with the idea of shifting energy and working with nonverbal parts of your brain, you will find yourself thinking intuitively, smoothly, and without effort.

If you use these exercises with the intention of cultivating your intuition, you will find that even the exercises that call on different intelligences in the reptilian brain and limbic system will help you build some of the skills included in the Ten-Step Program for enhancing your intuitive abilities in chapter 15. Whether you begin with the overall intention of learning how to use more of your whole brain or whether you start out wanting to develop your intuition, you win either way. With more of your whole brain available to you when you need it, how can you lose?

CHAPTER 9

The Physiology of Intuition: Your Body's Intuitive Responses

Do you find yourself losing concentration during certain times of the day? Perhaps it comes as a sudden touch of fatigue, or a subtle mental fuzziness. All of a sudden, you feel droopy. Your eyes may tear. You can't stop yawning, or you sigh. Maybe you find yourself staring out the window, your mind faraway from the tasks at hand. If somebody speaks to you, you find yourself startled by the sound of his voice. Or you don't understand what was said the first time and ask the speaker to repeat himself.

These are signs that your body is entering an ultradian rest response. If you observe yourself carefully during the day, you will find that this pattern recurs approximately every hour and a half. Noticing this pattern can help you tap into your intuition during the times when your physiology is naturally attuned to it. In this chapter, we will tell you how to do this and we will discuss some other physiological changes associated with intuitive states. During these periods when you lose concentration or get tired, the four main regulatory systems that link mind and body realign. These four physiological systems are:

1. The autonomic nervous system that regulates most of your body's important functions.

2. The endocrine system that regulates production of your pituitary, thalamus, hypothalamus, and thyroid hormones, among others.
3. The immune system.
4. The system of information substance chemicals (neuropeptides) in your brain.

Your drowsiness and loss of attention are telling you that these important changes are taking place. These feelings of distraction occur in part because of a shift in cerebral lateralization, that is, the right hemisphere of your neocortex becomes dominant during the ultradian rest response. The parasympathetic nervous system becomes activated, too, producing changes in moods and feelings. This is a time when you are more likely to say, "Aha!" or get a rare, sudden insight into yourself.

According to Ernest Rossi, author of *The Psychobiology of Mind-Body Healing,* "during the ultradian rest response, your body goes into an intuitive mode. You are more receptive to impressions from your unconscious."

If you try to ignore these signals by pretending that they do not exist, you may find yourself feeling irritable, uncomfortable, and depressed. If, however, you recognize and accept your body's messages, you can use the ultradian rest period for relaxing, creative intuitive work.

TAKE AN INTUITION BREAK

This is the best time to take a break rather than forcing yourself to push through the fatigue. You can think of it as your intuition break, time to take a deep breath, close your eyes, and allow impressions from your intuitive right hemisphere to flow through your mind. If you are working on a project and would like help from your intuition, this is the time to ask for it. It is also a good time to meditate or work with some of the techniques in this book.

As you become more aware of the physiology of intuition, you will find that your body's natural rhythms can help you ease into an intuitive state. You can meditate productively at any time during the day, but by recognizing the onset of your ultradian rest response, you can enhance your results by spending time in silence while your body does its neurophysiological work. By meditation, we mean spending some quiet time with yourself, perhaps as little as ten minutes a day. Along with meditation, an ultradian rest period is an optimum time to do visualization, self-healing, or any other technique that makes you more conscious of information from your unconscious mind. (This is also a good time to do the exercises contained in the following chapters.) Not only will you be more receptive to your intuition during this period, but the inner work will flow without any effort on your part. Says Rossi, "This is the time when it's easiest to access your own intuition, your own internal imagery. Thoughts are most likely to be closer to the unconscious. This is a time when the unconscious wants all the energy it can get. If you train yourself to just watch and observe and not intrude, you're going to fall into what is called reverie or hypnagogic state, what I call its more naturally intuitive state."

The ultradian response is a time when all the mind-body communication systems are most fluid, most flexible, and also most vulnerable to being damaged if we interfere with them too much. If we let the ultradian response have all the energy, it can most efficiently do all the healing it needs to. Rossi observes, "Most forms of healing, including shamanism and the holistic forms of healing are rituals for helping you to get into this ultradian response because it's so easy to entrain."

In *The Psychobiology of Mind-Body Healing,* Rossi proposes that you take a break every hour and a half. The traditional English workday reflects this pattern with coffee served at 10:30 A.M., lunch at noon, and tea break in midafternoon. "You work until, say, 10:30. Then an hour and a half after that it's lunchtime. Throughout the day you should take those breaks, even though most of us don't take them as seriously as we need to," Rossi says.

You can start by observing your own rhythms and noting down the signals your body presents to you at particular times of the day. Become familiar with your own patterns so that you can recognize and tap into your own ultradian rhythm. You may want to keep a list like the one provided below for a couple of days to identify your own ultradian indicators.

A BRIEF HISTORY OF ULTRADIAN RESEARCH

As far back as one hundred years ago, scientists reported periodic changes in physiological processes and noted their effects on human productivity. The Basic Rest-Activity Cycle was identified in 1969 after EEG experiments on sleeping subjects revealed ninety-minute patterns of low- and

SAMPLE ULTRADIAN RHYTHMS LOG

TIME	RHYTHM	SIGNAL
11 A.M.:	Can't concentrate.	Reread document three times. Nothing sinks in.
1:30 P.M.:	Lunchtime.	I ask Mary to repeat something a few times.
3 P.M.:	Drowsy.	Want to take a nap.
4:30 P.M.:	Drowsy.	Keep staring out window.
6 P.M.:	Drowsy.	Fall asleep on train.
8:30 P.M.:	Drowsy.	Watch TV but can't pay attention to programs.

high-frequency brain-wave activity. During the rapid eye movement (REM) stage, scientists noted changes in heartbeat and respiration, and some muscle contraction and expansion. Although it is harder to observe the Basic Rest-Activity Cycle during waking hours because of other distractions, these sleep researchers concluded that the same cycle occurs during waking hours, as well.

In the 1970s, the U.S. Department of Health, Education, and Welfare, the Veterans Administration, and the military spent millions of dollars to research ultradian rhythms because they suspected these cycles might be connected to periodic decreases in workers' efficiency. The government studied the effects of shift changes, continuous tasks, and long-distance flights. The flight studies noted the existence of twenty-four-hour circadian rhythms in some of the human regulatory systems that, when out of synch, produced jet lag symptoms such as disrupted sleep cycles. The ninety-minute ultradian rhythms were identified by Daniel Kripke, a psychologist working at the U.S. Naval Base in San Diego.

California psychotherapist Rossi first noticed the onset of ultradian rhythms in patients working with his mentor, hypnotherapist Milton Erickson in the mid-1970s. One of the foremost hypnotherapists of the twentieth century, Erickson spent two to three hours with each patient instead of a standard one-hour session. "I used to wonder, when is he going to begin the hypnosis?" Rossi says. "Sometimes it was at the beginning, sometimes at the end, and sometimes in the middle of the session. It was so subtle that it took me years to figure out his timing."

Rossi observed Erickson's patients closely and began to make a list. The elements on this list eventually became twenty-four hypnotic response readiness indicators. He noted that one patient might look away and stretch. Another patient might look directly at Erickson when he would ask a question, yet say, "Huh?" to indicate that he had not heard a thing. These were all indications that the patient's concentration was fuzzy and that he was turning inward. Those were the moments when Erickson would do hypnosis. Because he was sensitive to the patient's subtle clues, Erickson called his work the naturalistic approach.

Rossi noticed that the list of these ultradian rhythms corresponded to his list of hypnotic response readiness indicators. He asked Milton Erickson if he knew that he was tapping into the ultradian rhythm when he induced hypnosis, but Erickson had never heard of it. "He was a genius of observation," Rossi comments. "He was picking up this rhythm intuitively. By noting the subtle shifts of a person's mind-body responses, he perceived that was the time they needed to go inward."

Naturalistic hypnosis might, in fact, be a natural physiological process, part of your body's normal rhythm. More than a century ago, the French psychologist Pierre Janet, one of Sigmund Freud's teachers, attributed the spontaneous lowering of mental energy as the source of psychological problems. During that state of lowered mental energy, impressions from the outside world imprint themselves with a particular vividness. A traumatic event can become the nucleus of a neurosis. Rossi believes that you can use your ultradian rest period to heal those traumatic state-dependent memories. Ultradian rhythm experiments are now under way at a South Carolina clinic and the Himalaya Institute. One project seeks to determine whether people experience psychosomatic symptoms when they ignore their ultradian rhythms. "I do have experimental evidence for everything I do say," Rossi says, "But the evidence was not designed to test this hypothesis." Rossi's theoretical model is the integration of findings that already exist. "After a century of observation, we now have a psycho-biological framework," he says, pointing out that with the outlines of a theory, "we know where to pursue some research." One key research project would be to scientifically study whether a person receives a hypnotic suggestion more easily when he enters the ultradian rest rhythm.

YOUR NOSE KNOWS: THE ULTRADIAN NASAL CYCLE

Another exercise that uses the body's natural cycles to help you attune to the right neocortex is to simply lie on your right side. Within two or three minutes reflexively, your right nostril will become more congested and your left nostril will open up because most of the air is entering it. That reflexively turns on the right hemisphere of your neocortex, the center of your visual, associational, and intuitive processes. Sleeping on your right side will activate that hemisphere and may bring you more vivid dreams than if you sleep on your left side, your back, or your stomach.

Rossi offers this theory based on recent laboratory experiments on the relationship between yogic breathing and the neurophysiology of breathing. Yogic exercises stress alternate nostril breathing as part of cleansing and preparing both body and mind for deep meditation. The nasal cycle was first identified in 1895 by R. Kayser, a German rhinologist who noticed changes in the mucus of both the left and right nostrils during changes in breathing patterns. When the left nostril was open, the right one was congested, and vice versa. More recent studies show that the nasal cycle, too, conforms to the ultradian pattern of approximately ninety minutes. Conducting a simple experiment on himself, Rossi has found that by lying on his back and meditating or resting after performing mental work, his own dominant, or open, nostril shifts from the right to the left. This would indicate a natural lateral shift from the left to the right brain, a finding that has been confirmed in the laboratory.

The ultradian nasal cycle, then, is what Rossi calls "a window on cerebral hemispheric activity." By voluntarily changing the airflow through your nostrils, you can change your center of activity in the neocortex and can affect changes in your autonomic nervous system, as well. "Western science," notes Rossi, "finally validated the basic principles that underlay thousands of years of subjective, empirical experience by Eastern adepts!"

INFORMATION SUBSTANCES

In chapter 3, we discussed the chemistry of gut feelings. According to one theory, gut feelings are created by the chemical interaction of neurotransmitters. Neurotransmitters, also known as information substances, are chemicals that activate different processes in your brain.

The question of whether the neurotransmitter creates a particular mental or emotional response—like a gut feeling—or whether the thought or feeling activates the chemical process is one of those questions like "Which came first, the chicken or the egg?" Dr. Mary Schmitt, the neurophysiologist who conducted the Mead School experiments, says that it's too simplistic to say that a particular neurotransmitter creates a specific response. "Neurotransmitters interact with one another. One transmitter will do one thing at one nerve ending and something else at another nerve ending." She points to the relationship between schizophrenia and dopamine as an example. When a person has schizophrenia, there is an imbalance of dopamine in the limbic system. That often reassures people who have schizophrenia in their family because they know there is a chemical cause. But Dr. Schmitt asks, "Is the imbalance in dopamine the cause of the schizophrenia or does the schizophrenia cause the imbalance in the dopamine?"

Research into neurotransmitter activity is still in its early stages but these information substances in the brain could provide researchers with a key to the age-old mystery of mind-body communication. "How is mind different from body? You could study them as separate realms," Rossi says, "But the really interesting thing is how they are translated into each other. How is the information conceptualized in the realm of thoughts, words, feelings, emotions, behavior transduced into the molecules of the body? We have a path of information transduction from mind right down to the genes and molecules and back. So that old dichotomy of mind versus matter is sort of irrelevant." *Mind-Body Therapy*, by Ernest Rossi and David Cheek, explores these questions in greater detail.

The neurotransmitter serotonin, which quiets brain activity, may also be one of the informational substances critical to intuitive awareness. Dr. Arnold Mandell, a professor of psychiatry at the University of California at San Diego, told *American Health* magazine that meditation may inhibit serotonin functions. In turn, the brain's temporal lobes (which coordinate space and movement perception and the limbic system) generate greater electricity as the neurons' synaptical discharge speeds up. Ideas, experiences, and feelings take on new meaning in this heightened state of processing.

COGNITIVE OPERATORS IN THE BRAIN

Whatever form your intuition takes, it speaks in wholes. That is, your "Aha!" moment, the flash you see in your mind's eye, or the gut feeling or inner voice lets you glimpse the total picture. "There is something about the intuitive process that is more unitary than a process that involves discrete elements," says Dr. Eugene d'Aquili, a Philadelphia neuropsychiatrist and anthropologist who studies brain evolution in relationship to universal cultural institutions. Based in part on the triune brain model, Dr. d'Aquili's biogenetic structural approach draws connections between brain physiology and social sciences. "If someone says something that affects us very strongly, we have a kind of chill that goes down our spine. I very strongly suspect that this is the language of the nondominant hemisphere operating through the limbic system which is, in a sense, affirming what is being said. Usually that occurs when there is a general sense of the rightness of it. That is an intuitive affirmation."

Intuitive insights can be explained as a function of one of the six cognitive operators in both hemispheres of your neocortex and your limbic system. Cognitive operators are neural structures that organize experience in different ways. An operator is a term from mathematics referring to the means by which mathematical elements are made to relate to one another. The way you perceive the world depends on which operator predominates at a particular time, but they all work together, just as your left and right hemispheres work simultaneously, flashing on and off, with alternating periods of dominance. The six cognitive operators are:

1. Holistic, which lets you see reality as a whole. Dr. d'Aquili believes it is located in the parietal lobe of the right hemisphere. The parietal lobes are the top lateral aspects of your brain, that is, at the crown of your head.
2. Causal, which lets you see reality as causal sequences of abstract elements. Dr. d'Aquili places this operator in the left hemisphere.
3. Abstractive, which lets you form general concepts from empirical information. This is located in the left hemisphere.
4. Binary, which lets you find meaning by creating polarities, or dyads, such as good-bad, either-or, right-wrong. This is located in the left hemisphere.
5. Formal quantitative operator, which lets you abstract concepts of quantity and generates mathematics. This is located in the left hemisphere.
6. Value, which assigns value to cognitive functions. Dr. d'Aquili believes the value operator uses the interconnections between the right neo-

cortex and the limbic system, thereby calling on visual and affective awareness.

INTUITION AND THE HOLISTIC OPERATOR

Intuition is a function of the holistic operator and the degree to which it predominates may help answer the question of whether you consider yourself to be an intuitive person, that is, whether you strongly rely on that function. For Dr. d'Aquili, intuition is a degree of holistic perception much as the color pink is a degree of red. Dr. d'Aquili describes holistic perception as an aesthetic-religious spectrum. The different degrees of perception are like the colors of the rainbow in this metaphoric model. At the low end is the aesthetic sense. When your sense of how things are unified or connected is more pronounced than your sense of how they are separated, you would have what Dr. d'Aquili calls an aesthetic sense of beauty. From this aesthetic sense, holistic perception extends through romantic love—the sense that the two of us are greater—and into the area of religious awe.

Cosmic consciousness is the next level of holistic perception. It is different from religious awe, which is a sense of some divine presence. Cosmic consciousness is knowing that the world is unitary and ultimately meaningful. In a state of cosmic consciousness you are aware that all life is connected, but you are able to recognize separate physical units. The highest state on the holistic operator's scale is absolute unitary being, which is the direct experience of absolute unity. Dr. d'Aquili defines this level as a mystical state in which the sense of other is obliterated. In this state, you perceive only the connection and are not able to see separation.

RELIGIOUS INTUITION

On those very rare occasions when the holistic cognitive operator functions without the other five, you can experience complete unity. This powerful, altered state of consciousness in which all sense of the individual and all sense of duality disappears has been described by mystics for centuries and is the goal of Eastern meditation and rituals. Because it is nonverbal and subjective, it cannot be described in terms acceptable to the language of the other five cognitive operators. Very few people achieve this state, yet those who have experienced it, even briefly, report that it transforms their view of life. Dr. d'Aquili calls it "religious intuition" because once you know firsthand that absolute unitary being exists, you know without knowing how you know that this spaceless, timeless, infinite state is reality. It becomes your strongest sense of what is.

SPILLOVER AND INTUITIVE FUNCTIONING

Along with the other physiological changes associated with intuitive states are those that take place in your two nervous systems: the ergotropic and the trophotropic. The ergotropic, energy-expanding system consists primarily of your sympathetic nervous system and some complementary brain-stem functions. Your fight-or-flight response and other highly charged states of arousal come under its domain. The trophotropic, energy-conserving system consists primarily of your parasympathetic nervous system and the other mechanisms that keep your body functioning.

The right neocortex is identified with the trophotropic system. The left neocortex is identified with the ergotropic system. When either nervous system receives maximum stimulation, neuroscientists have found there is a spillover. This spillover spreads to the other nervous system so that both are stimulated at the same time. This spillover also affects your brain so that both the intuitive and reasoning functions are at their peak. In this spillover state, you may find the solution to that logical paradox. Problems that seemed insoluble may appear to solve themselves. This intensive state of consciousness can be induced through meditation or religious ritual such as chanting or trance dancing. (Although both meditation and religious ritual can produce this peak spillover state, each approach works through a different nervous system. Meditation affects the trophotropic nervous system while religious ritual affects the ergotrophic nervous system.)

BRAIN-WAVE RESEARCH AND INTUITION

Changes in brain waves have been measured during intuitive activity, providing yet another indication of the genuine physiological changes that take place when you are in an intuitive state. Studies of brain waves show that a person's EEG changes when he goes from one state of mind to another. The EEG is a measurement of the alternating electrical activity of the brain. The frequency (or number of cycles per seconds of this alternating current) is given in Hertz. The amplitude or strength of the signal is given in microvolts. One Hertz equals one cycle per second. Generally speaking, the delta range begins from 1 to 4 Hertz. The next is the theta range from 5 to 7 Hertz. The alpha range is from 8 to 12 Hertz. Beta is from 13 to 25 Hertz. Any frequency over 25 Hertz is called "fast beta" (see p. 144).

Delta waves are seen during sleep or can pinpoint areas of the cerebral cortex where brain damage has occurred. Low amplitude theta can indicate the onset of drowsiness, whereas high amplitude theta bursts can accompany emotional states (fear, anger, or the "aha!" moment of intuitive insight). Alpha can mean many things, depending on whether it is observed from only one hemisphere at a time, as in various cognitive tasks, or from both at the same time (relaxation or the beginnings of meditation). Beta is generally seen during awake attention with the eyes open. It may be dominant on one side of the cerebral cortex or the other in combination with alpha, depending on the cognitive process or on the right or left handedness of the subject. Simultaneous fast beta has been observed among spiritual healers and among meditators in advanced trance states.

Brain waves are like personal handwriting. Everyone's patterns are somewhat different. I may listen to music in alpha, and you may listen to music in beta. As I listen dreamily to the melody, you listen to the words and analyze which instrument is being played. You may even produce a theta flash on every down beat.

In the 1970s, Jean Millay pioneered research in the field of brain-wave synchronization between the left and right hemispheres. From 1970 to 1980, she conducted studies in biofeedback training that taught people how to synchronize the brain waves of both hemispheres to a relaxed alpha state. Using a "Phase Comparator" machine designed by Tim Scully, Millay found that thirty out of thirty-two participants reported that the biofeedback training "helped them to feel more relaxed and peaceful." In a paper called "Brain-Mind and the Dimensions beyond Space-Time," Millay reported, "years later, some claimed that the experience had helped them to increase their ability to focus attention, and that this ability was sustained even without the biofeedback instruments. Some of the participants also described flashes of intuitive insight after increased phase synchrony."

Thanks to more sophisticated technology, Millay was able to expand the

BRAIN WAVES

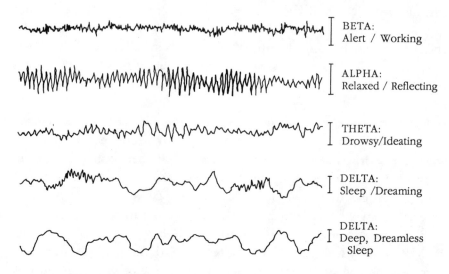

BETA:
Alert / Working

ALPHA:
Relaxed / Reflecting

THETA:
Drowsy/Ideating

DELTA:
Sleep /Dreaming

DELTA:
Deep, Dreamless
Sleep

range of her studies so that her next series of experiments compared the brain waves of two people's left and right hemispheres. Couples who found that they could synchronize both hemispheres and attune to their partner's frequency reported "intense, nonverbal feeling states." Notes Millay, "Musicians felt that it was like playing music, staying in tune and in time. Those who practiced martial arts compared the experience to the type of focus used during aikido exercises. Romantic couples felt that sexual feelings were evoked. They discussed 'the closeness of feelings' and the 'connections through the heart center.' "

Because some couples appeared better able to send and receive information telepathically during synchronization exercises, Millay hypothesized that "an electromagnetic connection" could " 'explain' telepathic communication." She conducted more than four hundred formal telepathic and one hundred formal psychic remote-viewing experiments, as well as extensive informal research. In her telepathy experiments, she asked a subject to draw a picture that his partner was looking at in another room. The sender would select an envelope containing a 3 × 5 card with a picture pasted on it from a group of one hundred or more. For eight minutes, the sender would draw the picture on another card and write down his impressions. The receiver, sitting in another room, would sketch and write about whatever came to mind during the eight-minute period. Independent judges were asked to evaluate each set of cards for shape, color, line drawing, word, mood, concept. Ten basic shapes, colors, and moods were used as a guide to evaluate these characteristics. Shape proved to be the most dominant similarity, followed by colors. Subjects who showed a strong preference for language showed greater similarity in words.

In 1978, Millay conducted the first formal biofeedback studies on interhemispheric and interpersonal brain-wave synchronization. In this series, twenty-two individuals pairing up into eleven teams attempted telepathy while using biofeedback to synchronize their own hemispheres to alpha as well as synchronizing their EEG output to that of their partners. These experiments did not produce statistically significant results. There was no correlation between the subjects' ability to synch up to each other's alpha and correctly transmit and receive telepathic messages.

Millay did find that partners who were able to get into a phase of what she calls "absolute synch," that is, they were able to closely match the phase angle of their EEG output as well as the frequency, produced more telepathic "hits" than those who merely synchronized their phase to the alpha range.

Millay compared the results of the telepathic study with the results of brain-wave synchronization scores by the same teams. There was no one-to-one correlation between the accuracy of each telepathic response and interpersonal synchronization tested. However, she did find that teams with the best above-average telepathy scores also had the best team average synchronization scores. Those teams that scored below chance on the telepathy test also had the lowest average brain-wave synchronization scores.

In "Brain-Mind and the Dimensions beyond Space-Time," Millay observed that "the mind is not limited to the four dimensions of space-time." This, she believes, is why the mind is capable of knowing things that the brain's sensory system does not pick up.

> The research on brain function among the most respected researchers from many disciplines has led us to the realization that the brain is at least a four-dimensional object (it keeps track of its own space and time). But as it does so, it produces the legal evidence of life, the EEG. This is the brain's electrical activity. Biofeedback research has demonstrated that individuals can exert voluntary control over this *fifth dimensional* electrical activity of their brains as well. This means that the MIND . . . must encompass dimensions of even more complexity.

She concluded, "This is one of the reasons that the mind can pick up information beyond the limitations of space-time. This shift in conceptualization toward a multidimensional mind allows a natural place for the psi phenomena we have observed. There is no longer a need to call these phenomena 'paranormal.' "

BRAIN-WAVE RESEARCH AND PSYCHIC FUNCTIONING

Experimental psychologist Norman S. Don has been conducting research into brain-wave patterns at the University of Illinois and the Kairos Foundation in Chicago for the past ten years. "We have found that the moment of insight, or the 'Aha!' experience produces brain-wave correlates in the left occipital lobe, which is the visual cortex. At that precise moment, we can see harmonics in the brain-wave patterns."

Also, since 1983, Don has been working with several psychics with outstanding reputations to study the brain-wave effects during psychic functioning. Don has learned that there are clear determinations of different states of consciousness as shown in the EEG patterns. What's more, the brain-wave patterns are clearly different when the psychic correctly determines something.

Although his research is not yet complete, Don's findings note strong individual differences among the participating subjects. Among the predominant patterns that most of his subjects show is more activity in their right hemisphere, some of it in the alpha range. He has also found brain-wave patterns that are simultaneously slow and fast in different parts of the brain. "Over large portions of the upper scalp, both in the right and left hemispheres, we see theta and delta patterns and direct current [DC] effects. In the right hemisphere, we are observing along with the theta and delta, very fast brain waves, from 13 Hertz up to 70 in some cases."

What does it mean? For Don, it means "causality is shattered." There is no way to explain psychic phenomena in terms of cause and effect. For people who need physical evidence, these findings show that intuition— both with and without precedent—produces measurable activity in the brain and therefore, does exist.

After ten years of research, Don is still amazed: "What's really happening God only knows, but the brain waves of ordinary people during insight experiences, and of psychics when their information is accurate, are unique. Their brains are in special states."

CHAPTER 10

Knowing Your Reptilian Brain

Before you start reading this section, we want you to take the next few minutes to make yourself comfortable. Find whatever you need to create a safe nest for yourself: a pillow, perhaps, or a plump, soft chair, or a cozy couch. Anywhere where you can say, "This is my place." Think of a dog or cat that takes a little blanket or towel, walks around it a few times, shoves it over a little bit, then tries to lie down in one position and then another. Then, finally, it releases a sigh. That sigh means, "My brain feels safe, comfortable, content, fine. The world is fine." It may seem funny to compare yourself to a pet, but the part of your brain that needs to feel safe and comfortable before you can learn or work functions the same for you as it does for such a pet.

The reptilian brain, also known as the primal, or old, brain, is, in evolutionary terms, the oldest part of your triune brain. Located at the base of your neck, it absorbs information in the form of energy that flows up the spinal column and through your pores. From the reptilian brain, absorbed energy makes its way into the higher brain systems, the limbic and the neocortex. Information from the other senses—your eyes, ears, nose, and mouth—enters the neocortex and limbic system. Of course, all of your brains and all your intelligences are working simultaneously all the time, but when the reptilian brain does not feel comfortable and safe, it sends distress signals up through the top two brains, which can make it impossible for you to concentrate on the work at hand. You may be aware that something is bothering you, but you might not know what it is. It could be as simple as someone else sitting in your favorite chair or leaning too far across your desk. Whether or not you are aware of the cause, you cannot afford to ignore those signals. That feeling of discomfort can prevent you from skillfully using the information that your other brains are processing.

It's unlikely that you have ever compared yourself to a snake or lizard, but many of our nonverbal, instinctive behavior patterns are generated in this reptilian brain. In his studies of many different reptiles, Dr. Paul MacLean has found that human beings share as many as two dozen behavior patterns with lizards! These include selecting and preparing homesites; establishing territory; showing place preferences; using color and adornments to mark, display, and defend territory; hunting; homing; hoarding; defecating at specific sites; the formation of social groups; and the creation of social hierarchies. The next time you choose new carpet, curtains, and bedspreads, remember that the komodo dragon decorates her home, too. And the part of your brain that moves instinctively to decorate is very similar to hers.

Working from the triune brain model, Elaine de Beauport finds three distinct intelligences at work in this old brain. *Basic* reptilian intelligence consists of moving toward and away from things, and the ability to imitate. This is how young children learn behavior and how we, as grown-ups, often react in social situations. Also basic to the reptilian brain is territorial identity and the need for safety. *Routine* intelligence is the brain's ability to create habits, patterns, and routines. When you drive to work the same way every morning for fifteen years and find that even after your office moves you are still heading off on the old road every morning, that's your routine intelligence taking command. It takes time and repetition for your reptilian brain to learn a new routine. *Ritual* intelligence is the brain's ability to create a routine that is enhanced with meaning.

Becoming conscious of your patterns, habits, and routines is the key to unlocking the secrets of your reptilian brain. As you become aware of how powerful this particular creative intelligence is, you can begin to focus your attention on creating new patterns and changing old ones by shifting your point of focus, or energy, to that part of your brain. A survey by several psychological disciplines found that the basic issue for most people entering psychotherapy is self-esteem. Self-esteem, the need to recognize yourself and feel yourself recognized, originates in the reptilian brain. You need to take care of your essential needs to be whole so that you can handle whatever comes along and feel connected to the people for whom you care. To feel connected to other people, you have to really value yourself—not because you're better than anyone else but because you are the only one who can value you. If you are always searching for a place to feel safe, you will never experience real brilliance. By real brilliance, we mean having the conscious ability to use your network of multiple intelligences, not simply being able to score high on tests.

It is very hard, if not impossible, to access your intuition when your reptilian brain does not feel safe. You need to be grounded in a strong sense of who you are, with a strong sense of your own territory and your place in it. You have to know that you exist, that you are whole, and that you deserve to be here before you take the risk of being sure of something as ephemeral as intuition, something to which you cannot give concrete form. Because one of the prime prerequisites for intuition is trust, be aware that you cannot experience trust if you have no sense of self. You need to know that you exist on this elemental, reptilian level before you can have that trust.

LEARNING FROM REPTILES

Did you ever have a reptile for a pet? A chameleon from the circus, perhaps, or some other lizard? Lizards don't do very much. They don't play. Nor do they engage with the outside world. In the evolution of your brain, one of the differences between reptiles and mammals is that mammals are able to connect emotionally with each other and with the outside world. With few exceptions, reptiles hatch eggs and then ignore their young (unless they eat them).

So if reptiles don't do much and don't respond, what can you learn from them? The next time you go to the zoo, or to the home of someone who has a pet snake, lizard, turtle, or alligator, spend some time observing the animal's movements. See how it establishes its territory and moves its energy toward some things and away from others. Notice how it slowly is drawn to a particular spot in the sun, and how it recoils from other spots. Try to get a feel of that slow, slow reptilian pace because you will want to keep it in mind when you do the following exercise.

EXERCISE FOR FINDING YOUR REPTILIAN ENERGY

Set aside fifteen minutes for this exercise.

Once again, be sure that you are completely comfortable in a safe place. Breathe deeply and exhale fully. Let your breathing slow down. Feel yourself getting heavier and heavier as you let go and move deeper into your mind.

Go inside your mind and begin way back when you first opened your eyes this morning. Watch yourself as you go through your day from the moment you stepped out of bed. Notice your *energy,* your *point of focus,* not your thoughts or your feelings, but your *energy.* This is almost impossible to describe in words because we are talking about a nonverbal intelligence. You will have to experiment until you sense it for yourself. Now, see what you are drawn to. What is your energy drawn to during the course of the day? As you get out of bed and begin your morning, what do you see your energy moving toward? What do you see it moving away from? As you look to your family or the other people with whom you live what do you feel yourself moving toward? From what do you move away? As you go to your place of work, what people or what parts of the environment do you feel your energy moving toward? Where do you notice your energy recoil- ing? Allow yourself to sense your energy and what seems to repel it in the places and activities at work. As you see yourself moving toward your home again at the end of the day, toward what do you move, and from what do you recoil? As you get ready to go to bed, what do you move toward, and from what do you move away?

You may start to notice certain patterns of which you were not aware, like being drawn to sunny spots and moving away from dark ones, or moving toward quiet and away from noise. Can you identify your own energy trail? Are you drawn toward clean places while you recoil from messy spots? How about certain colors and smells? You may never have realized that certain places or people gave you the creeps because your reptilian essence simply recoiled. There is no reason for any of these patterns so don't judge yourself, just observe. And practice. Do this exercise several times so that you can identify your reptilian essence and recognize it when you find yourself drawn to or pulled away from a person or place.

What is the difference between an intuitive warning and a reptilian recoiling? As you become able to observe yourself, you will become familiar with your reptilian patterns that are repeated over and over again in certain situations. When you feel one of those energy patterns pulling you somewhere, it is coming from the reptilian brain. Intuition occurs higher up in your brain system and feels livelier.

RECOGNIZING YOUR PATTERNS

Observe yourself in the morning. Do you get out of bed sleepy-eyed and follow an unvarying routine—slippers, bathroom, splash face, brush teeth, shower, shuffle to kitchen, make coffee, shuffle to bedroom closet, get dressed, shuffle back to kitchen, drink coffee—all on automatic pilot? If you shave, do you notice that you can't remember shaving unless you touch your face a few minutes later? Notice, if you will, how many parts of that routine you actually perform with no conscious thought. This hazy, automatic pilot routine is actually a behavior pattern created by your reptilian brain. In thinking back to how you start your day, do you recall your state of mind as kind of pleasantly dazed? That mild, stoned buzz is another characteristically reptilian state.

How many such routines do you follow throughout the course of the day? Can you break them down into miniroutines such as just shaving, or just brushing your teeth? Have you noticed whether you leave the water running when you shave or brush your teeth? Little habits that irritate you when someone else does them differently are also reptilian patterns. During the course of one week, notice one particular pattern and try to change it. Sit in a different chair at dinner time or sleep on a different side of the bed and notice how you respond. If you find that something inside you resists changing these small, everyday routines, you will realize how strong these reptilian rhythms can be.

This annoyance at the disruption of an established pattern can also flare up when your personal territory is invaded. Is someone sitting in your chair? Using your desk at the office? Drinking from your favorite glass? Parking in your regular space? Cutting you off in traffic? Sitting on your regular seat in the bus or train? Again, notice the little things that disturb your equilibrium and don't criticize yourself. You need to feel safe and calm in order to function. Learn to respect your basic, territorial intelligence and give yourself the conditions that you need in order to feel at home anywhere.

This isn't easy. Most of us have been told by our parents and teachers not to be selfish, to give up our seat for someone else, or to give someone else a toy that we loved. In itself, giving up a seat or a toy is not a catastrophic event. But over time, the reptilian brain can encode these messages that say "don't do this, you can't do that" into a composite message that says, "I have no right to exist, I can't do anything, and I'm not going to take care of myself because I'm not worth anything." To care for your inner reptile, you may wish to look at what deeply nourishes you and create rituals around those things that will give you a warm sense of personal satisfaction. Every day find one thing—an event, a place, a work of art, or a friend, perhaps—that really gives you a strong, good feeling. Create a ritual for yourself around that person, place, or thing. It can be as simple as giving yourself five or ten or fifteen minutes to simply enjoy being around whatever it is that nourishes you, so that when you are finished you can say, "I really feel good that I did that! I deserve to spend some time each day doing something that makes me feel happy and strong." Because many of us go through our days feeling deprived and exhausted and since we don't take care of our reptilian needs, establishing these minirituals will recharge our energy. Nobody taught you to do this in school but this positive energy is stimulating to your brain. By feeding and taking care of your inner reptile, you are really taking care of your whole brain.

YOUR PERSONAL SANCTUARY: AN EXERCISE

When you find yourself tired, under stress, or anxious, you can use your territorial intelligence to create a place of inner safety that will always be available to you. When you are frightened, threatened, or feeling worried, you can shift your point of focus to this personal sanctuary at any time and feel calm just by being there. Should you have trouble with this or any other exercise, practice several times. When you start working out or learning a new sport, you are using your muscles in new combinations for new activities. Similarly, in these exercises, too, you are using parts of your brain that you have never consciously tried to work with before. As with any exercise program, if you give yourself time to practice, you will get results.

Set aside twenty minutes for this exercise.

The first thing to do is make sure that you have all your energy focused. Close your eyes and visualize the outside form of your body enlarging.

Then actively put all of your energy inside your margins and see yourself being molded with energy on the inside. Allow this energy to become very peaceful and very still. Breathe deeply and when you exhale, let any tension you feel flow right out. Be conscious of a great slowing down. Allow yourself to be totally aware of yourself as a solid and growing and evolving and unique and beautiful energy form. If there is any tension in your body anywhere, just send some consciousness to that area. Take a few more deep breaths and give yourself permission to just relax. This may be the only time today that you are focused on yourself as being comfortable, peaceful, solid, and completely here.

Now go inside your mind and allow yourself to choose the perfect spot for you. Make it as clear as you possibly can with all of the color, the feeling, and the sensing that you possibly can. Include any smells you really love. Make your perfect sanctuary look exactly as you want it to look. Let your mind go to create whatever you choose so that you can feel perfectly safe, in a place where you know you can always go and be you and feel completely rested. This is a place where you will only allow in thoughts, ideas, images, other people, and other things when you choose. You can create this place exactly as you want it to be. This is your perfect sanctuary.

As you get ready to leave your special spot, know that you can always return, alone or with someone. If your intuition scares you, you can go straight to your place of inner safety. It belongs to you and you can take it with you wherever you go. Whenever you feel scared or unsure or unsafe, remember that you have within you your safe place.

CHAPTER 11

Knowing Your Limbic System

Wrapped around the top of the reptilian brain, and connected to the mushrooming neocortex above it, the limbic system, also known as the limbic brain, is the center of all your emotional activity. Love, anger, depression, and fear are among the feelings that originate there. Although you probably never thought of your feelings in connection with your brain, the limbic system is truly the heart of your mind.

The limbic system is located behind your face and connects your feelings to the ways in which you express them. When your limbic system experiences sadness, you feel as if you want to cry and tears start to come out of your eyes. When you smile or growl to express your feelings, your face becomes the outward projection of your limbic activity.

The limbic system, also known as the paleomammalian brain, evolved after the reptilian brain. It is called the brain of connection because it evolved physiologically so that members of one species of mammals could feel sensitivity for other members of the same species. As we pointed out in the last chapter, mammals differ significantly from reptiles in the way they care for their young. Whereas most reptiles hatch their offspring and leave them, mammals nurture and protect their cubs, becoming savage if one of their young is attacked. In his studies of animal behavior, Dr. Paul MacLean has discovered that the presence of the limbic brain is the common denominator in all mammals, and he notes that this brain has "the capacity to generate vivid, affective feelings of what is true, real, and important."

Elaine de Beauport identifies six intelligences at work in the limbic system, more than in the two other brains. Connected with the senses of taste and smell, *oral* and *nasal* intelligences are powerful anchors for emotional states. *Sexual intelligence,* too, combines sensory-based and emotional information. The limbic brain is the center of pleasure and pain, with accompanying *mood* states that can range from anger to exquisite happiness. Your sense of *motivation* is a limbic state, as is your ability to be *affected* by another person, an event, or a place. We described the essence of the reptilian brain as moving toward and away from people, places, and things. The essence of the limbic brain is the ability to be charged with excitement and to connect and disconnect emotionally.

Dr. MacLean uses the analogy of biological computers to describe how the three brains function, each with its own "subjectivity and intelligence, its own sense of time and space, and its own memory, motor, and other functions." But the limbic brain can also be compared to a pharmacy, because it is the most chemically volatile of the three brains. Neuroscientists, medical researchers, and psychologists are now studying the limbic system and its effect on your physical health. The new field of psycho-neuroimmunology, which deals with the mind's impact on the body's ability to heal, focuses primarily on limbic activity because nearly all of your physiological processes are regulated in the limbic system. As more people accept the role that the mind-body connection plays in sickness and healing, words such as *hypochondria* are going out of fashion. If you accept the presupposition that your mind, specifically your limbic brain, affects your body, then you cannot readily dismiss someone's symptoms as being "just in his mind." (Because the limbic brain is the main mind-body transducer, we are mentioning its connection to healing. But the role of the mind in healing is a vast subject in itself, which we are not able to discuss at any length here. Many excellent books describe the interrelationship between your mind, body, and healing and we have listed several in the Bibliography.)

Becoming conscious of what your limbic brain does and learning how to shift your point of focus into different feeling states can improve your physical, mental, and emotional health. Because the immune system is connected to your limbic brain, it responds to limbic stress in a variety of ways that can depress your body's ability to stay healthy. When you learn how to release and express emotional energy, you not only energize your limbic system, you can improve your natural psychoneuroimmunological responses. Because your intuition can take the form of a feeling state, increasing the range of your emotional sensitivity will also enhance your ability to recognize and interpret your intuitive feelings.

THE SUBJECTIVE BRAIN

Simply accepting that your limbic brain supplies you with valuable information may require that you shift values and suspend some disbelief. Because most of us are taught to believe that only the left half of the neocortex is capable of valid mental activity, we have trouble accepting the idea that other intelligences—reptilian, limbic, and intuitive—are of equal importance. Unlike the left neocortex, which is concerned with external facts, the limbic brain gives you information about your internal world as well as the external world. To become fully functional in emotional intelligence, you need to prioritize your beliefs. You must be willing to accept that information acquired through your subjective brain, which is not the brain you took to school, is valid. Feeling is a powerful way of getting information. When you decide to close down your feelings you are shutting off an important channel of data.

You probably have been conditioned to believe that feelings are not as important as factual thoughts. Feelings get you into trouble because they affect you and because your feelings affect other people. You may have decided, as many people do, that you do not want to deal with your feelings at all. Or if you do, you judge them, saying, "Oh, that's only a feeling, it doesn't really count" or "I was feeling really angry the other day and I know I shouldn't feel that way." Whether you choose to acknowledge it in your linear left brain or not, you are affected by your feelings. When you give priority to that internal dialogue with your voice of reason, you are allowing the voice of the left brain to impose its linear perspective and you are not letting yourself benefit from the information that your limbic brain is giving you. This same self-censoring process can occur when intuitive intelligence presents you with information.

Because the left brain is the center of language, it has words to tell you that its thoughts are more important than those feelings. But feelings and thoughts are both synaptic responses, created by an electrochemical process. One metaphorical difference is that thoughts are concrete and tangible. They begin with a capital and end with a period. We can usually manage them because they have a beginning, a middle, and an end. Feelings don't. They overtake you. They are vague, ephemeral, intangible, and foggy. It's difficult to have a feeling that you can really grab onto because feelings tend to dissolve when you attempt to hold on to them. But feelings and thoughts do have equal value. They are both valuable ways in which your brain absorbs and processes information, and both can be components of your intuition.

THE LANGUAGE OF FEELINGS

The only language of feelings is crying, laughing, snarling, growling, screaming, and smiling. As you build your skills of self-observation, learning your own language of feelings can become a bridge to greater intuitive awareness. All expressions of emotion release tension. As the range of your emotional vocabulary expands, you will become more attuned to your own subtle tones and nuances. "You can develop a kind of emotional or intuitive language that is like the beginning of words in linear thinking," says Francis Ford Coppola, who compares his own emotional language development to that of a two- or three-year-old who is learning words. "I can imagine an entire emotional language that would really operate on such a powerful level in the art of anticipation and planning. It would use intuitive glimpses as the basis of a whole method of thinking and feeling and would be the same as using simple words to develop language. You could cultivate this intuitive, emotional language so that it became the equivalent of what analysis is to deductive thinking."

To begin building your feeling language skills, you need to find out who you are as a feeling being. You are capable of having all kinds of emotions from quietness to ecstasy but how many have you had recently? You may not know what they are to start with, because you probably have not paid sufficient attention to them to name them all. You probably recognize sadness, frustration, and anger. You may recognize depression but it could also be stillness. How do you recognize joy? Have you experienced ecstasy lately?

You don't have to necessarily name a feeling to experience it. Ask yourself simply, What is it like to feel? Do I know how to let myself feel sad, so that the sadness vibrates through me? Or do I believe that I have to think about that feeling and decide to do something about it? See if you can let yourself experience one emotion without judging it, thinking about it, or resolving it in some way. The next time you feel sad, allow the feeling to wash through you. If you want to, you can identify it by saying, "Sad, sad, sad, sad." It may seem silly, but doing this will actually help the feeling to pass. If you let it, the feeling will move through you and you will not feel stuck. If you debate yourself and try to figure out what to do about a feeling, it will hang around for a while and you will be frustrated. Another way to learn how to feel is to watch a child. Children cry, laugh, scream, hit their heads on the floor, smile, dance, and giggle so quickly that they seem to be experiencing these feelings almost all at once. Do they have to learn how to feel? No. They just let go. That's what you, as an adult, can learn from them.

Identifying your feelings can help you become more comfortable with the whole subject called emotion. As we did in the first part of this book when we asked you to break down the subject of intuition into different types of experience and characteristic, we are asking you now to take a similar approach. If the prospect of experiencing your feelings makes you anxious, working with smaller pieces of emotional information will make it easier. You don't have to be overwhelmed by feeling your feelings, you can let them in one at a time. Invisible and powerful, emotions can be scary when you don't know how to feel them, express them, and let them go. If a particular feeling makes you uncomfortable, take note of it. How, specifically, does that discomfort make itself known? Pick a feeling and stay with that feeling long enough to see what information it is giving you. Then, if you can, talk, draw, write, or dance about what that feeling has told you. I feel sad about . . . I feel happy because . . . I feel angry when . . .

Try to become aware of one feeling a day, keeping in mind that by doing so, you are building your data bank of self-knowledge. Keep working to develop clarity. The clearest sense of who you are is through your feelings. When you are secure in your ability to know what and how you feel, you will find yourself more fluent in your own personal nonverbal language of feelings, and concomitantly more aware of how you process intuitive feelings, as well. When you become an intellect in the world of feeling, you will find it completely natural to rely on your emotions as a source of information about yourself, other people, and the world.

LET YOURSELF WANT: AN EXERCISE

Since you are probably reading this book because you want to know more about your intuition and would like to be more intuitive, you may find it helpful to open up your motivational intelligence. Now shift your point of focus from your goal or outcome—developing your intuition—to your motivational intelligence, the part of you that really *wants* to be more in touch with your intuitive abilities. Wanting is part of the energy of the limbic system and feeling your wanting can move you closer to your desired state. Motivation is focused wanting. It is powerful, energizing, and concentrated, like a laser beam. It is the energy that moves you. When you are motivated, everything falls into place and everything you do has a purpose. Begin by remembering a time when you were highly motivated. Let that serve as your point of reference so that you can recognize what we are talking about.

Set aside fifteen minutes for this exercise.

Now, make yourself comfortable. You may want to listen to some relaxing music as you take a few deep breaths and release any tension. Give yourself permission to feel yourself wanting. You can let yourself want to be able to access your intuition or you can let yourself want anything else in the world: a house, a stereo, a lover, an adventure. This exercise is intended only to open you up to the feeling of focused wanting. It is not about having goals. It is about sensing the difference between your outcomes and goals and feeling your wants. This is the time for you to ask yourself, "What do I want? What do I really want?" and to keep asking yourself. Don't stop asking "What do I want?" The more that you ask, the deeper you will go. Close your eyes and go deep inside yourself and feel your wanting. You may not have words for it at first. You may have pictures. You may have senses. You may have never given yourself permission before but this is a very real, important, and growing part of you. You may never have asked yourself this before. Sometimes the first time you ask yourself, the answers are slow to come. If you find this exercise hard, you may not have validated and supported your own feelings of focused wanting. Give yourself plenty of time. You can want anything. It's okay to want.

You can do this exercise with a friend. Take turns and spend five minutes asking each other, "What do you want?" Don't let your friend stop wanting. Keep asking for the full five minutes. The person who is asking the questions can write down his partner's responses so that you will each have a record of what you want.

LOVING YOURSELF: AN EXERCISE

As we mentioned earlier, to value and trust your intuition, you must be able to love yourself. For most of us this may sound easy, but it's very hard to do. From the perspective of your limbic system, you can access, re-create, and strengthen how love feels. All your emotional memories are stored in your limbic library and you can reactivate them at will. Remembering a feeling from the past and allowing it to flood your limbic system re-creates that moment so that it lives in your feeling state again. So powerful are your emotional memories that by reactivating them you are, in a sense, making the past into the present.

Set aside twenty minutes for this exercise.

Take a few minutes to get comfortable. Breathe deeply and release any tension in your body. Now think of a time when you were completely and thoroughly loved. And think of a time when you gave love completely and thoroughly. Find a memory that is so strong that you feel the openness and expansiveness of that love rushing through your body. If you have ever loved or been loved, then you know how to create it. You can retrieve the memory of love that you have stored in your limbic library and let yourself experience that feeling now. Feeling love does not involve judgment. It is not about cause and effect. Love vibrates within us and vibrates with other people. You get stuck when you use the left brain of the neocortex to create boundaries and limits, such as when you say, "I can't love him because he did that" or "I don't love her because she doesn't give me what I want." If you do get stuck saying that, you can stop and move your point of focus to that part of your brain that recognizes and feels love as limitless. You can connect with that feeling and let it give you information about who you are: I love when . . . I love to . . . I am loved when . . .

When you know that you can unlock that love and feel yourself loved at any time by activating your limbic awareness, you will come to respect your feeling intelligence. And you will enjoy using it to give love to yourself. Valuing your intuition is an extension of that self-love.

CHAPTER 12

Knowing Your Neocortex

By now, you should be familiar with this top brain, the newest of the three, and you should know something about how each of its hemispheres functions. The left half, or left brain, is the brain you took to school, the seat of rational, analytical, and sequential intellectual processes. The right half, or right brain, is the center of random, nonsequential intellectual processes. Elaine de Beauport identifies the three right-brain intelligences as *intuitive, visual,* and *associational*. Visual or spatial intelligence is the ability to create, hold, and manipulate images in your mind's eye. Associational intelligence is the ability to notice or perceive connections between disparate circumstances, people, or things. You could call it improvisational intelligence because that's the essence of what it does. It is practically impossible to separate associational from visual and intuitive intelligence because they work together so much of the time and are very much part of the same thing, although you can have moments when you are thinking visually that have nothing to do with intuition. And you can spontaneously come up with a new combination of two different concepts without intuition, too. But often, when you suddenly connect two unrelated ideas, it comes as a flash of insight that feels like an intuitive grasp of a concept. Such an intuitive flash may take the form of an inspired minibrainstorm. You might even see this new combination in a mental image and would therefore not really be able to distinguish between the associational and the visual. Nor could you identify specifically the point at which you knew without knowing how you knew that such a connection was possible. We will present exercises that allow you to work with all of your right-brain intelligences so you can see this for yourself.

Although we have given the left brain a hard time in this book, we have done so, in part, to compensate for what we see as an exaggerated cultural perception of its superiority over the other brains and their innate mental abilities. For most of us, indoctrination into the myth of the superiority of the left neocortex began when we were too young to know the difference. Now, as an adult, having experienced intuitive knowing at least once or twice in your life, you have to demystify how you think about how you think if you are to begin to use your whole brain. That means first accepting that rational thinking is not the only way to process information, and second, learning how to shift your point of focus into these other intelligences so that you experience them for yourself.

Nor are we advocating that you surrender logic to intuition. The two must work together so that you can verify your intuitive perceptions. You need the skills of the left brain to balance your inner vision so that you can make a concensual reality check to see whether your intuition is on target in the world of external events. To the degree that you believe that your left brain is superior and that its beliefs, values, and assessments of the world are the only correct ones, you will need to surrender these beliefs, at least for the moment, to move into your right-brain ways of knowing. If you have read this far, you know that you can't expect linear, logical, analytical processes to do everything for you. You can't expect your left brain to feel, to create a sense of safety, or to intuit—it simply cannot do those things.

THE VOICE OF REASON EXERCISE

If you don't believe us, you may want to try an exercise that will help you to revise your relationship with the part of yourself that tells you, "logic is the only way to view the world." When you hear that logical inner voice, it's as if you had Mr. Spock from "Star Trek" inside your head. Whenever you have an intuitive flash, hunch, or gut feeling, Mr. Spock pipes up with, "But that isn't logical, Captain. And if it isn't logical, it doesn't count." Mr. Spock is a metaphor for your voice of reason.

Set aside fifteen minutes for this exercise.

Close your eyes and listen to that voice. What does it sound like? Is the tone deep or high-pitched? Is the tempo slow or fast? How would you describe the volume? Is the voice clear and well modulated or is it raspy and fuzzy? Notice as many audio modality distinctions as possible.

Is there an image attached to that inner voice? Do you see Mr. Spock? (You may experience the voice of reason in an audio representational system only or you may pick up a mental image, as well.) If you have a picture of Mr. Spock, notice whether it is black-and-white or color, its location in relation to where you are now, and the brightness or intensity of the colors. Notice any physical or emotional feelings you have in connection with the image and voice.

Now say hello to Mr. Spock and listen as he greets you. Tell him that you understand that he believes logic is the only valid method for processing information and that you agree that logic is important. Tell him that you value your intuition as an equal partner to logic and you are going to develop it. Tell Mr. Spock that you believe it is important to be able to use all of your inner resources, not only your analytical abilities. Explain to him that you do not intend to demean logic or take away any analytical strengths, merely that you want to expand your intellectual skills.

What does Mr. Spock say in response? How do you feel when you hear his answer? If you feel uncomfortable because Mr. Spock does not agree with or accept your intention to cultivate your intuition, try shifting some of the submodalities. Lower the volume and deepen his tone of voice. Slow the pace. If you are working with a mental image, you can move Mr. Spock farther away from you and dim the color brightness while you change the audio submodalities until you feel comfortable. Explain again that you value your intuition and plan to develop it. By shifting the submodalities, you can create a new balance between the part of yourself that wants to expand your intuition as well as the voice of reason. The outcome in this exercise is for you to feel confident that you are entitled to your own intuitive abilities. Remember, your voice of reason is part of you, but it is not all of you. You can modulate it so that it functions in a helpful way and does not overpower you or prevent you from developing your intuitive thinking abilities.

THE VOICE OF INTUITION EXERCISE

Now that you have identified your voice of reason, you may also want to spend some time locating and becoming familiar with your voice of intuition. When we use the word "voice" we don't want to imply that you need to be aware of words only, although intuition can occur inside you as a voice. Very often people ask us, "How can I be sure that I am hearing or sensing my intuition?" By identifying and becoming familiar with the characteristics of your intuition, you will become more confident. You are the only one who can know where and how your intuition functions for you. You may want to read this exercise a couple of times before you practice it for the first time. With this exercise and the one that follows, you may also want to have someone read it to you or tape-record it and play it back for yourself.

We want to help guide you to an inner place where you can extract some essence of understanding that can be applied to a specific situation. That essence of understanding is intuitive. You will want to be able to ask your intuition for guidance whenever you need it.

Set aside fifteen minutes for this exercise.

Get into a comfortable position and relax. Take several deep breaths and imagine all the tension in your body leaving you as you exhale. As you inhale, imagine energy coming into your body that allows you to expand, to let go, to change, to be more relaxed, and to feel. As you continue to breathe deeply, allow your consciousness to follow the sound of your breath in and out of your body. Let yourself become still enough and quiet enough inside to allow yourself to follow the sound of your breath to its beginnings. As you exhale . . . to its endings. As you inhale again . . . follow the sound of your breath to where it starts in your body. As you exhale, find where it ends. As you relax more with each breath cycle, and as you pay attention to where the sound begins, see if you can locate the quietest place in your breathing cycle. Follow the sound of your breathing to its source.

In this quietness, you have probably noticed that there are many different kinds of voice sounds moving through your awareness. Certain thoughts talk about things that have happened during the day. Others talk about what you are going to do and what you are experiencing now. Quiet those thoughts for a moment at the beginning of a deep breath and push them off to the side knowing that they are not gone forever. If they are important to you they will come back later, when you have finished this exercise. Right now, focus your full attention on where in your body the sound and feeling of your breath begins and ends. Let yourself return to that focus when you hear your thoughts.

Take another deep breath and let go. Now ask your intuition if it is willing to communicate with you. If your intuition says no, you need not be alarmed or discouraged. No is still an answer that indicates that you have intuition and it is able to communicate. Ask your intuition what conditions it needs to be willing to communicate. Be flexible in establishing a dialogue with your intuitive voice. Let it know that you are willing to listen when it is ready to communicate. Establish a signal. For example, if you feel a warm spot in your chest or throat area when your intuition speaks, tell it to make that warm spot noticeably warmer if its answer to a particular question is yes, and colder if its answer is no.

Without judging the answer, allow yourself to stay connected to that sense, feeling, or voice that you just had. Let your attention now move toward your connection with that voice of intuition. If your intuition says yes, it is willing to communicate with you, then think of a situation in which you would like some intuitive guidance. The easiest way to communicate with your intuitive voice is to phrase your questions to have yes or no answers. Then ask your intuition about a specific situation. You can ask the same question several times if you are unclear about the answer. Pay attention to the sound of your voice of intuition as it responds. Experience the sensation, the vibration, and the fullness of it. Notice the volume, the pitch, and the tempo of this voice. How clear is it? Is it loud or soft? What happens when you increase the volume and raise the pitch? Notice what physical and emotional feelings occur in your body when your voice of intuition is speaking.

THE INTUITION STORE: AN EXERCISE

Set aside twenty minutes for this exercise.

Take some time to relax and feel yourself become quiet. Do whatever you need to surround yourself with complete peace and comfort. Let go of the day. Pack it up and send it out the door and up to the ceiling or out the window and move to a level of peace and stillness. You are moving out of the outside world and closer to your inner world. Take a very deep breath and forcibly let it out. With each exhalation, let go of more tension and thoughts. This is your time, a time of stillness and relaxation. It is time to move to a larger sense of yourself, in which all knowing is available to you. To do that, you need to let go of criticism, evaluation, and analysis, and move into vibration, image, and feelings. Peacefully, without struggle. With confidence.

Now see yourself walking down the street to a row of stores. You approach a store that looks exciting and interesting, and when you look up, you see the word *Intuition* over the door. With great excitement, you open the door and walk in. Inside, you find a room filled with all kinds of symbols and artifacts. Everything is in this store. You can choose anything you like to be your personal symbol of intuition.

Look at all of the shelves, high and low, as you start to pick up certain symbols that might represent intuition to you. Pick them up and put them down as you move through the store. Notice what you are drawn toward. To which symbol do you keep coming back? Which symbol do you keep picking up and holding, feeling as if it is yours and it belongs to you? It can be anything you choose. Spend a few more minutes happily walking around the intuition store until you find the symbol that is perfect for you. Pick it up and take it to the shopkeeper. Listen as he tells you that this is your symbol. It was meant for you. You can wrap it up and put it in a bag if you like, but it doesn't cost anything. It's yours. It was always meant to be yours.

Take your symbol under your arm or in a bag or however you choose and leave the intuition store. Take it to a special place, perhaps your place of inner safety or personal sanctuary, and spend some time with it. Look at it, feel it, sense it, experience it. Make it yours. Put it away inside of you so that you can get it whenever you choose. Take it with you everywhere so that you can look at it, feel it, and sense it when you want to know from within. You can feel comfortable and relaxed knowing that you have your symbol with you. When you are ready, open your eyes and come back to the outside world.

In the morning, when you wake up, take out your symbol and focus on it while you are taking a shower and getting ready to start the day. As you look at this lovely symbol of your intuition, affirm, "I am going to open up to my intuition today." You don't have to force it. Intuition is gentle. Simply by shifting your awareness to your symbol and acknowledging it by saying, "My intuition is going to open today," you will find that it is naturally, easily available.

SHIFTING FROM TRUST TO INTUITION

As we discussed in chapter 10, learning how to trust your intuition is a complicated step. Trusting it means not only recognizing it and relying on it when it gives you information, it also means trusting who you are. Just as you created a data bank of resources for intuition, you can create a data bank of resources for trusting yourself. In the two exercises that follow, you will be doing just that.

Self-trust firms up your inner territory and grounds you with solid premises for believing in who you are. During the first part of these exercises, you are shifting your point of focus to your reptilian brain where you declare "I am" and "I exist." Having moved to a place of trust, you will then shift your point of focus directly to your intuition and see, hear, and feel what happens. Remember, there is a part of your brain that "does" intuition naturally, at any given moment. By moving your awareness to your intuitive mind, you can access that process. Unlike rational processing, you do not have to "do" anything specific once you get there. You don't have to add or subtract or conjugate verbs or figure anything out. Rather, you need to be receptive to whatever information your intuition gives you.

For each of these exercises, you will need a partner. If possible, find someone whom you do not know very well. You will get a better sense of intuitive knowing because you will not be able to cite your past relationship with this person as a possible explanation for any information you receive. When doing this exercise with someone you hardly know at all, you must trust your intuition. Perhaps you can find a colleague at work or at school who will be curious enough to try this experiment. You and your partner will take turns doing each exercise. If you go first, spend a few minutes giving your partner reasons why you trust yourself. Your partner can write them down for you. When doing this exercise, someone once told us, "But I don't trust myself." If you feel like that, go back to the essentials: I trust myself to get up in the morning and brush my teeth. I trust myself to get dressed. I trust myself not to set the house on fire. I trust myself to get to work. I trust myself to get to work on time (more or less). I trust myself to eat a good lunch. I trust myself to call my mother on her birthday. I trust myself to feed the cat. I trust myself to drive safely. I

trust myself not to hurt anyone. I trust myself to do my laundry. You can
come up with at least ten of these, even if you don't believe that you trust
yourself. Your partner can keep asking you, "How, specifically, do you
trust yourself?" Spend at least five minutes giving yourself reasons to trust
yourself. Then close your eyes and accept that you know something about
trust. Start to talk to your partner about any impressions, feelings, senses,
or symbols that you have about her. Allow the person to give you feedback
as to the accuracy of your intuitive impressions. After you have expressed
whatever comes to you, take turns. You can then keep asking your partner,
"Why do you trust yourself?" and write down her answers. Then your
partner can describe her intuitive impressions about you.

If you doubt yourself or if you are critical of this wider sense of yourself,
then it will be difficult for you to get in touch with your intuition during
these exercises. By building your self-confidence first, you can make it a lot
easier to take your trust with you when you shift to intuition.

In the second exercise, spend at least five more minutes giving plenty of
reasons for trusting yourself. They can be the same reasons you used in the
previous exercise or you can find new ones. As you continue, you may be
surprised to find plenty of additional reasons to trust yourself. Have your
partner write down the first name of someone that you don't know and
hold the paper up so that you can see the first name. Ask your partner to
think about that person while you close your eyes and shift from trust to
intuition. Tell your partner any impressions, images, feelings, or sensations that come up for you in connection with that first name, and let her
smile, nod, or give you feedback without talking. When you are finished,
have your partner confirm which of your intuitive impressions were accurate. Then switch so that your partner gets to use her intuition about
someone whose first name you choose.

ACCEPTING YOUR INTUITION

You will probably be amazed by your own intuitive abilities when you try
the self-trust and intuition exercises. Be aware that your voice of reason will
not approve of your learning how to think in a nonlogical way and will
probably come up with all kinds of logical reasons why this exercise didn't
and can't really work. As we mentioned earlier in this book, the part of
your mind that says this is impossible is the part of your mind for which it

is, literally, impossible. If you need to explain this to yourself in language that your rational mind finds acceptable, you may simply wish to acknowledge that the intuitive mind does not separate and sequence time and space. Therefore, it can know things in a way that is not explainable in linear, step-by-step terms. If you still believe this is impossible and want to change that belief to one in which you accept what you have already experienced intuitively, you may want to talk to your voice of reason again and readjust the balance between your rational and intuitive awareness.

When in doubt, reinforce your self-trust.

CHAPTER 13

Intuition Notebook, Mind Map, and Treasure Map Exercises

This series of written exercises will help you to feel more comfortable with your intuition and other whole-brain abilities. We suggest that you begin a new notebook and use it exclusively for your intuition. If you keep a dream journal, you will want to continue to use it just for dreams. In your intuition notebook, you will be jotting down intuitive flashes, hunches, and gut feelings whenever they occur to you as well as experimenting with the workbook exercises.

We suggest that you reserve a separate section of the notebook for recording your intuitive experiences. That way, you will be able to refer back to them to confirm their accuracy. This will help you build trust in your own intuitive ability. You can also use this notebook as a guide to help you distinguish the difference between "true" and "false" intuitive experiences. As you become more observant of yourself, you may want to spend an extra few seconds writing a specific description of how each hunch or gut feeling looks, sounds, and feels. That, too, will help you identify the components of your intuitive awareness. You may begin to notice the emergence of any patterns which will enable you to fine-tune your understanding of where and when intuition occurs and how accurate it is.

Start doing the workbook exercises only when you feel relaxed and comfortable. Do not force yourself to do them as you would an assignment for work or school. If you feel like doodling or daydreaming, you may want to try one or two of these exercises and see what happens. The more relaxed you are when you do them, the more enjoyable and productive they will be. If you believe that keeping a journal is a chore, or too much like work, then don't feel compelled to keep an intuition notebook or to do these exercises.

We suggest that you get a notebook or pad that has colors or designs that appeal to you and that you write with different colored pens. This may seem silly, but it is anchored in our knowledge of how your triune brain behaves. By creating a workbook that you find attractive, you will be making it easier for your reptilian energy to be drawn toward it. Your visual, right brain is also stimulated by colors and shapes and it absorbs information by taking in the whole picture. If you feel excited by certain colors, then you will be activating your limbic brain, as well. Think of this notebook as something playful that you will enjoy using for the sheer fun of it. Know that while you are having fun, you are energizing your whole brain!

REPTILIAN BRAIN

1. *"I Am . . ."* This self-descriptive exercise will help to ground you and will give you a strong, clear sense of who you are. You can write "I AM . . ." at the top of the page or in its center. Then, write down whatever self-descriptions come to you: happy, sad, trusting, friendly, loving, angry, intuitive, logical, compassionate, curious, etc. When you run out of adjectives, say "I Am" aloud and complete the thought in writing. When you have finished, find a place to write "THIS IS WHO I AM." If you do this exercise several times, you will find that your picture of who you are changes.

2. *I Trust Myself.* At the top of the page, write "I TRUST MYSELF BE-CAUSE . . ." and fill several pages with reasons to trust yourself. This is a variation of the exercise for moving from self-trust to intuition that we presented in chapter 12. The difference is that you can do this one by yourself and can keep adding to it as you develop more reasons for self-trust.

3. *Love Your Reptile.* Give yourself a reptilian vacation day. Try not to make any conscious decisions about where you will go and what you will do. Let yourself be drawn toward and away from activities, food, people, and places. Use one page of your notebook for Reptile Day. Divide it into two

vertical columns. You can head them Toward and Away, Drawn To and Pulled Away, or Attract and Recoil. As you drift through the day or when you have finished, make a record of your energy trail by listing in each column what you were drawn to and what you pulled away from.

You can do this exercise for shopping, going to a party, redecorating, or locating a lost object. Head one page in your intuition notebook "Shopping" and mark the two columns. When you are in the store, let your mind drift and allow yourself to be drawn to and pulled away from different items. You will be surprised by what you find when you let your reptile shop for you. When you get home, write down those things from which you moved away and those toward which you were attracted. Likewise, at a party, you can let yourself move toward certain people and away from others, suspending judgment and conscious thought. Let your reptilian brain lead you through the crowd. When you get home, set aside a page for the party and write down to whom you were drawn and from whom you recoiled in each column. Likewise, when you want to redecorate, start a page in your intuition notebook and divide it into two columns. Then move around your house or apartment and see which objects attract you to them and which ones cause you to recoil. Never mind that Aunt Susie gave you that orange lamp and she's really sweet so you have to keep it. Your reptilian brain does not think like that. In fact, it doesn't think! Allow it to move you and keep a record of whatever attracts and repulses you. This exercise uses your intuition as well as your reptilian intelligence. It is a good preparation for the next exercise.

When you are comfortable with the reptilian brain exercises, you may want to try locating a lost object using your reptilian and intuitive intelligences. The linear way in which you look for a lost object is to ask yourself, "When did I last have it?" and retrace your steps. In this exercise, you allow yourself to see the object in your mind's eye. Then intuitively move toward it. Your reptilian energy will kick in and pull you toward the lost object if you don't stop it. Because this is a new way to go about finding something you lost, you may have problems working with it. It will not work if you start retracing your steps, asking yourself, "When did I last have it?" You cannot use both methods at the same time. Don't be discouraged if it doesn't work the first time you try it. Like any new process, it takes practice to learn how to do it.

LIMBIC BRAIN

1. *A Feeling Page.* Choose five feelings. Write one on each page. Then look at each page and experience each feeling as a body sensation, image, picture, and thought. For example, if you choose excitement, queasiness, anticipation, joy, and dread, ask yourself for each one, "Where do I get this feeling? What does it look like? Does it have a color? A shape? A sound? A vibration? A phrase or slogan?" Write, sketch, paint, or draw your impressions. Let each feeling go, then move to the next page.

2. *Limbic Library.* Play music that makes you feel happy and remember those times when you were happy. Make a list, first with your dominant hand, then with your nondominant hand. Play music that makes you feel loved and loving. Remember those times when you felt love. Again, make a list, first with your dominant hand, then with your nondominant hand.

3. *Motivation.* Give yourself permission to experience focused wanting. At the top of the page, write "I WANT . . ." Spend fifteen minutes feeling your wanting and write down everything that comes to mind.

NEOCORTEX

1. *Associational.* Set aside one page for each of the following combinations of words and see how many associations you can come up with. Many intuitive ideas are concepts that combine disparate elements in a unique way. As we indicated earlier, associational, visual, and intuitive intelligences work together. Keep in mind that media and advertising slogans often use creative word associations to make new and creative connections. For example, a television news story about cloning was slugged "Designer Genes." You may want to think up some combinations in slogan form. As you play around with these phrases, you may wish to write down any new sets of words that come to mind so that you can work with them later. (Example: What associations can you create using the words *chicken* and *whisper*? I'll have a whisper of chicken, please. What's wrong with you, you whispering little chicken?)

Elephant/child	Mona Lisa/lamb chop
Sunset/computer	Rocket ship/brain

Art/bath   Drink/flowers
Seagull/kingdom   Telephone/carnival

2. *Decision Making.* Choose something about which you have to make a decision. Write it at the top of two separate pages. On one page, you can write a list that contains all the logical reasons for and against this decision. You may even want to use Pro and Con columns to help you organize your thoughts. On the second page, list all your hunches and gut feelings around this decision. This exercise gives you consciousness about how your brain works and helps you focus on how your left and right hemispheres each function in the decision-making process. How you decide, ultimately, is up to you. And whatever you do decide, you will have called both your logical and intuitive abilities to help you make the choice.

3. *Visualize Intuition.* Breathe deeply and relax. Visualize intuition. Does it have a shape? A color? A size? A voice? Where do you feel it in your body? Write or draw all the images, words, ideas, and impressions that intuition brings to your mind after you have breathed deeply and relaxed. This exercise will make you more sensitive to what your intuition looks and feels like.

4. *Intuition Hall of Fame.* Breathe deeply and relax. In your mind's eye, create a banquet at which you are the guest of honor. You are going to be inducted into the Intuition Hall of Fame for intuitive thinking in all areas of your life. Visualize yourself going to the podium and receiving an award. Listen as you make your acceptance speech telling about all the times your intuition has helped you. Now, open your eyes and make a list of every intuitive flash, hunch, or feeling that you have had. Make a separate list of intuitive experiences that you would like to have. Make sure you include the "little," everyday intuitive events like finding a parking space and knowing that someone was going to call you before they actually called. In your intuitive accomplishments list, don't forget to include learning your native language, any dreams that came true, and any gut feelings you may have had about people you met for the first time that turned out to be true. Give yourself all the credit you deserve for being intuitive.

MIND MAPPING

As you do these exercises, you may find that your lists become cluttered as you get new ideas and try to squeeze them onto the page. Or you may find that you add words by writing on different parts of the page then drawing arrows to connect them. If so, you may enjoy mind mapping as an alternative to the traditional list or outline formats.

Mind mapping, a creative outlining technique that starts from the center of the page and branches out, lets you flow from idea to idea without having to squeeze in additional lines after you have finished working on a section. Developed in the 1970s by British psychologist Tony Buzan, author of *Use Both Sides of Your Brain,* mind mapping allows you to add new ideas as they occur to you. And as you add new concepts and thoughts, you can keep the whole picture in view. This nonlinear brainstorming tool creates a symbolic picture which your right brain absorbs and processes as a whole. It also frees up your associational, creative, and intuitive awareness. Because you do not have to worry about squeezing a word or a line into a previously completed section, you can relax and allow free-form ideas to flow through your mind.

Robert Stempson has developed a mind map (see p. 176) on the advantages of mind-mapping techniques. When making your own mind map, begin by placing the main topic in the center of the page and circle it. When you get a second idea, you place it in a smaller circle and connect that circle to the central one. It's easier to read if you print rather than write in script and much easier to absorb if you use different colors for sets of ideas. Write down your main ideas first, then use circles and branching lines for clarity. You can use your intuition notebook for mind maps or you can work on a larger piece of paper so that you can expand the branches and subtopics. Let your mind go free. Don't judge or evaluate what comes to you. Have fun with it.

Mind mapping is not a substitute for traditional outlining. It is an alternative that gives you new choices and possibilities for writing down your ideas. One of the main differences between a traditional outline and a mind map is that a mind map does not indicate sequence or priority. You can number your circles and branches after you have finished to establish sequence. When you look at a traditional outline, you have to read it step-by-step, whereas when you look at a mind map, you take in the whole picture and can zoom into a particular section of subtopics.

Although you can do a mind map on any subject, for your intuition notebook you may want to do one on intuition. Write "INTUITION" in a large circle in the center of your mind map. Then branch off and write down what you consider to be the most important resources for you to

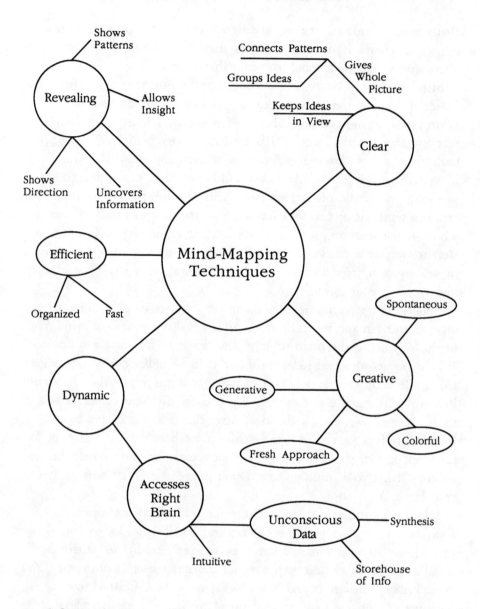

experience intuition. This will give you a different picture of your intuition. You can also use a mind map as an applied intuition tool because it will help you to concertize your intuitive impressions. Choose a subject about which you want some input from your intuition and place it in the center of the page in a circle. Then close your eyes, breathe deeply. Tell yourself that you want to receive guidance from your intuition on this subject. As ideas, impressions, and feelings come to you, use the branch and circle technique to write them down. It doesn't matter where you start. Each step is a new beginning. Each idea will generate another.

TREASURE MAPPING

A treasure map is another visual technique that combines associational, spatial, and intuitive thinking. Psychotherapist Gay Larned, who uses treasure mapping in her counseling work, describes it as "treasure for your unconscious." In actuality, a treasure map is a collage that you create around an outcome theme: self-worth, love, independence, success, or happiness, for example.

To begin your treasure map, spend about one month leafing through magazines and newspapers. Clip any words, phrases, and images that attract your attention. Once you start thinking about your treasure map, your intuition will lead you to pictures and groups of words that seem to be speaking directly to your outcome theme, many in places you never expected to find them.

When you begin to assemble your treasure map, have ready a picture of yourself and a large denomination bill of play money to symbolize prosperity coming into your life. We like to include a picture of a personal symbol from nature for good luck. Some people like to choose a picture of Jesus, a crucifix, or a pyramid. You can use whatever represents such qualities as truth, beauty, purity, compassion, wisdom, and a spiritual dimension to you. It may seem silly, but every image and word that you place on your treasure map is a symbol of a quality or resource that you want in your life. In his book *The Intuitive Manager*, Roy Rowan tells the story of the time Nobel Prize—winning scientist Niels Bohr put a horseshoe above his door for good luck. A neighbor said, "But surely you don't believe it works."

"True enough," said Bohr. "But I understand it works whether I believe it or not."

Whatever the theme of your treasure map, including a personal symbol that represents these magical qualities will help you bring them into your life.

When you have at least one hundred images, phrases, and words, buy a sheet of foam core about 19 × 25 inches and a glue stick or a bottle of white glue. Then you can begin to assemble your collage. Play with it. Move words and pictures around until you feel it really looks great. Even after you have assembled it, you can continue to add an occasional phrase or picture that appeals to you.

When you have completed your treasure map, place it in a location where you will see it every day. It should be someplace where it will not attract negative comments because that will make you doubt its value and will undermine its effectiveness. Whenever you look at it, you will be seeing the whole collage as a unit as well as the groups of words and pictures. Each word and image is a visual affirmation of a quality you want in your life. A treasure map imprints itself on your whole brain: You will find yourself attracted to and excited by it (stimulating the reptilian brain and limbic system). You will read its messages (left brain) and absorb its colors, shapes, and images (right brain). As these criteria for achieving your outcome theme begin to imprint themselves on your unconscious mind, you will find that intuitively you begin to meet people and go places where these criteria can begin to appear, seemingly by magic. You may even feel that your dreams really are starting to come true. One woman we know created a treasure map around the theme of finding her perfect partner. In the middle of the map, she put a picture of a man and a woman holding hands in front of a fire. A few months later, as she and her new boyfriend were sitting in front of their new fireplace, she remembered the picture from her treasure map. When they both got up to look at it, they laughed. The picture of the man she had placed in her treasure map months earlier looked exactly like him!

Be as specific as possible and don't be afraid to want the moon. Your treasure map is a picture of who you want to be and what you need in order for that picture to develop fully. It reflects the wishes of your present state. As with any of the other exercises, we advise you not to feel obligated to do it. If you do not feel comfortable for any reason, then stop. If you are not having fun, then it isn't working.

CHAPTER 14

A Return Visit

Now that you have moved through all three brain systems and have experienced a wide range of your own mental abilities, return to the room of your mind. Walk around the room and notice any differences. Do you find new mental abilities that were not apparent to you before? Identify them. What do they look like? What shape is each one? What color? What size? Which ones are closer to you? Which ones are farther away? Is there anything partially hidden from view? Toward which ones are you drawn? Are there any from which you pull back or recoil? Are there any you would like to touch? If so, what does each one feel like—soft, hard, scratchy, or smooth? Do you have any physical sensations or emotional feelings as you observe each mental ability? Where in your body are these sensations and feelings located?

Now, find your intuition. Is it larger or smaller than it was before? Do you feel drawn toward it or do you feel like moving away from it? Describe your intuition now. What color is it? What shape? What do you feel when you move your intuition closer to you, make it larger, and brighten the colors? Do you notice any difference? Do you feel more or less comfortable with your intuition being larger, closer, and brighter?

You may ask your intuition now if it is willing to communicate with you. Listen carefully to its voice. How would you describe it? Is it low, high, or medium in tone? How high or low is the volume? How fast or slow is its tempo? Does your voice of intuition sound stronger and more confident to you than it did the first time you identified it? How, specifically, can you describe stronger and more confident in terms of pitch, tone, and volume? When your voice of intuition speaks to you, what sensations do you notice in your body? What emotional feelings do you have in response to it?

Look around the room. Are you more or less comfortable than you were the first time you entered? Is there anything that you would like to have in this room that would make you feel more comfortable. A door, perhaps, or a window to serve as a symbol of connection between your inner and outer world? Feel free to add whatever you think your room needs so that you will know that this room is your secure place. You can come here whenever you need to reacquaint yourself with all of your wonderful mental abilities. The more time you spend here feeling comfortable about everything in your room, the easier it will be for you to return. When you find yourself drawn back here on occasion, allow yourself as much time as you need to look and walk around, observing, thinking, feeling, and sensing. The room will change each time you visit, reflecting your new insights.

CHAPTER 15

The Ten-Step Program for Enhancing Your Intuitive Abilities

In workshops at Programs for Human Development and during interviews for this book, dozens of people have asked if we could come up with some pointers to help them become more familiar with the intuitive process and how it works. Although everyone's intuition functions in a unique way, we believe it is possible to clarify and delineate aspects of intuitive functioning into a sequence of steps so that anyone who wants to can follow them. Although we believe that following these steps will make you more conscious of how your intuitive mind works, we do not insist that this is the only way to go about learning intuitive thinking. Nor is this sequential method akin to a teaching tool for a subject like calculus. If this were calculus, we could put the first step on the board. You could take it home and practice it and then we would say, "Now we are going to do the second step in calculus."

Intuition doesn't work that way. You bring your inner self, your inner energy, and your inner wavelengths to the whole process. From the perspective of taking intuition out of the realm of your unconscious and bringing it into conscious focus so that you can define, identify, and break it down, the Ten-Step Program can be very helpful. It can also help you create a spectrum of intuitive experiences and perception so that you can find different ways of looking at what's on that spectrum and pick out the aspects of intuition with which you feel most comfortable.

But don't expect this to work like a logical ten-step system in which step 1 fits into the groove of step 2, which fits into the groove of step 3, which fits into the groove of step 4. Logic and intuition follow different intellectual forms. You can't understand intuition the same way you can understand a logical process. You have to experience it to know that it's real. With this Ten-Step Program for intuition, you will experience intuition as a whole even though its sequential format might imply that you can experience a part of intuition by doing one or more steps. Not so. Even more contradictory, using this Ten-Step Program may involve your selecting certain steps and omitting others, or trying some steps in a different order than the one presented here. You will still experience intuition as a whole, for that is the only way it presents itself. You either know intuitively or you don't.

In working with this program, you need to begin with the understanding that what works for you may be different than these ten steps. Continue to experiment until you find the right combination. Rather than thinking of these steps as strictly 1, 2, 3 through 10, you may want to think of them as a personal alphabet with which you can create a new language of awareness to help you access your intuition.

If you are naturally intuitive—by which we mean that you know and trust your own intuition and feel comfortable doing that—you will probably not want to work with the Ten-Step Program. A naturally intuitive person may even laugh at the very idea. "Are you kidding?" one man said. "You can't do a ten-step program for intuition. It's either there or it's not there." For him, and possibly for you, this is probably true. Even if it is, you may want to spend a few minutes looking over the Ten-Step Program to see if anything in there can be helpful to you. We don't expect you to sit down and say, "Now I am going to do step 6 because I just finished step 5," if that is not how you work. But you may find that one or two steps make it easier for you to focus in on some aspect of the intuitive process.

Several other people have asked us if we could distill the Ten-Step Program down even further to just three essential steps. For us, those three most important parts of the process would be define, identify, and trust (steps 1, 2, and 5). If you simply concentrate on those three, you will find that you will learn to acknowledge, value, nurture, validate, and develop your inner resources intuitively as the rest of the program falls into place.

You probably have spent more time learning how to drive your car than you have learning how to use your whole brain. Once again, we urge you to practice working with these steps and not to impose unrealistic expectations on yourself. You didn't learn how to drive a car during your first lesson, and you are not going to be able to transform your thinking process in one sitting, either. Read the Ten-Step Program a couple of times, then think about it. You may find that one or two particular steps draw your attention and you may want to go back to those chapters in the book where we discuss them more fully. Or you may want to pick one particular step and focus on it. The Ten-Step Program is a guide, not a set of orders. It is intended to help you. It is up to you to find how it can best serve your needs.

THE TEN STEPS

1. *Define* intuition for yourself. Break it down into types of intuitive experience. Recall any intuitive experience that you have had and use it as a point of reference for the future.

2. *Identify* it. *Give it a form:* shape, color, sound, feeling. Visualize your mind as a room and find your intuition.

3. *Cultivate your intuitive resources.* Create a data bank of those qualities that you believe are components of your intuition. Take a picture of your intuition. *Model intuitive behavior.*

4. *Acknowledge* your intuition. Meditate by spending quiet time with yourself. Learn to hear your intuitive voice. Establish a dialogue by asking your intuition if it is willing to communicate with you. Even if you hear it say no, it will enable you to identify that intuitive voice. You can find out under what conditions it will be willing to communicate.

5. *Trust* it. Become aware of how you respond to your intuition. Do you "undermind" yourself? Do you suffer from intuition anxiety? Do you judge your intuition as weird? Create a place of inner safety, a personal sanctuary. Learn how to shift your point of focus so that you experience feeling safe and secure.

6. *Nurture* it. Deep breathing, yoga, and relaxation exercises are especially valuable. Learn how to defocus your attention from tense, stressful situations so that you can be receptive to input from your intuition. Make a mind map and a treasure map to stimulate free-form, creative ideas.

7. *Value* it. Respect your intuitive intelligence as another mental ability. Affirm that you deserve to make full use of your whole brain, including your intuition. If your voice of reason opposes this intention, engage in a dialogue with it. You may want to refer to the voice of reason exercise in chapter 12. Understand how intuition functions as part of your whole-brain intelligence network and affirm for yourself that you will recognize and support the information it sends you.

8. *Release* it. Then wait for it to guide you. Ask for advice or direction and learn how to identify the response. It may be a voice, a flash of insight, an emotional impression or gut feeling, or simply a sense of knowing where to go and what to do.

9. *Validate* it. How did information from your intuition serve you? Was it accurate? Did it work? Was it timely? Helpful? Use your rational intelligence to assess it.

10. *Thank* it. At first, the idea of saying or thinking "thank you" to a part of your own mind may seem strange. But it's important. Don't you work better when someone thanks you for a job well done? As you become more familiar with this step, you will find that you naturally feel appreciative when your intuition transmits helpful signals. Thanking it is part of learning to appreciate yourself and reinforces the intuitive process.

PART IV

THE
SCIENCE
OF INTUITION

*"Our science is totally incomplete
and will remain so until we include
the study of consciousness as a
casual element in the universe."*

—WILLIS HARMAN

INTRODUCTION

When we talk about the science of intuition, we are referring to research into intuitive phenomena and a theory known as the new science. In the previous section we presented experiential exercises based on interpretations of the triune brain model in which we asked you to shift your point of focus, or energy, to activate your different intelligence systems. The new science identifies that point of focus as the starting place for all mental phenomena. It studies how that point of focus, or consciousness, actually functions. Neuroscientist Dr. Roger Sperry defines consciousness as "that state of awareness typically present in our normal waking state but lacking in a dreamless sleep or coma."

In the first section of this book, we broke the subject of intuition into smaller categories so that you could consider this ephemeral, elusive subject in smaller segments, or chunks of information. Now, we are going to move up from intuition to a larger category—the mind. As we take a look at some pioneering scientific research into the nature of the mind, we hope that you will begin to think about your intuition within a larger framework. In this section you will step beyond intuition itself and observe it as a component of consciousness. If you take the time to do this, you will get a more comprehensive sense of your intuition. You will also find that this new perspective enhances the exercises.

Throughout this book we have asked you to think about how you think. In this section, we are asking you to stop for a moment and think about what science means to you. We, who are not scientists, have talked to many scientists to see how they define science. The definition that most appeals to us is the one given by Dr. Leigh Lipton, who holds advanced degrees in physical chemistry, biological chemistry, and medicine: "Science is *not* pouring one solution into another to see what happens; only a suicidal maniac would do that. Science, for me, is the art of being able to define terms. Let's agree that 'science' is the art of explanation. Once that is understood the term loses a great deal of its mystery."

A CONTROVERSIAL SCIENCE

We wanted to find out how scientists have approached intuition and consciousness. As we began our research for this section of the book, we quickly found out that this is such a controversial field that most scientists do not even consider it to be an acceptable field of study. Many are completely unwilling to accept the new theories, experiments, and findings as in any way valid. One of the reasons is that consciousness, or mind, is subjective and cannot be systematically calibrated and measured. Science has certain models about how reality works. The spontaneous, random events that characterize intuitive phenomena cannot be explained in terms of cause and effect as science presently understands them. Instead of saying, "That's beyond our ability to observe," mainstream scientists often say, "That doesn't exist." Because scientists have become the high priests of our society, most of us tend to accept scientific opinion as fact. We fail to question it because we believe that "scientists know everything." If most scientists say that intuitive phenomena do not exist, then we think that must be true, even if it means denying our own personal experiences.

It's important to recognize that there is plenty of disagreement about intuition among scientists themselves. And there are reasons for this controversy. In an article titled "The Persistent Paradox of Psychic Phenomena: An Engineering Perspective," published in the February 1982 *Proceedings of the IEEE,* Robert Jahn, dean emeritus of the School of Engineering and Applied Science at Princeton University, cited "demonstrable fraud, naïveté of technique, including inadequate controls, faulty equipment, and poor experimental replicability" as some of the technical and procedural reasons why research into the psychic component of intuitive functioning has come under attack by the scientific establishment. He also pointed out that there has been "little improvement in comprehension over many years of study" and mentions the "elusiveness of effects under close scrutiny." In addition, the difficulty that scientists have had in producing consistent results makes this field of research particularly vulnerable to criticism.

The underlying issue of credibility is itself on the line here. Many scientists believe that the psychic component of intuitive perception is impossible and are committed to relegating any findings that indicate otherwise to the bottom of what Jahn calls the "hierarchy of credibility." Intuitive knowing without a sensory-based precedent is simply inconsistent with the "prevailing scientific world view." Again, we would like to point out that the operative word here is *prevailing* and that it prevails, in our view, because most scientists have been rewarded for brilliant performance in the skills of the left neocortex. The brain you took to school is the brain that gets high marks in science and math. It's the brain that can only see its own sequential, rational processes and cannot by its very nature accept as valid any information that comes through a complementary, nonrational intelligence, especially when the source of that information cannot be readily explained in sensory-based terms. Jahn observes, "Over recent years, a sizable spectrum of evidence has been brought forth from reputable laboratories in several disciplines to suggest that at times *human consciousness can acquire information inaccessible by any known physical mechanism and can influence the behavior of physical systems or processes*" (emphasis added). Since 1978, Jahn has been conducting psychic research experiments at Princeton's School of Engineering and Applied Science. Although he notes many of these experiments cannot be replicated, he states, "anomalous yields are well beyond chance expectations."

This point leads us back to beliefs. If you are committed to the belief that intuitive processing (with or without sensory-based precedent) is inferior to logical processing or downright impossible, then no amount of evidence will persuade you otherwise. Several scientists have expressed their frustration with so-called objective observers who insist, after seeing several successful experiments, that they are being tricked, conned, or seduced because they do not want to believe what they are witnessing. It is not our intention here to prove to you that the psychic component of intuition exists or that these findings are legitimate. Our intention is to report on the state of scientific research into these phenomena. If your intention is to disprove or disbelieve, you can find many reasons to do so without our help. However, if you need to learn more about the arguments against this research, we would like to refer you to *A Skeptic's Handbook of*

Parapsychology, edited by Paul Kurtz. This book thoroughly details many of the positions against scientific studies of psychic functioning.

When skepticism is used as a way of reserving judgment until you have verified the information for yourself, it can be a valuable mental tool. But too much skepticism can be dangerous, and can serve to stifle scientific curiosity. The nature of mind, as well as its specific intuitive aspects, is still unknown and those few scientists who are willing to be pioneers on the frontiers of consciousness need to be encouraged, not suppressed because their findings do not coincide with existing knowledge. "We don't like to admit that science is incomplete," says former astronaut Edgar Mitchell. "We glom onto ideas and stick with them. Most humans are not questing to find new ways."

The conflict between those who insist on the status quo versus those who are willing to expand their parameters of knowledge so that humanity can progress has been an archetypal struggle throughout the history of science. Those who dared to venture into new territory were punished by their colleagues, ostracized by their society, and occasionally even executed for their heresies. Today, notes one physicist and engineer who has been active in psychic research for several decades, "Some of these scientists will go to the grave trying to make themselves right. Until you have looked through Galileo's telescope, you can't tell him he's wrong."

CHAPTER 16

The Cutting Edge—Remote Viewing Experiments

In a remote viewing experiment, a subject is asked to describe a location or picture—called a target—from which she is physically removed and of which she has no previous knowledge. Like all scientific research into the psychic component of intuition, these experiments, conducted in the United States since 1972, are highly controversial.

Remote viewing, also known as remote perception, is defined by Robert Jahn of Princeton's School of Engineering and Applied Science as "the acquisition of information about geographical targets remote in distance and time and inaccessible by any known sensory means." Over the years, researchers have found that despite the spatial separation of the subject from the target, it is possible for subjects who have never before attempted this to pick up accurate, descriptive information about their unseen (or hidden) target. Experiments conducted at the Maimonedes Medical Center in Brooklyn, New York, in the mid-1970s showed that subjects were even able to do this in their sleep. Impossible, you say? Once again, we need to point out that the rational part of your mind that says it's impossible is also the part of your mind for which it is, in fact, impossible. Scientists conducting remote viewing research have found that people do intuitively receive pictorial, nonanalytic information in these experiments. Physicist Russell Targ who initiated remote viewing experiments at SRI International (formerly Stanford Research Institute) in Menlo Park, California, in the early 1970s, says, "In the experimental mode, we have extremely strong evidence that people can obtain information about the present and the future that they have not previously experienced. And we can show people how to gain access to and incorporate that kind of information into their lives."

Targ's experiments intrigue us primarily because they provide scientific corroboration for our thesis that intuition, both sensory based and non-sensory based, is a natural mental ability that can be learned and improved on with practice. Targ and coauthor Arthur Hastings point out in their article "Psychological Impact of Psychic Abilities" that one prerequisite for remote viewing is that the experimental environment be as comfortable as possible and the subject be as relaxed as possible. The subject, who can intuitively obtain visual images or other impressions about the target location or target image, talks to an interviewer or analytic navigator who asks questions about the impressions that the viewer receives. The viewer accesses the visual and intuitive right-brain intelligences while the inter-viewer uses the verbal, analytical left-brain intelligences. "This division of labor parallels the two main modes of brain functioning," noted Targ and Hastings, who added that "only very experienced viewers seem able to handle both tasks simultaneously."

A BRIEF HISTORY OF REMOTE VIEWING

In their book *Mind-Reach,* Targ and coauthor Harold Puthoff described their first remote viewing experiments with Ingo Swann, an artist and psychic. A skeptical colleague on the East Coast had provided Targ and Puthoff with longitude and latitude coordinates that were specific down to the degrees, minutes, and seconds. Neither Targ nor Puthoff had checked a map or globe and maintain that they were unfamiliar with the location. So was Swann, who closed his eyes and reeled off a description of hills, a flagpole, some lawns, and a couple of buildings. He sketched his impres-sions. Several weeks later, the skeptical colleague who had submitted the coordinates confirmed that Swann's sketch and description were accurate!

Another of Targ and Puthoff's participants was Richard Bach, author of *Jonathan Livingston Seagull.* Bach, who was not a professional psychic, participated in his first remote viewing experiment at Stanford Research Institute in 1975. In this experiment, Puthoff used a random selection process to choose a sealed envelope with a card naming the target location.

Puthoff proceeded to that location. Meanwhile, Bach was seated in the laboratory. After thirty minutes, the time estimated for Puthoff to arrive at any of the secret target locations, Bach described a "gray building with a pointed roof." As interviewer, Targ asked a number of questions to elicit more details. Bach replied, "The roof is all scalloped in different colors." In fact, the target was a Methodist church that did have a scalloped roof with stained-glass insets. Later, an independent judge was given Bach's description and a list of several target sites and asked to match the site with the description as a way of verifying the subject's accuracy, which he did.

Two main criticisms against these remote viewing experiments concerned the interviewing and verification procedures. It was possible, said skeptics, that the interviewer questioning the subject could provide sensory clues about the target site. In addition, they say, some of the independent judges were able to locate the targets because clues, such as a reference to a site visited the day before, sometimes tipped the judges to the correct site. Edgar Mitchell, who observed many of these remote viewing sessions, says that he is satisfied that correct scientific procedures were followed. He noted that scientists who did not believe that remote viewing abilities were possible "would break out in a cold sweat and say, 'I don't know how you're tricking me but you're tricking me.' "

Although the 1970s experiments at SRI International were among the first in the United States, remote viewing may have started as far back as 550 B.C. In *The Mind Race,* the second book about the SRI remote viewing experiments, Targ and coauthor Keith Harary noted that Herodotus wrote about an experiment in which King Croesus of Lydia dispatched several messengers to different parts of his kingdom. On the one hundredth day of their journey, they were to consult the nearest reputable oracle, including the famous oracle at Delphi, as to King Croesus's exact location. Paracelsus, the sixteenth-century German physician and alchemist (whose real name was Theophrastus Bombast von Hohenheim), also noted that it was possible for people to see "friends and the circumstances by which they are surrounded, although such persons may be a thousand miles away . . . at that time."

THE RHINES' CARD GUESSING EXPERIMENTS

The remote viewing experiments conducted in laboratories today evolved from the first experiments into *psi* phenomena conducted at Duke University from 1927 to 1967 by Dr. J.B. and Louisa Rhine. *Psi* is explained as "the unknown factors in parapsychology which do not appear to conform to the *known* laws of science" (italics added). Parapsychology, of which Dr. J.B. Rhine is known as the father, is the study of psi. The Rhines coined the term *parapsychology* to describe their research because it went beyond (*para*) the range of traditional psychology in its attempt to explore the hidden realms of what are generically called psi phenomena. In their laboratory work, the Rhines separated psi phenomena into two categories: psychokinesis (PK), in which mental energy can be shown to affect physical matter, and what the Rhines called extrasensory perception (ESP). In their thousands of ESP experiments, the Rhines used a deck of five cards, called Zener cards. Each card had one symbol: a circle, a cross, wavy lines, a square, or a star. Subjects in the Rhine experiments had to name which card was being shown in another location. After years of research, Louisa Rhine notes that it was "still an almost unrecognized fact" that "perfectly sane and healthy persons" could and often did experience extrasensory knowing. Her husband, Dr. J.B. Rhine, noted that extrasensory and psychokinesis functions were "function[s] of the total personality, not of an abstracted, isolated, momentary mental state."

ANYONE CAN LEARN TO DO REMOTE VIEWING

One important difference between today's remote viewing experiments and the Rhines' is the discovery that intuition can be learned. Targ and Hastings point out that "an important finding of our research is that remote viewing abilities are apparently latent and widely distributed in the general population. In fact, according to our data, many people are able to learn to do remote viewing with only a modest amount of training and practice."

In *Mind-Reach,* Targ and Puthoff described how they stopped demonstrating their experiments to outside observers because they found it was more effective for the observers to become participants and experience remote viewing for themselves. In a series of five experiments, two government scientists successfully described several target sites. One skeptical scientist, who did not believe in remote viewing abilities, described a "kaleidoscope picture of triangles, squares, and more triangles." The target site was a seventy-five foot transmission line tower and matched his description. Of course, he found it hard to believe that he had done so well because remote viewing was, in his view, impossible. He went on to successfully describe and draw another target site: a small merry-go-round. When he was taken to the target site, he immediately recognized it and cried, "My God, it really works!"

WHY REMOTE VIEWING SUCCEEDS BETTER THAN ESP CARDS

In the past fifteen years, variations of remote viewing experiments have emerged as the predominant form of testing intuitive perception because they are more responsive to free-form, subjective, nonanalytic mental processes. In giving subjects a repetitive, forced-choice test, such as the Rhines' card guessing experiments, parapsychologists found that subjects got bored and lost their ability to score well (the "decline effect"). Remote viewing calls on a subject's right-hemispheric visual pattern-recognition abilities and its receptivity to brief flashes of what Targ and Hastings call "gentle, fleeting impressions, feelings, and images." Although learning how to do remote viewing does not require that you believe in your own psychic ability, they say that it does necessitate that you become aware of subtle differences in thought and feeling. Unlike the Rhines' original ESP experiments, the purpose of remote viewing sessions are not to test a subject's ESP as such; rather, it is to validate, accept, and encourage the subject to discover his own intuitive perception. In their book *The Mind Race,* Targ and Harary report that after eight to ten trials, subjects in their remote viewing experiments were able to obtain accurate information by odds that were considered 100 to 1 greater than chance, as compared to the hundreds of thousands of trials needed to obtain the same results in the Rhine experiments.

VARIATIONS OF REMOTE VIEWING EXPERIMENTS

In one variation of the "sealed envelope" exercise, the subject is asked to describe a target site *before* the subject, also known as the beacon, had chosen it. Although it seems incredible, many subjects have found no difficulty in doing this. Princeton's School of Engineering and Applied Science now specializes in these studies, which Jahn and his colleague Brenda Dunne call precognitive remote perception (PRP) experiments.

Dunne, now the manager of the Princeton's Engineering Anomalies Research Laboratory, conducted remote viewing experiments at Mundelein College in Chicago between 1976 and 1979. (In 1977, a CBS News crew recorded and later broadcast the proceedings of a successful remote viewing experiment at Mundelein.)

In *Margins of Reality*, authors Jahn and Dunne corroborate some of the earlier findings that indicate remote perception is possible even when the subject is separated from the target by thousands of miles. In a typical PRP experiment at Princeton, the subject is asked to give his impressions of a target site before the second participant (whom Jahn and Dunne call an "agent") visits or selects the target. Their findings reveal descriptions that range from nearly photographic accuracy to differing degrees of specific descriptions about the target scene, to what Jahn calls "total irrelevance." One of the idiosyncracies of the PRP experiments is that subjects often describe details of the target scene that are actually of minor significance— such as decorative features of a building—while ignoring details of greater importance—such as the building's overall structure. To facilitate the descriptive process, Jahn and Dunne have developed thirty binary questions that give the subject a yes or no choice about such criteria as whether the target site is indoors or outdoors, light or dark, day or night, colorful in general or containing highlights of color. Jahn and Dunne then quantify the information into statistical, analytical form, noting even as they do so that one of the curious paradoxes of parapsychological research is that the information is received in impressionistic bits and pieces. In order for it to be considered "scientifically credible" they have to reduce it to quantitative form. Another step in the verification process is evaluation by one or two judges who were not actually participants in the experiments. Jahn and Dunne show the judge pictures of several different targets, including the one used in the experiment. The judge then matches a picture with the subject's description of the target. Statistical analyses are used to determine how the rate of evaluation differs from chance. Jahn and Dunne point out that because the judges are human, and therefore subjective, their biases toward or against parapsychology or the particular experiment may affect their ability to evaluate the target picture, as may their individual perceptual abilities. They express frustration with the need to reduce a complex, nonanalytic process down to a single, statistical unit because that robs the detailed descriptions of their complexity. The problem of how a scientist can effectively deal with subjective experiences as data is one of the big methodological difficulties of conducting research into intuitive phenomena.

Another problem stems from the random, unique nature of the intuitive impressions themselves, combined with the overall subjective quality that makes each individual's responses different. With this in mind, Charles Honorton, director of Psychophysical Research Laboratories (PRL) in Princeton, New Jersey, conducts his experiments with the goal of under-standing the basic conditions that generate intuitive perception. "The classic question is, Under what conditions does it occur?" Honorton says. "According to one theory, it occurs more frequently than we can become aware of it because our physical senses act more like filters than windows and effectively screen it out." PRL also maintains statistical profiles on the people who participate in their experiments as well as a file of Myers-Briggs questionnaires completed by everyone who participates in the experiments as a receiver. "We use the Myers-Briggs type indicator to get a sense of the personality variables involved in this kind of perception. Ninety-three percent of the people who participate in our experiments show up as intuitives on the Myers-Briggs. Myers-Briggs statistics taken among the general population show that 75 percent of the general public show up as having a dominant sensation function." One reason why intuitives participate in these experiments is because they tend to be more interested in understanding their own nature and are more likely to volunteer. Those who also score highest in the feeling/perceptive categories tend to have the greatest success in Honorton's experiments.

Honorton began research in this field at Maimonides Medical Center in Brooklyn, New York, in the 1960s and 1970s. A subject who made no claims to any particular intuitive or psychic abilities would go to sleep in a cubicle, electrodes wired to his head. A researcher watching the EEG readout would notice when the subject was dreaming and awaken him so that the details of the dreams could be noted. While the subject was dreaming, a sender located in another part of the sleep research laboratory would pick a picture from a group at random and would concentrate on mentally sending images about the picture to the person who was asleep whenever the EEG readout indicated that the subject was beginning to dream. The subject would be awakened whenever the dream cycle started so that he could describe any dream impressions. The next day, the subject would look at a group of pictures that contained the target picture and would try to identify it from the fragments he remembered from the dream state on a "blind" basis, that is, without knowing which pictures in the group had actually been sent. So successful were these experiments that researchers at Maimonides began to experiment with precognitive dreaming by asking subjects to dream about a picture that would not be selected at random until the following day. They also tried sending target pictures from faraway cities and discovered that untrained, inexperienced subjects were successful in this experiment as well as in the precognitive research. Their findings to a large extent mirrored those of Targ and his associates at SRI International, indicating that in sleep as well as during the waking state, it is possible to accurately perceive information about a remote location regardless of the space-time differential. Their research also corroborated the Rhines' belief that the ability to acquire accurate information by means other than the five primary senses is a natural ability for most people. As a result of these findings, the Maimonides team suggested that becoming aware of what you dream can be an important way of becoming sensitive to these abilities.

THE GANZFELD

During the course of his work at the Maimonides Medical Center, Honorton initiated a new kind of remote viewing experiment called *ganzfeld* stimulation, a mild sensory deprivation technique. The receiver was comfortably seated with his eyes covered with table-tennis ball halves to eliminate patterned visual perception. Earphones played white noise, either static or the sound of the ocean. The subject was then instructed to describe any images, thoughts, feelings, sensations, or sounds that passed through his mind. *Ganzfeld,* which means "total field," was first used by psychologists studying its effects on behavior and vision while a subject was in a normal, waking state. Honorton's experiment, however, called for a sender in another part of the laboratory to select some slides from a group at random and mentally transmit images about those pictures to the receiver in the ganzfeld room. To transmit the images, the sender concentrated and visualized the images, sometimes sketching the image on a scratch pad. Sketching and drawing are right-brain activities that help focus the sender's attention while he is mentally projecting the image.

After the session, the subject was given a group of slides and asked to identify the ones that had been sent during the experiment. As with other remote viewing experiments, ganzfeld stimulation showed that many people had natural intuitive abilities. Like other remote viewing experiments, it also indicated that in some cases the subject was able to identify the selected target picture before the sender actually chose it.

Critics, however, were quick to attack Honorton, focusing their criticism on the postsession judging process in which the subject identified the slides he had seen. In seeking undetected flaws in his experimental process, skeptics said that greasy finger marks left on the slide could provide a sensory cue. So Honorton began using untouched duplicate slides for the verification process and got the same results. He now uses videotape for both static and moving (dynamic) images, thereby removing any possibility of cueing through physical marks on the images. In discussing his critics, Honorton comments, "People see what they believe more than they believe what they see."

Another criticism leveled at Honorton was that he did not work with control groups. Drs. William and Lendell Braud at the University of Houston set up an experiment in which half the subjects were placed in the ganzfeld coccoon and the other half were not. Both groups were instructed to describe their impressions of an unseen target. In comparison to the ganzfeld group, which successfully described and identified the targets, the control group generally failed. These experiments showed definitively that the ganzfeld stimulation technique can significantly enhance a subject's intuitive awareness.

In 1979, Honorton founded PRL and continued his work with the ganzfeld. His laboratory has been funded by grants from the Fetzer Foundation and the James S. McDonnell Foundation, which also funds the Princeton School of Engineering Anomalies Research Laboratory. James McDonnell was a founder of McDonnell-Douglas aircraft.

Experiments at PRL today differ from the original experiments at the Maimonides Medical Center in that they now use a computer to select one video at random from a pool of 160 videos that includes static and dynamic images. The sender then mentally transmits images from that video to the receiver in the ganzfeld room. The receiver describes his impressions to an experimenter for thirty minutes then watches four videos and intuitively tries to identify the one used during the session.

Honorton says that the overall success rate for identifying the correct target after receiving impressions is 1 in 3. This is higher than the success rate attributed to chance, which is 1 in 4. In the one dozen different laboratories around the country where experimenters are using the ganzfeld technique, the overall success rate is 43 percent compared to the 25 percent that can be attributed to chance. "We can rule chance out as a reasonable explanation for successful perception of a remote image," Honorton says. "There is no longer any controversy about that. We know it's not chance. The controversy about these experiments is over what does cause this kind of perception."

POTENTIAL APPLICATIONS OF REMOTE VIEWING RESEARCH

The potential applications of this research are open-ended. Honorton, whose research is privately funded, has suggested an experiment to see if a subject could find where to dig for oil. Several years ago, the *New York Times* reported that H.L. Hunt had used a psychic before a series of oil exploration ventures. One United Nations official suggests, half-jokingly, "If enough people learn how to transmit visual information, we won't need fax machines any more. We'll have mental fax!"

The potential applications of this research for military use have not gone unnoticed either. "Since 1972, the U.S. government has sponsored programs to investigate, develop, and apply an intuitive perceptual-information-processing technique called *remote viewing*," wrote Targ and Hastings. Some of Targ's original research at SRI International was funded by NASA, the U.S. Navy, and according to some published accounts, the Central Intelligence Agency (CIA). According to Military Spending Research Services, a nonprofit organization that monitors defense contracts, SRI International is one of the largest civilian recipients of military research grants in the country. Embarrassed by the controversial publicity generated by ESP publications, executives at SRI International told Targ to stop publishing his results. Targ says he left SRI International over this issue and is now doing research in remote sensing of wind shear using lasers at Lockheed Missiles and Space Company. Although one vice-president of SRI International assured us that the organization was no longer conducting remote viewing research, the physicist who is directing their present remote viewing program and several other scientist alumni of SRI International confirmed that SRI International is continuing these government-funded experiments despite official claims to the contrary.

Part of the controversy over remote viewing concerns how remote viewing abilities could be applied in defense and espionage work. For example, if a subject in a California laboratory can pick up impressions about a target several thousands of miles away, as has been demonstrated, why can't that subject pick up impressions about a military target such as an underground missile silo in the Soviet Union? "Psychic Spying: Are You Safe?" sounds like a *National Enquirer* headline or the topic of a "Geraldo" show, but if a subject can accurately describe a target location that has not yet been selected, why can't he describe where a particular Soviet agent will be in a few hours, as well? One physicist who has participated in several of the government's psychic research programs says, "We are playing catch-up with the Soviets in the field of psychic spying, which is politely called remote viewing. In fact, the U.S. government is so concerned about the psychic gap that any time our officials believe that they are close to information that gives them an edge they publicly discredit that research. You will see articles published in scientific journals about a particular subject and then suddenly, it goes dark and you can't find anything more written about it."

Other scientists believe that this is psychic conspiracy hype that serves to sensationalize legitimate research. However, almost all of the scientists familiar with this area of research to whom we spoke reported that because the Soviets already accept that this type of intuitive perception is a natural, inherent ability, they are spending their time and money developing ways to use it rather than trying to prove it exists, as is being done in U.S. research facilities. One example of Soviet sophistication in this area is the account of Soviet cosmonaut Vitaly Sevastyanov, who says that while in space he was able to mentally signal his fellow cosmonaut when he wanted a tool. The other cosmonaut would then hand it to him. During preflight training in a centrifuge, Sevastyanov said he knew before a particular piece of equipment failed that it was going to do so and he also knew which back-up systems were needed.

One source claims that the Soviets have been experimenting with telepathy and hypnosis as a form of behavior control. The CIA has been conducting mind-control experiments using hypnosis for many years.

There is no way for us to confirm or deny such hypotheses and we mention them here only in the interest of reporting on what is being said in the psychic research community.

While we cannot verify the hypotheses about telepathic hypnosis, we do know that the U.S. government has been taking this area of research seriously for more than twenty years. In August 1966, a now-classified report at the Northrup Space Lab detailed experiments in the biological entrainment of the human brain. Entrainment entails using biofeedback signals to synchronize subjects' brain waves during telepathy experiments. In 1977, the *Chicago Tribune* reported former CIA Director Stansfield Turner's statement that the agency had financed remote viewing experiments in 1975. According to the newspaper account, Turner said that the subject of the experiment had died and the experiment was discontinued. In 1981, at a hearing of the House Subcommittee on Intelligence Evaluation and Oversight, Congressman Charles Rose reported that the results of certain remote viewing experiments at SRI International had been confirmed by aerial photography. He noted that there was no way it could have been faked and called remote viewing a "hell of a cheap radar system." Rose expressed concern that the Soviets might have a psychic edge. Also in 1981, a House of Representatives Science and Technology Committee report urged more funding for research into "the physics of consciousness." It noted that "a general recognition of the degree of interconnectiveness of minds could have far-reaching social and political implications for this nation and the world."

A STEP BEYOND: PSYCHOTRONICS RESEARCH

The interconnections between mind, body, and the environment and the interaction of matter, energy, and consciousness are the focus of a small group of electronics engineers and scientists involved in psychotronics research. As its name implies, psychotronics is a combination of "psychic" and "electronics" and is defined as "science, which in any interdisciplinary fashion studies fields of interaction between people, between body, mind, soul, and their environment (internal and external) and energetic interrelated processes, namely consciousness." What that means simply is that psychotronics researchers accept intuitive phenomena as real and are developing electronic instruments that interface with the consciousness or mental intention of the operator. The engineers themselves acknowledge the importance of their own intuitive input into the process. As one psychotronics engineer comments, "I like to call this intuitive engineering. You open yourself up and ask questions, then shut up long enough to listen and let the answers come."

Psychotronics engineers accept the existence of psychic phenomena and build devices that reportedly function in an interactive fashion with psychic energy. Their interests extend well beyond the parameters of remote viewing into the area of psychokinesis in which mental energy can affect a physical object.

Some remote viewing researchers dissociate themselves from the psychotronics community. They find it hard to accept psychotronics as a legitimate science, saying that there are no scientific ways to verify the competency of psychotronics research. The mainstream scientific establishment goes even further and regards psychotronics as a lunatic fringe of science. Yet members of the United States Psychotronics Association and the International Association for Psychotronics Research are expanding the definitions of science as well as exploring how mind, energy, and matter interact. The Seventh International Conference on Psychotronic Research held in Carrollton, Georgia, in December 1988 provided a forum for leading Soviet psychotronics researchers to present papers with such titles as "The Effects of the Geological Environment on Man," "Possibilities of a Psychotronic Approach to Learning," and "Some Physical Phenomena Associated with Psychotronics." The conference provided a meeting ground and a forum for Soviets and Americans to exchange ideas and learn about ongoing research in both countries.

ANOTHER STEP BEYOND: INTUITIVE CONSENSUS

Using a method that he calls "intuitive consensus," William Kautz, director of the Center for Applied Intuition in San Francisco, has been conducting scientific studies using individuals with highly developed intuitive skills as a source of new information for testable hypotheses in geophysics, archaeology, medicine, and history. Kautz started this research in 1973 when he was a scientist at SRI International. He founded the Center for Applied Intuition in 1977. When conducting intuitive consensus research, Kautz interviews a panel of people he calls "expert intuitives." "Intuition is the human process of acquiring knowledge directly, without recourse to reason or sensual perception, or even memory in the usual sense of memory. It is direct knowing. I use the term *expert intuitive* to mean someone who has the skill of doing that with very high competence," Kautz says.

The objective of his research is not to test the psychic component of intuition, which he accepts, but to obtain a consensus of information about a particular subject using a scientific method of inquiry. Kautz believes that information acquired through intuitive knowing without a sensory-based precedent can generate new ideas that can be tested through ordinary scientific methods, as well as technical information that may not be otherwise available. Although many people, especially those in the sciences, would argue that Kautz's use of psychics falls outside their accepted definition of intuitive, Kautz maintains, "The underlying process between psychism, clairvoyance, telepathy, mediumship and some other types of creative performance is intuition."

At first glance, Kautz's background would appear to make him an unlikely prospect for this specialized and subjective field of research. As a student of mathematics and electrical engineering, he received his doctorate from the Massachusetts Institute of Technology. In 1951, he became a staff scientist at the Stanford Research Institute, where he worked in computer science and communications before venturing into life sciences and geophysics research. Kautz describes himself during that period as "very much the straight-line scientist." But his personal experiences led him to reevaluate his negative attitudes toward this whole realm of intuitive phenomena. After he and his wife received highly accurate information during a psychic reading, Kautz asked himself how he could apply similarly derived information to his scientific work. He formulated some scientific questions and conducted an interview with Jane Roberts, who channeled a disembodied entity called Seth. (The series of books known as "the Seth books," published under Roberts's name, are now considered classics of channeling literature.)

Kautz follows scientific methodology when conducting his intuitive inquiries for research, formulating hypotheses around which he focuses his questions. "We carry our questions to intuitive sources just as a scientist carries his into the lab. We collect the intuitive information carefully then we work with it in a very logical way to come up with new ideas and hypotheses that can be verified. This is just what science does," Kautz says, pointing out that the main difference now is that the information comes from skilled intuitives instead of from the scientist's rational mind or from a physical laboratory. He observes that "the whole game in science is to grow new knowledge systematically from old knowledge and from observation, experiment, and deduction." The key step in this process is the formulation of good hypotheses. Kautz says that traditional science provides no systematic way to do this.

The expert intuitives working with Kautz are also known as channels, that is, they enter into light or deep trance and "channel" information that they are not consciously aware of. Some channels appear to be the mouthpieces for "entities" who live in other dimensions. Many people are suspicious of channeling because it cannot be explained in any rational way. Fraudulent channels, who fake their communications, and others who are naive about what they are doing, have contributed to the public's perception of channels as charlatans.

Certainly, the idea of channeling is alien to most of us. Specifically, what or who do channels channel? "We don't know, basically," answers Kautz. "This is not an area which traditional psychology has probed at all so there is no classical understanding of it." While many channels describe the source of their information as some higher knowledge, Kautz prefers to describe it as "the superconscious, or the collective unconscious," by which he means a reservoir of all human knowledge, past, present, and potential. He sees the conscious mind as reflecting the world that we are ordinarily aware of and the subconscious part as containing submerged personal memories. "Eastern religions refer to the superconscious as the Akashic Records. The early Christians called it The Book of God's Remembrance. There's a name for it in virtually all the world's great religions," Kautz says. Although many New Age philosophers like to refer to this source as energy, because that makes it sound more scientific, it is not a physical energy as we understand it because it cannot yet be measured.

But information derived intuitively can be verified objectively. In his study of the forces that trigger earthquakes, Kautz consulted seven expert intuitives and found that they all were in agreement on the following theory: In the days and hours preceding an earthquake, fossilogenic gases appear underneath the earth's crust. At the same time, high frequency radiation from space passes through occasional gaps in the ionosphere.

When the weather conditions are just right, the stratospheric and fossilogenic gases mix near the surface of the earth, often producing a chemical reaction. This reaction propagates downward into the earth to form a pressure wave that triggers the earthquake.

What's news here is that the atmosphere plays a major part in the triggering process. This theory, although incomplete, does not contradict current geological understanding of how earthquakes are triggered. It focuses attention on an aspect that has never been investigated and supplements what is already known. When this theory was formulated, this information was not available through standard geophysical surveys and could not have been deduced from the existing body of data, notes Kautz.

Having acquired this data, Kautz reexamined some neglected field reports on earthquake activity and found peripheral references to strange electrical activity in the atmosphere prior to the earthquakes. These references lend support to the intuitive theory. In 1978, Kautz and some colleagues at SRI International obtained funding for two government-sponsored projects to follow up on the initial research. They found good evidence to support the intuitive consensus. "Normally 10 to 20 percent of the scientific process is the validation," says Kautz. "This way, we saved the other 80 to 90 percent of the work by not having to search for the information in the first place. Intuition provides a means of obtaining knowledge directly without having to struggle for it. We feel we have a tiger by the tail."

But the scientific community doesn't see it that way. Kautz believes that only a small fraction is open to his work. "Most of them aren't interested, but the few who understand what we are doing say it's great," Kautz says. "Science today is material based and sensory based. There's no way it can work with subjective data. The problem lies with the limits of science rather than the field that we are investigating." In essence, Kautz's work and that of psychotronics engineers and remote viewing researchers fall outside of science as it is traditionally defined. The fact that establishment scientists say something doesn't exist doesn't mean it doesn't exist. It only means that science has no effective way to measure it. Which brings us back to what we noted at the beginning of this section: We need new definitions, new theories, and new approaches. A small number of scientists even go so far as to say we need a new science.

CHAPTER 17

The New Science

The new science introduced by neuroscientist Roger Sperry in 1964 is based on the premise that your consciousness—what we call your point of focus—can create physical effects in your brain as well as the other way around. Like most great ideas, the core concept of the new science is simple, but its ramifications are staggeringly complex. Although as few as an estimated 5 percent of scientists accept its basic tenets, the new science is taking hold in the behavioral and social sciences, particularly in cognitive psychology, which emphasizes the importance of such abstract mental processes as intuition, insight, and visual intelligence over external behavior. Whereas behaviorists believe that they can treat behavior without addressing the mental state, cognitive psychologists say that mental states organize and control behavior. Evolutionary theorists working in biology and related sciences are beginning to accept the new science, too. Because it believes that consciousness can cause physical change, the new science is also referred to as "the consciousness revolution."

Mainstream scientific thought is based on three primary assumptions: objectivism, which believes that the universe and everything it contains can be quantified; positivism, which accepts only that which can be physically observed as real; and reductionism, which, as its name indicates, reduces phenomena into smaller elements. The consciousness revolution differs radically from reductionist scientific thought because it contains the belief that the whole is greater than the sum of its parts.

NOT THE PHYSICS OF CONSCIOUSNESS

Much has been written about the "physics of consciousness," which applies the quantum theories of subatomic physics to attempt to explain mental phenomena, including intuitive perception and synchronicity. Such sophisticated interpretations are helpful to those who understand quantum mechanics, but those in the vanguard of the new science believe that, ultimately, physics cannot explain mind—including its intuitive aspect—because mind cannot be quantified, physically observed, and reduced. For example, Bell's Theorem of Nonlocality is often cited by New Age teachers as an explanation for the occurrence of intuitive phenomena in which no sensory-based precedents are apparent. Bell's Theorem states that two electrons that are joined and then separated from each other will vibrate at the same frequency even when they are in different locations. Many people who teach New Age philosophy cite this as scientific evidence for the belief that minds, too, can vibrate at the same frequency when physically separated. However, physicist John Stewart Bell, who developed his theorem in 1964, did not intend for his theorem to be applied to mental phenomena. In an interview published in *Psychological Perspectives,* Bell said, "I was never so ambitious as to assume that such a comprehensive description would also cover the mind. There is clearly some fundamental difference between mind and matter. If science is sufficiently comprehensive at some point in the future to discuss both these things intelligently at the same time, then we will learn something about their interaction."

The majority of those working in the hard sciences (physics and chemistry) would challenge Bell's open-mindedness, because they are committed to the positivist, objectivist, and reductionist model of reality. The new science, on the other hand, rejects the use of quantum physics to explain the mind because it does not believe that everything can be explained in physical terms. That belief is, in itself, a revolutionary idea.

DR. SPERRY'S CONSCIOUSNESS REVOLUTION

"When you walk down the street, your atoms and molecules don't tell you where to go," says Dr. Sperry, who won the Nobel Prize in 1981 for discovering the cognitive complementarity of left and right hemispheres of the neocortex. He uses this analogy to illustrate one of the main differences between the new science and reductionist scientific thought. "Neuroscience says it can explain all brain functions without reference to conscious mental states. The new science says this is not true and challenges the old view," says Dr. Sperry, who notes that in the 1950s and 1960s, neuroscientists "wouldn't be caught dead implying that consciousness of subjective experience can affect physical brain processing." In fact, in 1966, the prevailing mindset of neuroscience was described by British scientist Sir John Eccles, who wrote, "As neurophysiologists we simply have no use for consciousness."

When Dr. Sperry began his pioneering research into the brain, he accepted the traditional view that all brain functions could be explained in terms of nerve cell and biochemical activity. But over the years he gradually reevaluated his own position. For the last twenty-five years he has been trying to get his colleagues to redefine their own perspectives to include the assumption that mental states and experiences can have a controlling effect on the brain's physical functions. Thus consciousness, ideas, feelings, values, intentions, hunches, gut feelings, and beliefs can be considered emergent properties of the physical brain. Dr. Sperry notes, "When the brain is whole, the unified consciousness of the left and right hemispheres adds up to more than the composite properties of the separate hemispheres."

It is because he believes that the study of consciousness has wider ranging implications than the study of hemispheric functions that Dr. Sperry has broken ranks with many of his colleagues to write and lecture on the new science. "I gave up the right and left brain because it didn't compare in the implications. My colleagues thought I defected to philosophy and humanism, a scientist gone wrong," he says.

DOWNWARD CAUSATION

In seeking to define how the mind functions in terms of what he calls "downward causation," Dr. Sperry has ventured into new scientific territory. Put simply, downward causation means that the more highly evolved properties envelop and control the less evolved components. For example, if you decide to drive somewhere, your decision can activate a chain of events that will cause your car to move, according to the principles of downward causation. Seen from the perspective of upward causation, it is the movement of gasoline molecules that causes the engine to work, thus causing your car to move. It is important to remember that both of these perspectives are accurate and that they are complementary. One does not exclude the other. Microdeterminism, which sees events in terms of upward causality, is a valid scientific methodology. However, traditional science explains all phenomena in terms of upward causation and does not factor in downward causation when, in fact, both processes are at work simultaneously.

Dr. Sperry uses an airplane in flight as an example of upward and downward causation. Reductionist science can break down the elements of an airplane flight in terms of molecular and atomic activity. But reducing an airplane flight into molecules and atoms fails to take into account the role of the airplane's electrical circuits or the timing of its engines. In other words, there must be some organizing principles at work for the airplane to work. Its atoms and molecules cannot organize the airplane's different systems. They cannot make it fly. Subatomic physics cannot explain how the airplane's circuit plan is designed. That is done at a higher level, or macrolevel. Likewise, the circuit design in your brain is a complex, sensitive system in which your point of focus, train of thought, or other mental event affects the timing of the neurons. "Macrodeterminism says that the molecule is the master of its atoms and controls them," says Dr. Sperry.

In looking at mind in all its complexity as a biological fact, the new science asks us to reexamine our own thoughts, feelings, values, and beliefs, and to take them seriously as agents of change. "The new beliefs are a way out of our human predicament," says Dr. Sperry.

DR. SALK, INTUITION, AND EVOLUTION

For Dr. Jonas Salk, inventor of the first polio vaccine, consciousness is the key to our successful growth and continuing survival as a species. In his book *Anatomy of Reality: Merging of Intuition and Reason,* he wrote, "Man's mind is seen here as a metasystem, a metabiological system, serving the human biological and other ecosystems in the course of serving itself. To serve itself it must preserve, and serve, other biological systems that are relevant to itself. It must, therefore, 'know,' intuitively and cognitively, what is of value to itself and other systems."

In an article that was published in *The National Observer* on May 27, 1962, Dr. Salk asked, "Have we in a rather roundabout way arrived at the realization that science needs to become part of the conscience of man?" Two years earlier, Dr. Salk founded the Salk Institute in La Jolla, California, specifically to sponsor and encourage scientific research with a compassionate, philosophical overview. The term *biophilosophy* was coined to describe the Salk Institute's interdisciplinary approach, which combines laboratory research with humanistic concerns. Dr. Salk, who describes his work as "the science of the human side of nature," believes that humanity now has the potential for conscious evolution rather than simply evolving as a process of physical survival and that human evolution is a mental process as well as a physical one. To that end, he believes that researchers in the sciences as well as the humanities must work together "to make the decisions and choices that Nature has made until now . . . for the greatest value to human life and society as a whole."

Those decisions include formulating a blueprint for successful evolution that is primarily mental in nature. "The evolution of the human mind . . . depends upon the evolution of intuition and reason. It is important to recognize the binary nature of this relationship and to focus upon intuition and upon reason separately and together. Our subjective responses (intuitional) are more sensitive and more rapid than our objective responses (reasoned). Intuition is an innate quality, but it can be developed and cultivated," he wrote.

Intuitive thinking has played an invaluable role in Dr. Salk's scientific research for many years. When studying viruses, for example, he would visualize himself as a particular virus then intuitively sense how that virus behaved. He would also visualize himself as the immune system to get a sense of how the immune system would battle the invading virus. Only after he envisioned a number of scenarios about a particular situation would he design his laboratory experiments to test his intuitive perceptions. When encountering phenomena in the laboratory that he did not understand, Dr. Salk would frequently return to his original question and ask himself how he would behave as a virus cell or an immune system. Yet he is quick to point out that this mental process occurs intuitively; that is, he is not engaged in a conscious projection of his consciousness. "I feel as if this is all occurring at a level of my mind that I sense to be beneath consciousness and that seems to want to merge with my conscious mind. At the moment when the two converge, when they commune, I feel a rush of ecstasy, a sense of release, of satisfaction, of fulfillment," he wrote in *Anatomy of Reality*. While Dr. Salk, who describes himself as "practicing the art of science," acknowledges the importance of intuition in his own scientific work, he understands that there are other scientists for whom intuition is not significant.

And while he respects those differences in mental preferences, Dr. Salk believes that "the phenomenon of consciousness and self-consciousness, as well as of intuition and reason, manifests the same pattern of a functional binary relationship which characterizes all matter, and all natural phenomena, from the simplest to the most complex."

EDGAR MITCHELL'S THEORY OF CONSCIOUSNESS

Like Dr. Jonas Salk, former NASA astronaut Edgar Mitchell believes in a binary, or dyadic, model of the universe in which consciousness must be taken into account as a causal element.

As a scientist and an astronaut, Mitchell has been personally searching for answers to this fundamental dichotomy. He conducted in-flight experiments in extrasensory perception with professional psychics back on earth and reported a success rate that was phenomenally greater than that predicted by chance. In 1971, while on the *Apollo 14* mission, he looked back at the earth from his space capsule and knew intuitively that an intelligence was at work in the universe. Mitchell's epiphany in space did not end there. He returned to earth, left the space program, and founded the Institute of Noetic Sciences in Sausalito, California. "It is becoming increasingly clear that the human mind and physical universe do not exist independently. Something as yet indefinable connects them. This connective link—between mind and matter, intelligence and intuition—is what Noetic Sciences is all about." Mitchell chose the word *noetic* from the Greek word *nous,* meaning "mind, intelligence, and understanding." The word *noetic* encompasses the intellect's ability to reason, the perceptions of the physical senses, and the intuitive, spiritual, or inner ways of knowing. "The psychic component of the intuitive function, that is, the ability to perceive information in ways unexplainable, is a natural part of the universe. It is available to everyone. We have got to experience powerful intuition, psychokinesis, and healing to know that it is real. There is nothing magical or mystical about it. It is only that aspect of the unknown which we can't explain yet," Mitchell says.

While physicists believe that everything can be reduced to matter and energy and mentalists take the point of view that consciousness is the causal element, Mitchell believes that both are mutually necessary. "Like the north and south pole, you need both matter and consciousness for the universe to be complete." Mitchell sees mainstream science as primarily reductionist, breaking the atom down to elemental particles. Although that is valid for the physical spectrum, he believes that you have to take into account the nonphysical spectrum, as well. You have to ask, "What is the most elemental thing about our nonphysical essence?" For Mitchell, who holds a doctorate in aeronautics and who has spent eighteen years developing this scientific theory, it is information, that is, the ability and intent to distinguish between two simultaneous states. Like the north and south poles, energy then becomes the basis of physical reality and information the basis of consciousness.

Mitchell's model is unique in its integration of the principles of physics with principles of the new science. "Physics says that matter/energy is the creator of all while the religious camp says that mind is the creator of all. Everyone is trying to create a monadic model, one that posits one or the other as correct," he says. And he believes that in failing to recognize the binary or dual nature of the physical and nonphysical dimensions, scientists are restricting their own efforts to find answers.

For example, Mitchell points to the difficulty that physicists have had in trying to come up with a unified field theory. Scientists today have one set of equations for subatomic activity and a different set of equations for atomic activity. A unified field theory would allow them to develop consistent equations for both subatomic and atomic activity. "It's clear that they are interconnected and that the subatomic level affects what happens at the cosmic level. Tiny, subtle effects do have a major impact, but it's not clear that with the present state of knowledge scientists can write the same equation for both cosmic and subatomic levels," Mitchell notes. He adds that until science studies the fundamental interaction between microdeterminism and macrodeterminism, no scientist will be able to develop a unified field theory. "Scientists will never find the unified field theory until they look at human consciousness. Mind and mental phenomena are the last challenge of physics," he says.

THE SEARCH FOR A COMPLEMENTARY SCIENCE

Formulating a new scientific model for exploring consciousness is a primary focus of the Institute of Noetic Sciences. Willis Harman, director of the institute since 1978, was conducting research into future trends in government and business at SRI International when he realized "our basic assumptions about the human mind and spirit are really changing in a very dramatic way and that this is the most important thing about the future." But hard science does not have the methodology to investigate these phenomena, so Harman is proposing a complementary science. "You could call them a masculine and a feminine science. If women had set out to find out what we can learn about the universe, they would have turned mainly inward. For political and other reasons, men have turned mainly outward. We need a balance," he says.

This complementary science, which Harman also calls Science Two, is not antithetical to the science that is practiced today. It does, however, require a more participative research process. "If you want to explore it, you can't probe in the laboratory. You won't learn anything about it through quantum physics. You learn about it by looking into your own mind and comparing notes with people who are looking into theirs and you gradually build up a body of knowledge. Yes, it's a subjective science but all the important things in life are subjective." Quantum physics has made it clear that if you push reductionist science far enough, you run into the necessity to deal with wholes, and while Harman sees that as a big advance, he notes that "this doesn't mean that if you want to know about your own mind you should go out to a physics laboratory and do some work in quantum physics. You learn about your own mind by turning in the other direction."

A YOGA OF PARTICIPATION

By turning in the other direction, Harman means that a scientist needs to look inside his own mind. University of Michigan scientist Henryk Skolimowski proposes calling such a new scientific method a "yoga of participation." Traditional Western science practices what Skolimowski calls a "yoga of objectivity" in which scientists are trained for many years to view the world in an objective, analytical, and detached way.

In contrast to this yoga of objectivity, in which the scientist separates himself from what is being observed, the yoga of participation would have a scientist learn by identifying with what he observes. Dr. Salk has described how he identified with microorganisms when conducting his research. Nobel Prize–winning biologist Barbara McClintock also says that identifying with the chromosomes of the corn cells she studied was very important. "I was part of the system. . . . It surprised me because I actually felt as if I was right down there and these were my friends. As you look at these things they become a part of you," she is quoted as saying in the *Noetic Sciences Review.*

Universities teach science students the yoga of objectivity, which assumes that reality is objective and that you can study it by distancing yourself from it. The yoga of participation is interactive and intuitive. It assumes that the scientist will be sensitized and changed by identifying with his subject. To participate in this kind of research, you have to be willing to take the risk that your beliefs and knowledge base can be transformed. Harman indicates that you have to be willing to see with "new eyes, not eyes conditioned by the scientist's own culture."

Along with the objectivist thinking we have described, traditional science is also positivistic. That means that it assumes that only what is physically measurable is real. The complementary, new science, does not make this assumption. "There are two ways of contacting the universe and learning from it. One of them is through the physical senses and the other is through deep intuition. You need to use both. You don't learn anything about the nonphysical by physical probes, by definition alone," says Harman.

Reductionism, the third assumption on which traditional Western science is based, believes that all phenomena can be reduced to atomic and subatomic particles. The complementary science does not explain things solely in terms of how elementary particles move around the fields, or in terms of stimulus response, or the DNA molecule and the genetic code. "There's another kind of explanation that comes from the mind, including the hidden mind and the spirit," Harman says.

THE SPIRIT OF SCIENCE

Harman invokes the spirit of science as a guiding force, describing this research process as "an open inquiry in the scientific spirit." What makes it scientific? "You hold your hypothesis loosely and all validation is out in the public. You invite everybody to participate and you don't have any dogmas about it. There's no priesthood in this new science. What was wrong with religion was that there was a priesthood and what's wrong with science right now is that there is a priesthood," he says. If a scientist finds evidence that contradicts his conceptual framework, he will set those concepts aside and continue probing for answers, keeping in mind that the scientific path to intuitive knowledge may not follow the straight lines of hard science. "Any trained scientist can go into the laboratory and repeat a scientific experiment. However, that doesn't mean that just anybody can go through some kind of mechanical exercise and end up with intuition," Harman says.

To do that, you have to accept as a basic premise the idea that there is a nonphysical reality that cannot be explained in physical terms and most scientists simply are not ready to accept that. "This is a new heresy," Harman says. "But science itself was a heresy in its time and the scientific heresy changed the world." Copernicus, for example, proposed that the earth revolved around the sun instead of the other way around, thus transforming how all people on earth understood their position in the universe. Just as this empirical evidence caused people to question the authorities' version of reality in those times, today we have a new body of evidence that shows us that reality is not the way most scientists say it is.

"Our science is totally incomplete and will remain so until we include the study of consciousness as a causal element in the universe," Harman says. To do this, we need a new science, one that is capable of confronting what is both unknown and off-limits; a science that is capable of coming up with valid questions and, ultimately, answers about mind itself, about intuition, and about the substance and identity of this inner frontier.

CONCLUSION

At the beginning of this book, we indicated that your intuition works perfectly, whether or not you choose to cultivate it. We explained, too, that becoming more intuitive is a process of learning to notice how you think and respond. If, when you started reading this book, you were unfamiliar with the inner terrain of your own intuition, you may have been startled, dismayed, or even angered by this claim. If you were already comfortable with your intuition, then you probably had little or no trouble accepting this idea. Although we have presented specific techniques to help you to access your intuitive intelligence, we have also emphasized the importance of understanding your own definitions, experiences, and beliefs about intuition as a prerequisite for becoming sensitive to your own subtle, inner responses. These techniques and exercises are not simple push-this-button-and-release games. They are powerful tools to help you reach inside your unconscious mind and learn how to read those personal symbols, feelings, images, and impressions that make up your language of intuition. While certain characteristics and criteria are fairly universal to intuition, the language through which your own intuitive intelligence speaks is entirely your own. As you read this book and began to learn about your own intuitive language, you may have noticed subtle changes in how you began to react to experiences. Perhaps you paid attention to a strong gut feeling instead of disregarding it, or maybe you followed a hunch that you would have ignored earlier, or perhaps you had a dream that came true.

These are indications that your intuitive mind is actively processing the information in this book. Your ability to notice these signals and impressions is yet another signal of your developing intuition. We are aware that

some of the material we are presenting flies in the face of logic and that you
may have a hard time accepting it. You may even have argued with, or
dismissed some of what we discussed as impossible and absurd. Again, we
are compelled to point out that it is impossible and absurd to your rational
mind because your rational mind cannot think intuitively. However, in our
years of working with this material we have found that despite what your
logical mind believes, the truth nonetheless gets absorbed. The unconscious part of your mind intuitively recognizes its value and when your
intuitive mind absorbs it and integrates it, you start to notice differences in
your thoughts and feelings, your encounters with people, and your dreams.
In fact, you may find these new experiences and perceptions are coming to
you whether or not you consciously want or choose them!

In offering you information that gives you greater access to your own
inner resources, we feel that we are in a type of privileged position
described by Eugen Herrigel in his classic book *Zen in the Art of Archery.*
When discussing the relationship between the master archer who teaches
and the pupil, Herrigel says that the pupil (you, the reader) allows the
teacher (us, the writers) to "bring into view something of which he has
often heard but whose reality is only beginning to be tangible on the basis
of his own experience." In describing more fully how this is done, he
wrote, "Just as one uses a burning candle to light others with, the teacher
transfers the spirit of the right way."

Zen in the Art of Archery is, on the surface, a story about a German who
spends several years studying Japanese archery as taught by a strict Zen
master. He spends more than one year simply learning how to hold the
huge bow, and years more learning how to relax his muscles so that instead
of looking and aiming at the target, the arrow releases itself and finds the
bull's-eye. The book not only contains detailed explanations of the specific
physical processes involved in developing this skill, it also tells of the inner
work required to achieve a state of effortlessness. Similar techniques are
now being used to train Denise Parker, a young American archer who won
a bronze medal at the 1988 Olympics. Before a match, Parker visualizes
herself shooting arrows perfectly. When she actually faces her target, she is
able to enter the peak mental state that athletes call "the zone," in which
such specialized physical movements as shooting an arrow or pitching a
ball come effortlessly, writes Lawrence Shainberg in a *New York Times
Magazine* article, "Finding 'The Zone.'"

As Herrigel describes it, in order for the archer to be successful, his mind has to be attuned to the unconscious. Should he "deliberate and conceptualize, the original unconscious is lost." In intuition as in Zen archery, you can be successful only by focusing on the inner goal. The purpose of learning Zen archery is to train the mind so that it allows intuition to come through.

In searching for an appropriate metaphor to describe learning how to develop your intuitive sense, we believe there is none more descriptive and complete than the metaphor of *Zen in the Art of Archery.* Our goal has been to show you how to relax into the state of effortlessness required for your intuition to work. To do this, we have chosen language that is more colloquial than the traditional terminology for this process. We have quite simply urged you to "have fun" when practicing the exercises because for most of us "fun" is the complex equivalence of that spontaneous, effortless state in which intuitive knowing occurs.

In presenting you with ways to define, identify, and shape your intuition to give it a more concrete form, our intention, like that of the archery instructor in Herrigel's book, has been to nurture a free-flowing inner momentum between your conscious and unconscious awareness. Asking you to step back from your intuition, to look at it, talk to it, and touch it, offers you different ways to hold "the bow" prior to allowing "the arrow" to release itself.

A master archer needs only to relax into a "state of waiting without purpose" to fire the right shot. Just as he is intuitively able to distinguish his right shots from his failures, you too will become able to distinguish the "right shot" of your true intuition from off-the-mark anxiety, confusion, and wishful thinking. "You think that what you do not do yourself does not happen," Herrigel wrote, describing the conventional point of view. But to make full use of your intuition, just like shooting the straight arrow, you don't "make it" happen. You shift your point of focus, relax, and it comes to you. You can examine and approach your intuition from different perspectives, but like a master archer, you cannot reach your intuition by putting it aside or separating yourself from it. As the archer seeks to unite with the target, you and your intuition have to work as one. Ultimately, success in Zen archery is the same as success in intuitive thinking. You can shift your consciousness to an intuitive state but, in the end, intuition is an arrow that releases itself.

BIBLIOGRAPHY

BOOKS

Agor, Weston. *Intuitive Management: Integrating Left and Right Brain Management Skills.* Englewood Cliffs, N.J.: Prentice Hall, 1984.

Armstrong, Thomas. *In Their Own Way: Discovering and Encouraging Your Child's Personal Learning Style.* Los Angeles: Jeremy P. Tarcher, 1987.

Bain, Donald. *The Control of Candy Jones.* Chicago: Playboy Press, 1976.

Bandler, Richard. *Using Your Brain . . . For a Change.* Moab, Utah: Real People Press, 1985.

Bandler, Richard and John Grinder. *The Structure of Magic.* Palo Alto: Science and Behavior Books, 1975.

_____. *The Structure of Magic II.* Palo Alto: Science and Behavior Books, 1976.

Brown, Barbara. *Supermind, The Ultimate Energy.* San Francisco: Harper & Row, 1980.

Bruner, Jerome. *On Knowing: Essays for the Left Hand.* Cambridge, Mass.: Harvard University Press, 1979.

Buzan, Tony. *Use Both Sides of Your Brain.* New York: E.P. Dutton, 1974.

_____. *Make the Most of Your Mind.* New York: Linden/Simon & Schuster, 1984.

Calvin, William. *The Throwing Madonna.* New York: McGraw-Hill, 1985.

Campbell, Don. *Introduction to the Musical Brain.* St. Louis, Mo.: Magnamusic-Baton, 1983.

Campbell, Joseph with Bill Moyers. *The Power of Myth.* New York: Doubleday, 1988.

Chall, Jeanne and Allan Mirsky, eds. *Education and the Brain.* Chicago: University of Chicago Press, 1978.

Chitrabhanu, Gurudev Shree. *The Psychology of Enlightenment.* New York: Dodd, Mead & Co., 1979.

Corballis, Michael and Ivan Beals. *The Ambivalent Mind: The Neuropsychology of Left and Right.* New York: Nelson Hall, 1986.

Diagram Group. *The Brain: A User's Manual.* New York: G.P. Putnam, 1982.

Edelman, Gerald and Vernon Mountcastle. *The Mindful Brain.* Cambridge, Mass.: MIT Press, 1978.

Edwards, Betty. *Drawing on the Right Side of the Brain.* Los Angeles: Jeremy P. Tarcher, 1979.

219

Edwards, Harry. *The Healing Intelligence.* London: The Healer Publishing Co., 1967.

Ferguson, Marilyn. *The Aquarian Conspiracy: Personal and Social Transformation in the 80s.* Los Angeles: Jeremy P. Tarcher, 1978.

Franklin, Jon. *Molecules of the Mind.* New York: Dell Publishing Co., 1987.

Furst, Charles. *Origins of the Mind.* Englewood Cliffs, N.J.: Prentice Hall, 1979.

Gaddes, William. *Learning Disabilities and Brain Function: A Neuropsychological Approach.* New York: Springer-Verlag, 1980.

Gardner, Howard. *Frames of Mind: The Theory of Multiple Intelligences.* New York: Basic Books, 1983.

Gazzaniga, Michael. *The Bisected Brain.* Appleton, Wis.: Appleton-Century Crofts, 1970.

Gazzaniga, Michael and Joseph LeDoux. *The Integrated Mind.* New York, Plenum Books.

Gilot, Francoise and Carlton Lake. *Life with Picasso.* New York: McGraw Hill, 1981.

Goodspeed, Bennett. *The Tao Jones Average: A Guide to Whole-Brained Investing.* New York: E.P. Dutton, 1983.

Guinness Book of World Records. New York: Sterling Publishing Co., 1988.

Hampden-Turner, Charles. *Maps of the Mind.* London: Mitchell-Beazley Publishers, 1981.

Harman, Willis and Howard Rheingold. *Higher Creativity: Liberating the Unconscious for Breakthrough Insights.* Los Angeles: Jeremy P. Tarcher, 1984.

Herrigel, Eugen. *Zen in the Art of Archery.* New York: Pantheon Books, 1953.

Herrmann, Ned. *The Creative Brain.* Lake Lure, N.C.: Brain Books, 1988.

Hesse, Hermann. *Narcissus and Goldmund.* New York: Farrar, Straus & Giroux, 1968.

Hilton, Conrad. *Be My Guest.* Englewood Cliffs, N.J.: Prentice Hall, 1957.

Hooper, Judith and Nick Teresi. *The 3-Pound Universe.* New York: Del Publishing Co., 1986.

Hoy, David. *Psychic and Other ESP Party Games.* New York: Funk & Wagnalls, 1965.

Huffington, Arianna Stassinopoulos. *Picasso: Creator and Destroyer.* New York: Simon & Schuster, 1988.

Jahn, Robert and Brenda Dunne. *Margins of Reality: The Role of Consciousness in the Physical World.* San Diego: Harcourt Brace Jovanovich, 1987.

Jung, C.G. *The Portable Jung.* Edited by Joseph Campbell. New York: The Viking Press, 1971.

Jung, C.G. with Aniela Jaffe. *Memories, Dreams, Reflections.* New York: Random House, 1965.

Keynes, John Maynard. *Essays in Biography.* Edited by Geoffrey Keynes. New York: Horizon Press, 1951.

Krieger, Dolores. *The Therapeutic Touch: How to Use Your Hands to Help or Heal.* Englewood Cliffs, N.J.: Prentice Hall, 1979.

Krippner, Stanley and Joseph Dillard. *Dreamworking: How to Use Your Dreams for Creative Problem Solving.* Buffalo, N.Y.: Bearly Limited, 1988.

Kurtz, Paul, ed. *A Skeptic's Handbook of Parapsychology.* Buffalo, N.Y.: Prometheus Books, 1985.

Lesko, Matthew. *Information USA.* New York: Viking Penguin, 1986.

_____. *Government Giveaways for Entrepreneurs*. Chevy Chase, Md.: Information USA, Inc. 1988.

Levy, Steven. *The Unicorn's Secret*. New York: Prentice Hall Press, 1988.

Mazo, Earl, and Stephen Hess. *Nixon: A Political and Personal Portrait*. New York: Harper & Brothers, 1959.

O'Biso, Carol. *First Light*. Auckland, New Zealand: Heinemann, 1987.

Pascal, Blaise. *Pensées*. Translated by HF Stewart. New York: Pantheon Books, 1965.

Progoff, Ira. *At a Journal Workshop*. New York: Dialogue House, 1975.

_____. *The Practice of Process Meditation*. New York: Dialogue House, 1980.

Ray, Michael and Rochelle Myers. *Creativity in Business*. New York: Doubleday, 1986.

Reber, Arthur. *The Penguin Dictionary of Psychology*. New York: Viking, 1985.

Regan, Donald. *For the Record*. San Diego: Harcourt Brace Jovanovich, 1988.

Rogo, D. Scott. *Psychic Breakthroughs Today: Fascinating Encounters with Parapsychology's Latest Discoveries*. Wellingborough, Northamptonshire, UK: The Aquarian Press, 1987.

Rosanoff, Nancy. *Intuition Workout*. San Francisco: Aslan Publishing Co., 1988.

Rossi, Ernest. *Dreams and the Growth of Personality: Expanding Awareness in Psychotherapy*. New York: Brunner/Mazel, 1985.

_____. *The Psychobiology of Mind-Body Healing: New Concepts of Therapeutic Hypnosis*. New York: W.W. Norton and Company, 1986.

Rossi, Ernest and David Cheek. *Mind-Body Therapy: Methods of Ideodynamic Healing in Hypnosis*. New York: W.W. Norton, 1988.

Rowan, Roy. *The Intuitive Manager*. Boston: Little, Brown & Co., 1986.

Sacks, Oliver. *The Man Who Mistook His Wife for a Hat*. New York: Harper & Row, 1965.

Sagan, Carl. *The Dragons of Eden: Speculations on the Evolution of Human Intelligence*. New York: Random House, 1977.

Salk, Jonas. *Anatomy of Reality: Merging of Intuition and Reason*. New York: Columbia University Press, 1983.

Sharman-Burke, Juliet. *The Mythic Tarot Workbook*. New York: Simon & Schuster, 1988.

Sharman-Burke, Juliet and Liz Greene. *The Mythic Tarot: A New Approach to the Tarot Cards*. New York: Simon & Schuster, 1988.

Stassinopoulos, Arianna. *After Reason*. New York: Stein and Day, 1980.

_____. *Maria Callas: The Woman Behind the Legend*. New York: Simon & Schuster, 1981.

Targ, Russell and Keith Harary. *The Mind Race: Understanding and Using Psychic Abilities*. New York: Random House, 1984.

Targ, Russell and Harold Puthoff. *Mind-Reach: Scientists Look at Psychic Ability*. New York: Dell Publishing Co., 1977.

Thurston, Mark. *Dream Tonight's Answers for Tomorrow's Questions*. San Francisco: Harper & Row, 1988.

Time-Life Books. *Mystic Places*. Alexandria, Va.: Time-Life Books, 1988.

_____. *Psychic Powers*. Alexandria, Va.: Time-Life Books, 1988.

Trump, Donald and Tony Schwartz. *Trump: The Art of the Deal*. New York: Warner Books, 1988.

Vallentin, Antonina. *The Drama of Albert Einstein.* Garden City, N.Y.: Doubleday & Co., 1954.

Vare, Ethlie Ann and Greg Ptacek. *Mothers of Invention: From the Bra to the Bomb, Forgotten Women and their Unforgettable Ideas.* New York: William Morrow, 1988.

Wallace, Marjorie. *The Silent Twins.* New York: Prentice Hall, 1986.

Wynn, Wilton. *Keepers of the Keys.* New York: Random House, 1988.

ARTICLES

Aspaturian, Heidi. "Sperry on Consciousness." Pasadena: California Institute of Technology, 1988.

Bailey, Moira. "Researcher: Women's Intuition Has Some Validity." *The Coloradoan* (July 24, 1986).

Beck, Robert. "Instrumentation for Detecting, Recording, and Analyzing Natural and Man-Made ELF Signals and Human Brainwaves."

————. "Mood Modification with ELF Magnetic Fields: A Preliminary Investigation." *Archaeus* 4 (1986).

Beck, Robert. "Countersurveillance Basics: A New Age Survival Manual." *Bugging and De-Bugging Bulletin* 4 (1988).

Beck, Robert and Eldon Byrd. "Bibliography on the Psychoactivity of Electromagnetic Fields." *Archaeus* 4 (1986).

Black, Robert Alan. "Counseling Approaches." *International Brain Dominance Review* 4, no. 1 (1987).

Buckley, Karen Wilhelm. "The Role of Intuition in Transformative Change." Paper prepared for the International Management Institute (IMI) Intuition Network, 1988, copyright K.W. Buckley.

Catford, Lorna. "Intuition Is One of Many Strategies for Business Problem Solving: A Literature Review." Paper prepared for the International Management Institute (IMI) Intuition Network, 1988, copyright L. Catford.

Colman, Carol and associates. "Quarterly Supplement." *Inferential Focus IF 725* (Second Quarter 1986).

Colman, Carol and associates. "Focus: Transition to a New Order." *Inferential Focus IF 830* (September 24, 1987).

Colman, Carol and Kenneth Hey. "Remove Your Business Blinders—and View the Future." *Journal of Business Strategy* (July/August 1988).

Englebardt, Stanley. "Are You Thinking Right?" *Reader's Digest* (February 1988).

Franquemont, Sharon. "Intuition: Theories and Application in Business." Paper prepared for the International Management Institute (IMI) Intuition Network, 1988.

Graves, Florence. "The New Age of Consciousness: An Interview with Willis Harman." *The 1988 Guide to New Age Living,* 1988.

Greely, Andrew. "The Anatomy of Ecstasy. Shirley McClaine's Spiritual Dance." *American Health* (January/February 1987).

Harman, Willis. "Beyond Reductionism, What? The Need for a Basic Restructuring of Science." *Noetic Sciences Review* (1988).

_____. "Intuition As the Code Word for Global Transformation." Paper presented at the International Management Institute (IMI) Conference on Intuition, Geneva, February 1988.

Herrmann, Ned. "Diagnosing a Leadership Change in Progress." *International Brain Dominance Review* 5, no. 2 (1988).

Honorton, Charles. "Precognition and Real-Time ESP Performance in a Computer Task with an Exceptional Subject." *Journal of Parapsychology* 51 (December 1987).

Honorton, Charles, and Diane Ferrari, and George Hansen. "Meta-Analysis of Forced-Choice Precognition Experiments." Princeton: Psychophysical Research Laboratories, 1989.

Honorton, Charles, John Palmer, and Jessica Utts. "Reply to the National Research Council Study on Parapsychology." *Journal of the American Society for Psychical Research* 83 (January 1989).

IMI Intuition Network. Meeting notes. February 10, 1988.

Jahn, Robert. "The Persistent Paradox of Psychic Phenomena: An Engineering Perspective." *Proceedings of the IEEE* 70, no. 2 (February 1982).

_____. "Anomalies: Analysis and Aesthetics." Princeton Engineering Anomalies Research Technical Note PEAR 88003, August 1988.

Jahn, Robert and Brenda Dunne, and R.D. Nelson. "Engineering Anomalies Research." *Journal of Scientific Exploration* 1, no. 1 (1987).

John-David. "Tuning the Mind and Body." Paper presented at the Conference of American Association for Music Therapy, March 1988.

Kautz, William. "The Intuitive Historian: Reconstruction of the Life of Imhotep." *Phoenix: New Directions in the Study of Man* 4, nos. 1 and 2 (1980).

_____. "The Rosemary Case of Alleged Egyptian Xenoglossy." Paper presented at Founders' Days Conference, "Consciousness and Psi," Chapel Hill, N.C., April 1981.

_____. "Validation of Intuitive Consensus As a Method for Creative Problem Solving in the Sciences: Earthquake Triggering." Center for Applied Intuition (San Francisco), 1986.

MacLean, Paul. "The Triune Brain, Emotion, and Scientific Bias." In *The Neurosciences: Second Study Program,* Rockefeller University Press, 1970.

_____. "A Triune Concept of the Brain and Behavior." Hincks Memorial Lecture, Ontario Mental Health Foundation, University of Toronto Press, 1973.

_____. "An Evolutionary Approach to Brain Research on Prosematic (Nonverbal) Behavior." Washington D.C.: U.S. Department of Health, Education and Welfare, National Institutes of Health, 1977.

_____. "A Mind of Three Minds: Educating the Triune Brain." National Society for the Study of Education, 1978.

_____. "Brain Evolution Relating to Family, Play, and the Separation Call." *Archives of General Psychiatry* 42 (April 1985).

————. "Culminating Developments in the Evolution of the Limbic System; the Thalamocingulate Division." In *The Limbic System: Functional Organization and Clinical Disorders,* 1986.

MacLean, Paul and associates. "The Ecology and Biology of Mammal-like Reptiles." Washington, D.C.: Smithsonian Institution Press, 1986.

————. "Triune Brain." In *Encyclopedia of Neuroscience.* Edited by George Adelman. Boston: Birkhauser, 1987.

MacLean, Paul and John Newman. "Role of Midline Frontolimbic Cortex in Production of the Isolation Call of Squirrel Monkeys." *Brain Research, BRE 12559* (November 1987).

Millay, Jean. "Brainwave Synchronization: A Study of Subtle Forms of Communication." *Humanistic Psychology Institute Review* 3, no. 1 (Spring 1981).

————. "Brain-Mind and the Dimensions Beyond Space-Time." Copyright © 1987, J. Millay.

Miller, William. "Intuition and Total Quality." Paper prepared for the International Management Institute (IMI) Intuition Network, 1988, copyright W. Miller.

Powers, Richard. "Physiological Effects and Methods of Detection." *Geopathology* (1985).

Reber, Arthur. "Implicit Learning and Tacit Knowledge." *Journal of Experimental Psychology* (1988).

Rossi, Ernest. "Nonlocality in Physics and Psychology: An Interview with John Stewart Bell." *Psychological Perspectives* (Fall-Winter 1988).

Salk, Jonas. "Onward to a Union of Mind and Molecules." *National Observer,* May 27, 1962.

Schulz, Larry and Thomas Cunningham. "The Seasonal Structure Underlying the Arrangement of Hexagrams in the *I Jing (I Ching)*." *Federal Reserve Bank of America Occasional Paper Series* (March 1988).

Shainberg, Lawrence. "Finding 'The Zone'." *New York Times Magazine,* April 9, 1989.

Siebert, Al. "The Survivor Personality" newsletter.

Sharpnack, Nancy. *The Etherion Chronicles* premier issue (October 1987).

Smith, Emily. "Are You Creative?" *Business Week* (September 30, 1985).

Sperry, Roger. "Downward Causation: The Consciousness Revolution in Science." *Noetic Sciences Review* (Autumn 1987).

————. "Structure and Significance of the Consciousness Revolution." *Journal of Mind and Behavior* 8, no. 1 (Winter 1987).

————. "Psychology's Mentalist Paradigm and the Religon/Science Tension." *American Psychologist* (August 1988).

Stassinopoulos, Arianna. "Courage, Love, Forgiveness: Dr. Jonas Salk's Formula for the Future." *Parade* (November 4, 1984).

Steele, William. "Creativity: The New Biz Buzzword." *Working Mother* (November 1987).

Targ, Russell and Arthur Hastings. "Psychological Impact of Psychic Abilities." *Psychological Perspectives* 18, no. 1 (Spring 1987).

Timbal-Duclaux, Louis. "Five Techniques for Two Hemispheres." *International Brain Dominance Review* 4, no. 1 (1987).

Wiberg, Vince. "Geo-Acupuncture." *Page Two* (1986).

PSYCHOTECHNOLOGY AIDS

Psychotechnology aids are primarily audiotapes designed to alter your brain-wave pattern to induce a meditative or intuitive state. The one exception, the Synchro-Energizer, is a combined audiovisual experience that synchronizes your brain-wave pattern auditorily to produce a heightened state of awareness that includes visual effects.

    Synchro-Energize

    594 Broadway

    New York, N.Y. 10012.

Psychotechnology aids are powerful tools for increasing your intuitive awareness and must never be used when driving or operating machinery. We strongly recommend:

Condon, Thomas. *Expanded Intuition Training.* Berkeley: The Changeworks, 1986. Condon uses NLP techniques and multievocation hypnosis on this series of six audiotapes and workbook.

Condon, Thomas, Carol Erickson, and Steven Feinberg. *Deep Self-Appreciation.* Berkeley: The Changeworks, 1986.

———. *Natural Self-Confidence.* Berkeley: The Changeworks, 1986.

Monroe, Robert. *Hemi-Synch* audiotapes: "Focus 10 Relaxation," "Metamusic Trailing Edge," "Surf," and the "Gateway" series. All of Monroe's tapes have an underlying (not subliminal) pulse that synchronizes brain-wave patterns to relaxing alpha and deep, creative theta levels. "Metamusic" tapes have New Age music and the other tapes have guided visualizations and meditation. "Surf" plays the sound of the ocean. Faber, Va: The Monroe Institute, 1988.

    Other psychotechnology aids:

Charles, Brother. *Synchronicity.* Soundtracks with chanting and music are available in alpha, theta, and delta rhythms. Faber, Va.: M.S.H. Association, 1987.

John-David. *Brain Tune-Up, Anyone?* Contains alpha brain-wave patterns. Mild relaxation. Carlsbad, California: John-David Learning Institute, 1987.

Millay, Jean. *Mindmaster.* Biofeedback video game for personal computer. Santa Cruz, California: Mindware, 1988.

INDEX

ABOUT THE AUTHORS

Laurie Nadel has been writing professionally since 1969 when she began her career as a television newswriter in London. Returning to the United States, she worked as a writer/producer at ABC News before heading off to South America where she was a special-assignment reporter for United Press International and the *Newsweek* correspondent in Peru. Ms. Nadel became the first reporter to cover American oil operations in the Amazon jungle and covered the Chilean state of siege in Santiago. Upon returning to the United States, she worked as a reporter and consultant at the United Nations.

Ms. Nadel was a writer for CBS News for eight years, during which time she published articles on intuition and related subjects in *Family Circle, Natural History,* and *Signature* magazines. Her biography *Corazon Aquino: Journey to Power* was published in 1987. She is a member of the American Society of Journalists and Authors and is a certified practitioner of neuro-linguistic programming (NLP).

Judy Haims was one of the founding teachers of the Mead School for Human Development in Greenwich, Connecticut. Founded in 1969, the Mead School is the first in the country to incorporate whole-brain theory into the educational curriculum and to encourage young people to value their intuition as an intelligence. Well-known in the emerging field of whole-brain research and creativity training, Ms. Haims is a leading authority on the application of current brain research and has a consulting and counseling practice in Greenwich, Connecticut. She is on the board of directors of the Mead School and is coordinator of the Institute for Health and Healing at Wainwright House in Rye, New York. Ms. Haims was assistant director of Programs for Human Development in Greenwich, Connecticut. She has an M.S. degree from Columbia University.

Robert Stempson is director of Programs for Human Development (PHD) in Greenwich, Connecticut. PHD is an adult education center offering seminars and workshops in intuition, whole-brain learning, personal growth, and New Age subjects. A former curriculum director at the Mead School for Human Development, Mr. Stempson decided to form PHD so that adults could benefit from the same educational approach as the young students at the Mead School. Since 1982, thousands of people have taken PHD courses in meditation, visualization, the power of thought, coping with stress, communicating with dolphins, mind mapping, and developing intuition. Frustrated by the lack of Ph.D. programs in intuitive thinking, Mr. Stempson chose the initials PHD for his educational center, saying, "the courses offered here are those I would like to have taken for my Ph.D. degree."

Mr. Stempson studied Media Studies at the New School for Social Research in New York City, and also studied neurolinguistic programming with NLP founders John Grinder and Richard Bandler in 1981. "In learning how to look at images, I found that media studies was a form of perceptual psychology and that we can splice, edit, and juxtapose our own mental images," he says. In addition, Mr. Stempson also received a B.A. in Social Relations from Harvard University. He has a private counseling and consulting practice in Greenwich, Connecticut.